LANGUAGE IN SOCIETY 17

The Language of News Media

Language in Society

GENERAL EDITOR
  Peter Trudgill, Professor in the Department of Language and Linguistics,
  University of Lausanne

ADVISORY EDITORS
  Jack Chambers, Professor of Linguistics, University of Toronto
  Ralph Fasold, Professor of Linguistics, Georgetown University
  William Labov, Professor of Linguistics, University of Pennsylvania
  Lesley Milroy, Professor of Linguistics, University of Michigan, Ann Arbor

The Language of
News Media

ALLAN BELL

Copyright © Allan Bell, 1991

First published 1991
Reprinted 1993, 1994, 1995, 1996, 1999

Blackwell Publishers Ltd
108 Cowley Road
Oxford OX4 1JF, UK

Blackwell Publishers Inc
350 Main Street
Malden, Massachusetts 02148, USA

British Library Cataloguing in Publication Data
A CIP catalogue record for this book is available from the British Library

Library of Congress Cataloging in Publication Data
Bell, Allan
The language of news media / Allan Bell
p.   cm. — (Language in society: 17)
Includes bibliographical references and index.
ISBN   0–631–16435–9 (pbk)
1. Mass media and language. 2. Broadcast journalism – Language.
3. Newspapers – Language. 4. Sociolinguistics. I. Title.
II. Series: Language in society (Oxford, England); 17
P96.L34B45   1991   90–1289
302.23'014—dc20   CIP

Typeset in 10.5 on 12pt Symposia
by Colset Private Limited, Singapore
Printed and bound in Great Britain
by Athenæum Press Ltd, Gateshead, Tyne & Wear

This book is printed on acid-free paper

Contents

Figures and Tables

Editor's Preface

A series editor should be careful to avoid exaggeration when introducing volumes in the series, and I am conscious that Allan Bell is not the first author to write for the Language and Society series for whom I have made the claim that he or she is uniquely qualified to write on their given topic. It is difficult, however, to avoid observing that Allan Bell is the only scholar I have ever come across who is both an experienced and practising journalist and an academic sociolinguist with an international reputation. As a New Zealand-based journalist, Allan Bell is a writer who is familiar with both the electronic media and print journalism in many parts of the (particularly English-speaking) world; and, within academic sociolinguistics and linguistic variation theory, he is very well known indeed as a scholar who has produced solidly empirically-based work of very considerable theoretical importance. In particular, his 1984 media-based theoretical paper 'Language style as audience design' is widely regarded as a sociolinguistic classic.

The use of language in the presentation of news, and elsewhere in the media, represents a form of interaction between language and society which affects us all. His surely unique combination of knowledge and expertise has now enabled Allan Bell to produce a book which provides original and exciting insights into this area which will be of great importance for students and researchers in communications and media studies, as well as in sociolinguistics.

Peter Trudgill

*For the Memory of
my Mother and Father*

Introduction and Acknowledgements

It is my belief — and one of the themes of this book — that audiences are an important influence on media content. The book is addressed to an audience of all those who are interested in how media work, how language works, and particularly how the two interact. Its contents should be accessible to people who have a lay interest in these issues as well as to people who study such matters. I hope it will also be of interest to journalists and others in the news media to learn something about the nature of the linguistic work they do.

The book's disciplinary background is in sociolinguistics and discourse analysis, but it draws on a wide range of mass communications theory and research. The book should serve to introduce the study of mass media to students of sociolinguistics. It is less appropriate as an introduction to linguistics for communications researchers, although I have generally avoided technical linguistic terminology.

What is media discourse like? What can it tell us about media? What can it tell us about language? These are important questions for both sociolinguistics and mass communication research. They are also important for society at large. It is my belief that true, responsive communication among people and between peoples is worth striving for. The language of news media is prominent and pervasive in society, and it is worth understanding how that language works, how it affects our perceptions of others and ourselves, how it is produced, how it is shaped by values. This book addresses central issues in the nature of media language and discourse, its production and its reception. It does not, however, enter into the debate over what effect media may have on the use of language in society, for instance whether media language is debasing everyday language. 'The media and language' is the subject for another look.

To explain the background to this book: I have been both studying and making media language for nearly 20 years. I began research on media language in 1972, and several years later moved to work in journalism. For a decade I alternated employment as an editor and journalist with semi-employment as a researcher in sociolinguistics and mass communications. In that time I worked in monthly magazines, a weekly newspaper and a daily news service, covering especially environmental, scientific and agricultural issues.

Daily journalism leaves no time or mental space for reflection let alone research, but I am now able to combine rather than alternate the two strands of practice and theory. For this my thanks go to the Head Office of the New Zealand Department of Scientific and Industrial Research, where I work half-time as a journalist and media consultant, and particularly to Kevin Sloan for allowing me several months away to write full-time and so complete this book. My other working life is spent as a freelance researcher, and I am grateful to the Department of Linguistics at Victoria University of Wellington, which has adopted me as an honorary research fellow.

Participant observation is a method which has produced insights into the nature of news and its production. Much of what I write here is the fruit of a converse approach — observant participation. I have drawn many examples and observations from my own experience and news stories I have written, or from stories by journalists who worked with or for me.

The content of this book has been, as I say, a long time brewing. Some of the work (on style in news language) originates in doctoral study of 15 years ago, some (especially on discourse analysis of news stories, and news comprehension) I have come to quite recently. Calling up all one's intellectual debts over such a period is difficult. But first credit goes to my principal research colleague, Janet Holmes of Victoria University's Department of Linguistics. She has been a continuing co-worker and encourager in a number of projects, and has commented helpfully on most of this manuscript.

I thank other individuals who have contributed insights and encouragement on aspects of my work: William Labov, Walt Wolfram, Ralph Fasold, Joy Kreeft Peyton, Nikolas Coupland, Howard Giles and Gerhard Leitner. And I remember the late Werner Droescher, who started me off in linguistics at the University of Auckland, and the late Colin Bowley, who saw me through a doctorate there.

As well as presenting my own work, this book incorporates a wide range of other people's research and findings on media language. For this I am indebted to a score of scholars, whose published work I have drawn on freely but most of whom I do not (or did not) know personally: Oliver Boyd-Barrett, Harald Burger, Jack Cappon, Howard

Davis, Teun van Dijk, Mark Fishman, Johan Galtung, Herbert Gans, the Glasgow University Media Group, Erving Goffman, Barrie Gunter, Andreas Jucker, Hannes Kniffka, Denis McQuail, Marie Holmboe Ruge, Philip Schlesinger, Michael Schudson, Gaye Tuchman, Paul Walton and Ruth Wodak. They have all produced insightful work, and I hope my presentation does them justice.

To those hosts who have over the years taken in this 'freelance academic nomad' (I owe the title to Walt Wolfram), I am grateful: the Center for Applied Linguistics, Washington, DC, where I was a Visiting Research Associate in 1981; University of Reading, where I was Leverhulme Visiting Fellow in 1982; Victoria University's Stout Research Centre, for its hospitality on a couple of occasions; and Linguistics Departments at Georgetown University, Washington, DC, University of Pennsylvania, University College, London, and the University of Stuttgart.

Several chapters of this book report findings from a project on media coverage and public understanding of the climate change issue in New Zealand. I acknowledge funding contributed to this project by the Department of Scientific and Industrial Research and Ministry for the Environment. I am also indebted to Jenny Neale, Andrew Matthews and Peter Clare for their professional inputs to the project.

And an appropriately brief 'par' — 'graf' to the Americans — to thank those journalists and editors with whom I have worked. I have learnt most from those I had the most trouble with.

Other journalists have also taken time out to talk to me as a researcher about their work, especially Radio New Zealand's staff, and Lindsay Clark, formerly of Wellington's *Dominion* newspaper. Philip Carpenter has been a most patient publisher awaiting a work which has had the gestation period of several elephants. And Ann Bone's editing skills have helped to clarify the end product. I am indebted to Peter Trudgill, both for his general contribution to my work and in his role as editor of the Language in Society series.

The book is dedicated to my mother, who died just before it was finished, and my father, who died 30 years earlier. Finally, I thank Susan Jordan — companion for precisely as long as I have been working on media language — for her constant encouragement and support, and occasional insight and research assistance. She has been ably seconded by Sonny and Thorcas.

One point of writing style in this book: in using generic pronouns, my policy is roughly to alternate *she* and *he*, giving precedence to *she* in most contexts.

Allan Bell, Wellington

1

Media and Language

People in Western countries probably hear more language from the media than they do directly from the lips of their fellow humans in conversation. Society is pervaded by media language. Even in a nation as small as New Zealand, the media pour out daily almost two million words of that primary media genre, news, through some 35 newspapers, newscasts carried by a hundred radio stations and three television networks. In larger countries, the production multiplies. The American blockbuster Sunday newspapers print close to a million words each. The production of media language is huge, although only a fraction of all the face-to-face talk individuals produce. But media language is heard not just by one or two people but by mass audiences. It is the few talking to the many. Media are dominating presenters of language in our society at large.

Within the media, news is the primary language genre. It fills pages of the daily newspaper and hours of radio and television time. Even in broadcasting, where it occupies a small minority of airtime, news is seen by both media organizations and audiences as the focus of media content. Also common to all three daily media is the other dominant genre, advertising, which bulks larger than the news in many daily papers. Some of our data and examples in this book will be drawn from advertising, but most will come from the news since this is the most researched and arguably the most central (cf. McQuail 1987) genre.

News was not always so dominant. The year 1930 was early days for radio. The youthful British Broadcasting Corporation sometimes found there was a shortage of news deemed worthy to be broadcast. If this happened, no attempt was made to fill the gap. The announcer just said: 'There is no news tonight'. At that time, the BBC had a total news staff of four. It carried news only after six o'clock at night, by agreement with news agencies and the press, who feared for their monopoly. It was allowed to broadcast no more than 400 eye-witness accounts of events per year (quoted in Schlesinger 1987: 20). In this later generation, the declaration that there is 'no news tonight' comes as a shock, a challenge to convention, even to the shape of reality itself. Now there is always news – unless a strike makes us do without.

In the news are carried the stories and images of our day. News is determined by values, and the kind of language in which that news is told reflects and expresses those values. Audiences feel that the way in which language is used must affect the content of what we receive from the media. We will touch on some but not all of the questions which concern people about the media and their language. One question which we will not address here is this: whether, in a world saturated in media language, the way the media use language is changing language itself. In this book we examine the characteristics of news language not its effect on other language.

Mass communication has several characteristics which distinguish it from face-to-face communication and offer advantages to the linguist: multiple originators, a mass simultaneous audience, a fragmented audience, absence of feedback, and general accessibility to the public. We shall see that these characteristics have a profound effect on the shape of media language, on how it is produced, on audiences' ability to understand media content, and on communicators' ability to make themselves understood.

This book deals mainly with language as it is used in the mainline, daily news media – press, television and radio. A wider definition of printed media could call in magazines, books, posters, record covers, bumper stickers, T-shirts – each getting further from the core media. We could include records, cassettes, videos, films. We might cover newer media such as teletext – but it tends to reproduce press-style content and style in broadcast format. But I will confine myself to those media which have a mass audience, and a continuous or daily production cycle. The massness of the core media is characterized by their general availability to all people within a given geographical area. Anyone with a radio or television set or spare change to spend can receive the mainline mass media.

1 WHY STUDY MEDIA LANGUAGE?

First, because it is there. The uses to which language is put in the mass media are intrinsically interesting to us as language users and receivers. The linguistic means advertisers use to try and persuade us, the distinctive manner in which DJs speak, the way news stories are told: these are all interesting uses of language in their own right. How the media use language often seems larger than life, and research which just describes such uses has its own interest.

Secondly, as we have noted, media generate a lot of the language that is heard in society. This is reflected in frequent public comment about how the media use language. Criticism of the media's language use, and the presumed bad effects which those usages are having on everyday speech, are a commonplace of public debate – ironically, conducted in the media's own columns.

A third reason for looking at media language is that language is an essential part of the content of what the media purvey to us. That is, language is a tool and expression of media messages. Both the general public and researchers – to say nothing of the communicators themselves – concern themselves with the content of what is transmitted by the media and with the way in which language carries that content.

Fourth, media language offers the linguist advantages over face-to-face communication. In collecting data from ordinary conversation, one of the biggest problems faced by sociolinguistic researchers is Labov's 'Observer's Paradox' (1972a: 209): that we want to observe and record speakers talking the way they do when they are not being observed and recorded. In the media, this is a non-problem since media language is already intended for mass public consumption. The radio broadcaster is already doing all the necessary monitoring in order to cater to her public, and the fact that someone is recording her makes no change in her awareness of the way she speaks.

Another advantage is availability. Media language is easier to collect than conversation. It is also there in large quantities. The average newspaper may provide you with 100,000 or more words of text. The problem is not so much getting enough language to analyse but deciding how to restrict yourself to a manageable amount. Finally, media offer the potential for good quality recording of spoken language. Direct-line recording off radio or television means that recordings can be almost as good in quality as the originals, with none of the problems of interference, traffic, background television or children's noise which bedevil face-to-face recording.

In sum, assessing the range of research with which I am familiar, these seem to be the main reasons why researchers have studied media language:

- accessibility of media as a source of data for some language feature they want to study
- interest in some aspect of media language in its own right, such as headline language
- interest in the way the media use some language feature also found in ordinary speech
- taking advantage of how the media communication situation manipulates language in a revealing way, for instance in news copy editing
- interest in media's role in affecting language in wider society
- interest in what language reveals about the media's structure and values
- interest in what media language reveals as a mirror of the wider society and culture
- interest in how media language affects attitudes and opinions in society through the way it presents people and issues.

Some of the data and examples I use in this book are drawn from my own work, both as researcher and journalist, the rest are from other researchers. Most are from New Zealand and the United Kingdom, with a small proportion from Europe and the United States. Besides being the geographical areas I am most familiar with, these are also the ones where most research has been done and published. There is an imbalance here, with Asia, Africa and South America under-represented. The countries of the North dominate research on media as well as the production of media content, particularly through material in and on the English language. Writing from a country (Aotearoa/New Zealand) which lies socially and politically between the North and the South – a power in the South Pacific but an ex-colony of Europe – I regret the lack of alternative examples which means having to reproduce Western media dominance.

As well as being concerned with what makes media language tick in its own right, this book focuses on the light it can cast on two related questions: what do the patterns of media language tell us about language, and what do the patterns of media language tell us about news and media? That is, I am concerned to address central questions in linguistics and sociolinguistics, and central questions in mass communication research. Media language can tell us things both about media and about language.

These are some of the specific issues which researchers have addressed through their study of media language:

- What are the ideologies behind different television reports on a single event, particularly through the way the news actors are labelled (Davis and Walton 1983a)?
- What are the discourse structures of one story reported in 250 newspapers in a hundred countries (van Dijk 1988a)?
- What language styles are used on radio stations in New Zealand, and why do they differ from each other (Bell 1982a)?
- Is British television news coverage of industrial issues biased (Glasgow University Media Group 1980)?
- How acceptable is the standard of spoken English on BBC radio (Burchfield, Donoghue and Timothy 1979)?
- What linguistic resources does a presenter use to create a relationship with the audience (Coupland 1985, Montgomery 1988)?
- How do copy editors edit international news (Bell 1984a)?
- How well do people understand the same news story rewritten in different ways (Lutz and Wodak 1987)?
- How did broadcast language develop from the early days of radio (Leitner 1983e)?
- Has British news language become more American over the past 100 years (Bell 1985)?
- How do radio announcers manage to produce a stream of fault-free talk (Goffman 1981)?
- What is the conversational structure of news interviews on BBC radio (Jucker 1986)?
- How do newsworkers structure headlines and lead paragraphs (Kniffka 1980)?

2 MEDIA LANGUAGE RESEARCH AND THE DISCIPLINES

The study of media language has much to offer to the different disciplines on whose territory it touches, including linguistics, sociolinguistics, discourse analysis, semiotics, communication studies, sociology and social psychology. The principal questions within these disciplines can be illuminated by the study of media language, and that study can itself be illuminated by framing research questions from a variety of disciplinary traditions.

Sociolinguists have tended to regard media language as a second-class means of getting access to the real thing – conversational data (for example Labov 1972a: 211). I would suggest there are rather better reasons for turning to the media for language data. Mass communication provides a situation where data on certain (socio)linguistic issues can be found more readily, or phenomena observed more clearly, than in face-to-face communication. For instance, the way in which broadcasters shift their styles when they move from one station to another is crucial evidence in the issue of what causes style shift (Bell 1984b, and chapter 6 below). It indicates that style shift cannot be explained in terms of a mechanistic view of the amount of attention paid to speech (Labov 1972a).

In sociolinguistics there is also a phenomenon known as initiative or metaphorical style (Blom and Gumperz 1972, Bell 1984b). This occurs when a person adopts a style, or even a language, which is not just a response to the situation in which they find themselves but which actually redefines the situation as something different. This occurs, for example, when a speaker switches from local dialect to a prestigious national dialect in order to win an argument with a friend or family member. But data on such switches is very hard to collect, since by definition they occur rarely and in unexpected circumstances.

However, it turns out that broadcast advertisements provide a situation which matches closely the conditions that produce such style shifts (chapter 7 below): the need to influence the audience through language, and a short time to do it in. And advertisements are far more readily recorded. So broadcasting provides something of a laboratory instance of initiative shift, which simulates the conditions which produce it in face-to-face communication, and enables us to record it in adequate quantities from a readily available data source. In addition such a study provides a fascinating view of how language works in advertising and touches on concerns of the general public: what are the means which advertisers use to get at us?

To linguists, media language can provide data relevant to questions of theoretical importance. For instance, news stories are the common narratives of our time. Their discourse structure casts light on the way in which stories in general are told and structured (chapter 8). News production processes mean we can gain access to language on the production line as it is composed and edited by journalists and newsworkers. It illuminates the ways people compose and amend written discourse (chapter 4). The media can provide data for diachronic linguistics – the study of language change (chapter 7). In the print media we now have a precisely dated, large and consistent archive stretching back for several hundred years since the first recognizably modern newspapers were produced in Europe in the seventeenth century.

To the social psychologist, concerned with attitudes to language or the means by which individuals and groups interact with each other, the media offer a public data source, and their own field of study. The media carry many evidences of interaction between groups and the part language plays in this. They also carry explicit comment on language varieties and their acceptability in society. And they reveal in their own language usage the ways in which people can mould their language in order to cater to their different audiences (chapter 6). Concerns with intergroup relations and images which one group holds of another are well focused in the words media use to describe people and groups: are they 'terrorists' or 'freedom fighters' (chapter 9)?

To the sociologist of language, media are one of the main language-forming institutions in society, along with education and government. How does the use of language in the media affect groups in a society? Can the media contribute to a society's language planning goals? In the sociology of organizations, the issue of organizational control is neatly encapsulated in the ways in which media attempt to control how staff use language (chapter 3). And in the micro-sociology pioneered and practised so insightfully by Erving Goffman, we find a long study devoted to the language of radio presenters and what it can tell us about their self-presentation (Goffman 1981).

In communication studies, the study of media language is crucial to understanding the messages the media construct (chapters 8 and 9). The field of semiotics and cultural analysis, and communication studies in general, has long concerned itself with the language in which such messages are framed as a clue to the underlying structures of meanings, often in a search for bias and stereotyping. Such analysis benefits from close application of linguistic analysis, and may in fact be either misleading or unconvincing if it approaches language with inadequate methods (chapter 10).

Sociolinguistics and communication studies share a historical interest in similar research questions. Early paradigms put forward by pioneers in the two fields are uncannily close. Basic issues of communications research were encapsulated by Harold Lasswell in 1948:

Who says what in which channel to whom with what effect? (Lasswell 1960: 117)

Compare this with a prescription for the sociolinguistic enterprise:

Who speaks what language to whom and when? (J. Fishman 1965: 67)

3 THEMES OF THE BOOK

This book is based in the concerns and frameworks of sociolinguistics and discourse analysis. It does not introduce students or scholars of mass communication to those disciplines. A number of good introductory texts on sociolinguistics exist for that purpose, although discourse analysis is not so well served.[1] I have, however, tried to keep technical linguistic detail to a minimum, and to explain it when it arises, so the book should be accessible to those without a background in linguistics.

On the other hand, the book does aim to introduce linguists to media research. For those linguists who wish to inform themselves more about mass communications, there are a number of introductions, overviews and collections of key papers in print.[2] While no adequate introduction to the study of news media language exists in English (although in German, see Burger 1984), there are several important collections of papers on media language: Davis and Walton (1983b), Leitner (1983b), Baetens Beardsmore (1984), van Dijk (1985a). Later chapters in this volume present much of this research.

Finally, thumbing through my own book, I want to draw out three themes which run through the volume: the importance of the processes which produce media language, the notion of the news story, and the role of the media audience. Media language is the product of multiple hands, and the processes by which it is moulded and modified are both crucial and enlightening for an understanding of the eventual news text, its form and its content. This theme occupies us in chapters 3, 4 and 10. The idea of the story is central to news. Newsworkers – journalists, copy editors, and others directly involved in production – do not write articles. They write stories – with structure, order, viewpoint and values. The story, its generation, conventions and ideology, are our subject in chapters 4, 8, 9 and 10. Lastly there is the audience, whose role in news language seems peculiarly ambivalent. While apparently passive receivers of material determined by producers, audience members bring the power of their own choices, understandings and preconceptions to media reception. The nature of the audience, their role in influencing media language styles, and their comprehension of media content are the theme of chapters 5, 6, 7 and 11.

2

Researching Media Language

Good research on media language requires some familiarity with three things:

- language and how to analyse it
- media and research on media
- the specific media under study and their output.

Many small-scale and student research projects make use of media language data. The reasons are obvious: the media provide data which are good in quality, adequate in quantity, comparatively easy to access, and not modified by an observer effect. But media language research is littered with examples of flawed methods or mistaken conclusions which arose simply because the researchers did not acquaint themselves either with the basics of media, or with linguistic analysis, or with the media they were about to study.

In this chapter I background the structures, operations and content of the media as a prelude to the discussion of media language. I do this by looking at methods of conducting research on media language, particularly the decisions required to gather an actual sample or corpus of data. The chapter thus serves primarily as an introduction – but also as a guide – to how media language research is conducted.

News media form a kind of speech community producing their own variety of language, and the first rule of studying a speech community also applies here: get to know it. Direct, personal observation of media production processes is valuable, but a lot can be learned by close acquaintance with media output. The sociologist Erving

Goffman's long, perceptive essay on radio language (1981) was the fruit of close listening to radio output.

Availability is one of the attractions of media as a linguistic data source, especially for projects with severe time limitations. Buying a newspaper or recording a radio station are easier than many other kinds of linguistic fieldwork, which may require face-to-face interviewing in often difficult circumstances (Labov 1984, Milroy 1987). But the apparently easy accessibility of media language is deceptive. The obstacles to collecting media language may be different from those of recording face to face, but they are nonetheless real obstacles.

1 UNIVERSE AND SAMPLE

Any research beyond a small-scale glance at a couple of media texts means defining the kind of media language one wants to study and how it will be collected. This involves two steps: making a clear and consistent delineation of exactly what is to be collected, and limiting the amount of data to be gathered to manageable proportions while ensuring it remains representative. The first step defines the universe of discourse or the population, and the second draws a valid and reliable sample of that universe. Strictly speaking, defining the universe precedes any sampling, but in practice there is a to-and-fro between the two steps as you become more familiar with what you are working on, especially with the volumes of data which certain decisions will produce. This book draws on data from many other researchers as well as my own. The following list shows the kind of samples they used to gather the data, ranging from recordings of many months of broadcast news, or stories from a hundred different countries, to just a single news clip or radio programme:

Brunel 1970
    audio recordings of five French-language radio stations in Quebec, one on each day of the week
Glasgow University Media Group 1976, 1980
    video recordings of all 260 hours of television news broadcast in Britain throughout a five-month period
Bell 1977, 1982a
    35 hours of radio news, being a five-day, constructed week sample of all news broadcast in Auckland, together with additional recording of specific newsreaders

Burchfield, Donoghue and Timothy 1979
   extensive listening to BBC radio networks for a four-week period
Goffman 1981
   Erving Goffman's use of Kermit Schafer's lovingly gathered corpus
   of American radio 'bloopers', augmented by interviews, participant
   observation, 20 hours of recordings, and his own note-taking as
   a listener
Davis and Walton 1983a, 1983c
   video recordings of television news of a single event as reported in
   three different countries
Lerman 1983
   video recordings of commentaries on a Nixon Watergate speech,
   broadcast on the three United States television networks
Letiner 1983a
   audio recordings of three BBC radio phone-in programmes
Bell 1984a
   copy from local and international news agencies for a five-day constructed week
Hartley and Montgomery 1985
   four feature articles on the conditions of the poor in England,
   published between 1860 and 1931
Coupland 1985, Selting 1985, Montgomery 1988
   recordings of individual radio programme presenters in Wales,
   Germany and England
Jucker 1986
   seven hours of interviews extracted from BBC Radio 4 programmes
Corbett and Ahmad 1986
   a 93-day sample of editorials in one Melbourne newspaper
Bell 1988
   a constructed week in each decade from 1920 to 1980 of the London *Daily Mirror*
van Dijk 1988a
   clips of one story reported in 250 newspapers in a hundred countries
van Dijk 1988b
   several days' sample of six national and two regional Dutch newspapers, national news agency copy, and source materials
Bell 1989
   six months of news on climate change published or broadcast in
   New Zealand.

In sample design, language researchers can take advantage of the
long history of sampling media production in one tradition of com-

munication research – content analysis. The field of quantitative content analysis developed a range of sample designs in its heyday between the 1930s and 1960s. Leaving aside limitations of content analysis itself as an approach, the sampling methodologies developed are precisely of the kind needed for linguistic purposes, because they aim to control for the principal sources of fluctuation in media output. There are several standard surveys of content analysis and its techniques, including Holsti (1968, 1969), Danielson (1963) and Krippendorff (1980). The field has progressed little in the past 20 years, and Budd, Thorp and Donohew (1967) remains probably the clearest brief introduction, including a good chapter on sampling (and a 300-item annotated bibliography).

A sample must cope adequately with non-random fluctuations within the population, but not burden the researcher with a corpus of millions of words. In practice one often wants to satisfy a number of not quite compatible aims. In 1974 I designed and recorded a random sample of radio news in Auckland (Bell 1977, 1982a). It needed to be large enough to catch the stations' regular newsreaders, and to record one continuous week risked missing some them. But that played off against another requirement: collecting a sufficient amount of language from individual newsreaders. If I recorded non-continuous sample days, there was a risk of not gathering enough from the individuals. This problem is typical of those that come up in media sampling. I decided to gather a random sample of all news and record additional data from specific newsreaders.

Decisions on gathering a corpus of media language are required in three main areas: genres, outlets and outputs.

1   The genres are the particular kind of media content in which you are interested – news, classified advertising, game shows, weather forecasts, and so forth.
2   The media outlets are the publications, television channels or radio stations which carry the content.
3   'Outputs' are what the media outlets produce – specific newscasts, advertisements or programmes – and the time period to be covered.

2 WHAT'S NEWS: DEFINING GENRES

Study of media language usually begins with an interest in the language of a specific genre – in how a particular kind of news is reported, how headlines differ from other language, how advertising seeks to persuade. Media content includes many genres, most of which have a language component: news, letters to the editor, display advertising, documentaries, soap operas, music, sports commentary. Of course, not all genres can occur in all media – the press cannot print phone-in programmes nor can the radio broadcast cartoons.

Two genres are common to all the primary media of mass communication – news and advertising. These have also been the focus of most research on media and on media language. Nearly all daily media carry news – hence their collective label of 'news media'. Most carry advertising. The absence of advertising in some public service broadcasting, for example BBC radio and television and the Public Broadcasting Service in the United States, is an exception. However, even PBS stations devote a significant proportion of their airtime to crediting sponsors and to regular, lengthy fund-raising drives.

Press advertising divides into two categories: the familiar small-print columns of classifieds, and display advertising scattered throughout the news pages and designed to attract the reader. Broadcast advertisements come in chunks of sound ranging from 5 to 120 seconds long. They may be gathered into 'commercial breaks', as in television, or dropped singly into the flow of radio programming.

In a newspaper, everything other than advertising is called 'editorial'. [1] Most editorial content is written 'copy'. Some is visual, but may have a subsidiary language component (cartoons, graphs). We can divide editorial copy into three broad categories: service information, opinion and news. Service information consists of lists rather than continuous copy: sports results, television programmes, share prices, weather forecasts. It is often associated with specialist sections such as sports or business pages.

Opinion copy includes what are often called 'editorials' or 'leaders' – a statement of the newspaper's own views on an issue, usually appearing on an inside page under a reduced banner of the paper's 'masthead'. Most of the remaining opinion copy is regular contributed columns, letters to the editor and reviews. By journalistic tradition, opinion and news reporting are supposed to be kept separate. Opinion copy is usually flagged by devices such as a standard heading or 'mugshot' above a columnist's copy, and 'bylining' with the writer's name. Although numerous media researchers have shown that fact and opinion are by no means easy to separate, this has made little difference to how newsworkers perceive – or newspapers present – these categories.

Types of press news

For language analysis, I divide the genre of press news into four categories, which are generally the categories newsworkers themselves use under various labels:

- hard news
- feature articles
- special-topic news, e.g. sports, racing, business/financial, arts, agriculture, computers
- headlines, crossheads or subheadings, bylines, photo captions.

Newsworkers' basic distinction is between hard news and features. Hard news is their staple product: reports of accidents, conflicts, crimes, announcements, discoveries and other events which have occurred or come to light since the previous issue of their paper or programme. The one-off, unscheduled events such as fires and disasters are sometimes called 'spot news'. The opposite to hard news is 'soft' news, which is not time-bound to immediacy. Features are the most obvious case of soft news. These are longer 'articles' rather than 'stories' covering immediate events. They provide background, sometimes 'editorialize' (carry the writer's personal opinions), and are usually bylined with the writer's name. A newspaper's feature articles may be gathered together on feature pages, often together with opinion material. Features are often produced by a different group of journalists from those who write the day-by-day hard news. A lot of newspapers acquire their features from outside services provided by news agencies or major newspapers like *The Times* of London, and the *Washington Post/Los Angeles Times* service.

For both newsworkers and researchers, the boundaries between hard and soft news are unclear (see the insightful discussion in Tuchman 1978: 47). Indeed, journalists spend much of their energy trying to find an angle which will present what is essentially soft news in hard news terms. Journalists and media researchers both recognize hard news as the core news product, the typical against which other copy will be measured. Hard news is also the place where a distinctive news style will be found if anywhere. In features, journalists are allowed more liberty of style, and many features are written by non-journalists. Research problems can arise when language users' own basic categories are overlooked. The million-word Brown corpus of American English and Lancaster-Oslo-Bergen (LOB) corpus of British English appear to make no distinction between hard news and features, treating all news as 'reportage'. Burger notes (1984) that the German 'boulevard press' deliberately blurs the boundary of soft and hard news in its reporting.

My third category, special-topic news, normally appears in sections of the paper explicitly flagged for their subject matter. Such pages are generally produced by separate groups of specialist journalists under the control of their own editor, such as the business or sports editor. In research I always distinguish special-topic news such as sports or financial from general news. Many newspapers allocate news to pages according to its geographical origin – for example, local, national, international. I treat these as simple divisions of general news. And because politics is so much the dominant topic of general news, I count pages flagged as 'political' in with general news.

The fourth category is a miscellaneous or residual one which cuts across the first three. The 'body copy' – the main text of a story or feature – is classified in the first three categories. The adjuncts to it are headlines, crossheads (subheadings within a story), writers' names or bylines, and captions to photographs. All these are usually visually distinct, set in different typefaces or sizes to the body copy.[2]

Broadcast news

News and advertising make up the great majority of press content, but they occupy a small proportion of broadcast airtime. In television and radio, staple news consists of a number of short items of hard news gathered into a bulletin usually three to five minutes long. In addition, once or more each day, many stations broadcast news pro- grammes, between 15 minutes and two hours long. These combine short news items with longer, 'softer' backgrounders, interviews and the like, plus weather forecasts and other material. Broadcasting's equivalent of the feature is current or public affairs (commentary and documentary are more akin to opinion material). While the core of broadcast hard news tends to be gathered into short bulletins, the boundary between current affairs and news is a grey one, particularly for the audience.

Different sections of what listeners hear as a single, seamless news programme may in practice be compiled by two editorially indepen- dent sections of the broadcasting organization. A programme such as BBC Radio 4's *World at One* lunchtime programme carries bulletins originated by News personnel, while the surrounding, magazine-like material originates with Current Affairs. There is little liaison between the two groups and they are usually unaware of the specifics of what the other may cover in any given programme – this at least was the case at the time of Schlesinger's excellent study (1987: 248) of BBC news production in the mid-1970s.

Broadcasting like the press carries separate special-topic news, particularly on sport. But major sports or business stories may feature in the general broadcast bulletins, just as they do in the general pages of the newspaper. When these stories appear along with general news, I classify them as such.

Different media have different ratios of advertising to editorial copy. In some newspapers news makes up a majority of the content, but more often advertising predominates. News can occupy a surprisingly small proportion of some newspapers, for example in the blockbuster Sunday editions of American papers. With broadcast media the news always occupies a small proportion of airtime. In the Auckland radio project mentioned above (Bell 1977), news took up less than 7 per cent of all broadcast hours – an average of only four minutes per hour across the day. On television, the proportion is probably even lower. Yet news is regarded by both audiences and media personnel as significant far beyond this rather small amount of time (Wright and Hosman 1986).

Just as we distinguish body copy from headlines and other copy categories in the press, so some of the material which occurs in broadcast news must be separated out as potentially different. This includes the commercials which often interrupt news bulletins or programmes, opening or closing words, headlines, and weather forecasts. Even within the structure of a story, a variety of different material occurs other than that read by the newscaster. These 'injects' are of several kinds – voice reports from journalists, interviews with newsmakers, recorded public speeches, on-the-spot sound or film. These would be excluded if you were studying the core of scripted news as produced by the anchor person of a news programme or bulletin.

Where news copy comes from

One criterion which is rarely worth trying to apply is that of gathering only news which is written by the particular outlets under study. Most news outlets carry far more news originated by other organizations than by their own journalists. Almost all international news derives from the 'Big Four' news agencies: Reuters, Associated Press, United Press International and Agence France Presse. Domestic news from beyond an outlet's immediate geographical area comes mainly from internal news agencies such as the Press Association in the United

Kingdom or New Zealand, and the Associated Press in the United States. Even if it is not explicitly credited to an outside agency, any out-of-town news is unlikely to have been produced by an outlet's own staff. More complicated still, many stories ostensibly written by local journalists, and even bylined to them, consist largely of material they have rewritten (often only lightly) from press releases issued by newsmaking organizations. A large proportion of news which appears to be produced by local reporters is primarily the work of press officers working for companies, government departments or other organizations.[3] It is in practice virtually impossible to identify accurately which copy has been originated by a local newspaper or broadcast station. The only way to gather an assured sample of local journalists' production would be to undertake continuous detailed participant observation in the newsroom.

Genre is largely a matter of defining what kind of copy does and does not qualify as what you are looking for. A researcher may wish to look only at certain subgenres such as 'spot' news, features or headlines, or at certain topics such as industrial, economic or international news, or take only the front page. Defining what stories are about a particular topic provides its own set of questions. Even 'front page news' is not as straightforward as it seems in those countries, such as the United States, where the practice is to start stories on page one and continue them on later pages.

Once the limits of the target genre have been defined, the sheer amount of material available may mean one needs to sample only part of what has been identified. With news stories, a sample can be selected by methods such as picking all stories on certain page numbers, or by numbering stories within an issue or bulletin and selecting every nth story or using a table of random numbers to select stories at random.

3 NEWS OUTLETS

Once the genre under study has been clearly defined, the researcher considers what outlets – publications or broadcast stations – to look at. Consistently defining the differences between daily newspapers, weekly papers, news magazines, weekly magazines, and so on is not always easy. But here the sheer amount of media language available can come to the rescue. Unless one is aiming at complete coverage which requires assigning a classification to everything, it is enough to stick to the outlets which clearly qualify and leave the marginals aside altogether. There will still be plenty of language data for the research purpose.

Outlets are often selected at the outset of a study by the researcher's own interests. Typical criteria for what outlets one chooses are:

- geographical area, e.g. all radio stations broadcasting in a particular city
- audience type or size, e.g. daily newspapers with elite readerships, or with the high circulations
- time of day, e.g. morning newspapers, or evening television newscasts.

Often all these criteria would be used, as in a sample of all nationally distributed morning dailies with circulations over 500,000. Knowing something of the media one wants to work on is necessary, especially if a study covers countries other than one's own. It is particularly important to compare like with like and not, for example, to treat (as I have heard done) the British *Guardian* newspaper as equivalent to the United States communist paper *The Worker*. The *Guardian* is simply a phenomenon inconceivable in the current American political scene – a left-leaning national prestige daily.

Gathering historical media language data presents particular problems for continuity. Mergers and closures are a normal part of the press scene, but they make life difficult for the researcher trying to decide what publication in 1900 was equivalent to a particular title today. When I wanted to do historical analysis of language in the British popular press, I found the only tabloid with continuous publication, name and content since 1900 was the *Daily Mirror*. In the United States, the paper best described as the *New York Journal-American* had eight name changes in 15 years as it combined and recombined with other titles at the end of last century.

An example illustrates some of the complexities of defining outlets for even a medium-scale sample of media language. In 1987 a group of Wellington linguists decided to collect a random sample of press language as part of a general corpus of New Zealand English. We identified seven classes of publications which might be included in 'the press':

1 Metropolitan daily newspapers – nine of them, with circulations from the *New Zealand Herald*'s 240,000 to the *National Business Review* (10,500). The metropolitans are those papers published

in New Zealand's four main cities (Auckland, Wellington, Christchurch, Dunedin).

2 Provincial dailies – about 25 titles, ranging from substantial news-papers serving secondary cities to local rags with circulations below 3000.

3 Four high-circulation national weekly papers.

4 Newspapers serving small rural communities, published anywhere between three times a week and once a month.

5 The (sub)urban giveaways, some with high circulations and readership and published up to three times per week. (Circulation is the number of copies which a publication sells, readership is the number of people who read the publication – usually several for each copy sold).

6 Specialist papers (some published weekly) for particular interest groups or communities, such as university, religious and farming papers.

7 National magazines, such as the *New Zealand Listener* and *New Zealand Woman's Weekly*, which have high weekly circulations. While there are arguments for including these in a press sample, their page size, design and stapled format set them apart from the newspapers.

This list is not exhaustive, but similar classes of publications with claims to be regarded as news media exist in most countries. We faced several decisions. Should we include only daily newspapers, or also the several national weeklies whose editorial content, like that of Sunday papers the world over, tends to differ from the dailies? We decided to include both dailies and weeklies, but as separate categories, even though two of the weeklies are Sunday editions of daily papers. All the other categories above we excluded from the random press sample – but some we decided to collect as separate subsidiary categories in their own right.

Even with the population restricted to only the metropolitan and provincial dailies and the national weeklies, decisions still remained. One provincial, the *Wanganui Herald*, closed during the period we were looking at. Should it be included, omitted, or counted for the time it was published, thus complicating the way the sample was drawn? We omitted it altogether. In New Zealand, daily newspapers generally publish six days a week – but several do not put out Saturday editions. The *Marlborough Express* publishes only an advertising giveaway on Saturdays: we excluded it. The *Auckland Star* publishes the *Sunday Star* but no Saturday edition. Should that be included as a weekly in its own right, or as the weekend edition of the daily? We classed it as a separate weekly. And then there is the *Dominion Sunday Times*, now editorially a Sunday edition of Wellington's morning daily *The Dominion* and no longer the separate weekly paper, the *New Zealand Times*. Again, we decided to treat it as a weekly under its own title.

Most countries have their conventional subdivisions of the press. Where in New Zealand the daily press is divided between metropolitans and provincials, in the United Kingdom the split is between national and regional titles, for both daily and weekly press. The dozen or so national dailies dominate the British press in a way paralleled in few other countries. Most nations lack a true national daily press because of the difficulties of nationwide distribution. But technological advances, with transmission of made-up final pages to distant presses, have made a national newspaper possible even in a territory as vast as the United States – *USA Today*.

A further subdivision – particularly strong in Britain but acknowledged in many other countries – is between the 'quality' and 'popular' press (although 'quantity' versus 'quality', or 'popular' versus 'unpopular' might be less loaded terms). This groups newspapers such as the *Guardian*, *New York Times*, *Le Monde* and the *Frankfurter Allgemeine* versus the rest. The distinction generally reflects a somewhat different definition of what is news, different visual impact and typographical means. The elite press tends to use the larger broadsheet (A2) page, while popular papers print on tabloid size (A3) – and are often called 'tabloids'. The prestige press is regularly singled out for research, sometimes for international comparison (for example, Pool, Lasswell and Lerner 1970, Peterson 1981, Sparks and Campbell 1987).

Production versus reception

Establishing which outlets to gather news from requires a decision in principle between a receiver-oriented and sender-oriented definition. This has two aspects, the first of which was mentioned above: whether to collect only what is *generated* in your particular area, or all the news which is *received* there. In most places, a majority of media content originates elsewhere. Many publications and broadcast networks have national distribution, which means they are originated in one place and disseminated to many others. The BBC's four radio networks are heard throughout Britain, although they originate in London. Auckland radio at the time of my 1974 sample had six stations broadcasting from transmitters within the urban area. But nearly half the news originated from Wellington, the capital city and head-quarters of Radio New Zealand. From the audience's viewpoint, even the BBC World Service – today still rebroadcast live on Radio New Zealand's highbrow Concert Programme – is part of the news in Auckland. But from the sender's viewpoint, it is a British outlet.

The network situation is paralleled in many countries. In the United States, this means including network television newscasts originated on the East Coast as part of the news received in other states and time zones. Externally originated content is thus very common, and often the major media received in an area are located elsewhere. Such material is also usually not identified by audiences as different from locally originated material. For research purposes I generally count the major outlets received in a particular place rather than just those originating there – while taking note of the potential difference of those that originate elsewhere.

The second aspect of the production/reception issue is deciding whether to treat each outlet equally or to weight them by audience size. If each is represented equally, it is on the grounds that each is a separate producer of language. If outlets are weighted according to their audiences, the number of receivers is treated as the impor-tant factor in selection. The Auckland radio sample combined pro-duction and reception criteria. All stations contributed equally, that is, all the news they broadcast was part of the universe of discourse. There was no attempt at weighting what was sampled according to audience size or prestige by, for example, taking ten bulletins from a station with 100,000 in its audience but only one from a station with a 10,000 audience. On the other hand, all and any news the stations carried was counted, regardless of whether it was produced in Auckland, Wellington or London: a reception-based criterion. In the New Zealand press sample, publications were weighted according to their circulation. The NZ Herald therefore had over 80 more chances of being selected than the Dannevirke Evening News (circula-tion 2800).

The mix of production or reception-based criteria differs for dif-ferent sampling purposes. Knowledge of the media and the com-munity's use of them is essential to making the decisions. And a dash of common sense rejects, for instance, BBC World Service news as part of the universe of New Zealand English news language. But the fact that it is rebroadcast through local stations says something about cultural and linguistic attitudes in New Zealand (Bell 1982b). Often in fact one finds oneself sampling almost automatically according to reception criteria, without realizing that in sociolinguistic terms this is rather unusual.

Most countries have a published guide listing all newspapers, usually giving their circulations, whether morning or evening, and other information. Audience figures are usually readily obtainable. In the United Kingdom the Audit Bureau of Circulations (ABC) publishes quarterly newspaper sales figures. The New Zealand ABC produces annual audited circulations. In Britain there is also the Joint Industry Committee for National Readership Surveys (JICNARS) which publishes readership (as opposed to circulation) figures with some demographic breakdowns. In most countries there are also commercial organizations whose business is counting and analysing broadcast audiences. They are often prepared to make their findings available to bona fide researchers.

4 NEWS OUTPUTS

News output is the actual product of a news organization, the issues of a newspaper or bulletins of broadcast news. Decisions are needed on three questions: the time period the sample will cover, the days to be sampled within that period, and the specific issues or bulletins to be sampled within those days. Deciding on the time period is part of defining the universe to which a sample strictly applies. If the research aims to study radio news for a particular year, strictly speaking the universe to be sampled will probably be several weeks of that year. The period sampled should probably be shorter than at first intended rather than longer. The tendency with media language is to collect too much not too little, and so run the risk of drowning in data. Before finalizing the time period, it is wise to check on the accessibility of the material you want to gather. Archive collections of newspapers, even from the present and recent past, are usually not as complete as they are supposed to be.

Over any time period there are regular variations in media content which affect both deciding on the period and sampling within it. Seasonal variations such as school or other holidays must be considered. The amount of political news varies greatly depending on whether a nation's governing assemblies are in session or not. And major events, whether expected such as an election or unscheduled such as a disaster, can skew the content of news for days or even weeks on end. Different kinds of content are carried on different days of the week, reflecting weekly cycles of activity. A Monday newspaper contains little government news but a lot of sports. Weekend outputs usually differ from weekdays. The Sunday editions of daily newspapers tend to carry a different type of editorial content from the weekday editions. In broadcasting, the number and length of news bulletins are drastically reduced at weekends and their content changes markedly. In New Zealand, news broadcasts during weekends – and throughout the December–January summer holiday – often contain little more than a catalogue of accidents and sports results.

Once the time period is set, the next step is to decide on sampling days within it. Content analysis researchers have tested the reliability of different sizes and designs of samples across different time periods. To represent a month of news, samples consisting of every second day (that is, a total sample of 15 days) and every fifth day (a total of 6 days) provided content proportions similar to those of the entire month (Mintz 1949). Samples which took every tenth day (a total of three days out of the month) were inadequate, as were those consisting of a week of consecutive days. In testing samples to represent a full year of news copy, those of 6, 12, 18, 24 and 48 days of a year were all adequate (Stempel 1952). Samples larger than 12 days provided little additional reliability. A frequent sampling pattern is to take every nth day of a given period. Such samples of non-consecutive days have been demonstrated as reliable provided that n is not equal to 7, which would repeat the same weekday (Davis and Turner 1951). Again, consecutive weekdays were found to over-represent certain kinds of content.

A commonly used design, with the appeal of elegance, is the constructed week, which I adopted for the Auckland radio sample. First developed by Jones and Carter (1959), the technique involves selecting days by a random process from several weeks to make up a composite week of days from five (for a Monday to Friday universe) or six (Monday–Saturday) different weeks.

The final decision on news output involves the different editions of a daily newspaper, and the multiple bulletins of broadcast news. Most larger dailies publish two or more editions a day, and the changes from one to the next can be both major and non-random. In New Zealand, the early editions of metropolitan morning dailies circulate to country areas, and therefore carry some agricultural news which is dropped from the later edition. Again, familiarity with the media one wants to study is essential to making the right decisions. With broadcast media, a researcher may decide to collect only the principal news programmes of the day, such as British ITN's *News at Ten* or

NBC's *Nightly News* in the United States rather than all the lesser bulletins.

Radio – and to a lesser extent television – presents a problem which does not arise with the press once a specific edition has been selected: the question of repeated news items. When news is being broadcast every half-hour, as it tends to be on breakfast shows, many items are repeated in successive bulletins on the assumption that the audience is passing through in segments of about 45 minutes. In the Auckland radio sample, items were commonly repeated – verbatim – four or more times between 6 and 9 a.m. To include identical or almost identical repeats of a news item would unduly bias the quantitative analysis of some linguistic features if an unusual form happened to occur in a repeated item. So in that study, only the first occurrence of an item was included, which eliminated no less than a third of the total sample. This together with other exclusions such as headlines, interviews and the like, cut the 35-hour sample of five days of radio news by more than half to 17 hours – about 180,000 words. Even within that, for some purposes it was necessary to cut down the total amount by sampling only certain bulletins.

Allowing for non-random fluctuations between bulletins within the day needs a feel for how news varies as well as an acquaintance with the local news scene. The time of day when deadlines fall affects the kind of news carried. New Zealand, for example, wakes up about the time the major news-creating nations of Europe and North America finish their working days. News bulletins on morning radio thus contain a higher proportion of international news than at other times.

By a process of inclusion and elimination of genres, outlets and outputs, the universe for the Auckland radio news project was defined as:

> All scheduled, general-topic, hard news radio bulletins broadcast by Auckland stations between 6.00 a.m. and 12.00 midnight, Mondays to Fridays, for a five-week period in 1974.

Within that period, I drew a constructed week sample. It is interesting to compare such a sample with the data on which sociolinguistic research has been founded in the last two decades. The major foundation studies in sociolinguistics (for example, Labov 1966, Trudgill 1974) were based on drawing a random sample of speakers and recording them in interview. With media language we can proceed one step further and design a sample of the media's actual language output. We sample the speech rather than the speakers.

Large-scale random samples laid a foundation on which later sociolinguistic studies – either by the same practitioners or others – built (cf. Labov 1984). In my own research, techniques developed and knowledge gained from the Auckland study have formed the basis of later more specific samples and studies. I have often returned to features which were noted in the Auckland study and used a quick non-random sample to collect more data on them. In this way I have gathered about 15 different 'samples of media language in as many years in New Zealand, the United Kingdom and United States. They range from the large random Auckland sample to direct off-air noting of specific, easily audible syntactic variables which occur no more than once or twice a minute.

5 PITFALLS, SHORTCUTS AND THE LONG WAY ROUND

One of the advantages of media language – its accessibility – is easy to squander. Collecting a local broadcast or press sample day by day is a straightforward business – *if* it is planned ahead. But obtaining newspapers from other locations or after publication date is at best time-consuming and often impracticable. Trying to obtain television or radio language after the broadcast time is usually impossible: most stations do not record their own output. The logistics of large-scale international sampling are shown in van Dijk's (1988a) project which gathered 250 newspapers from 99 countries – but still did not fill the designed sample.

Most media language samples are of the media's present production, which in practice means planning to gather material in the near future. For some purposes the commercial agencies which supply companies with clips of published stories in requested categories can be used. Such services are usually inexpensive compared with the real cost of doing it oneself to track a specific topic over a long period or in a lot of papers. But they need to be used with care if a sample depends on accurate, comprehensive clipping which catches everything in the categories you have requested. For one clipping survey I commissioned, I ran my own independent check: the agency had picked up only 65 per cent of the specified clips, largely nullifying the value of the survey.

Archives and access

An excellent resource, especially for the study of syntactic change, are the press archives maintained in many countries, such as the British

Library's newspaper collection at Colindale, North London. But the completeness of archive collections needs checking out before committing oneself to a particular project. The New Zealand press sample described above was planned in 1987–8 to cover the year 1986. We designed the methodology and drew by random numbers the actual newspapers and dates to be sampled – only to find that the copying facilities at the principal national archive were inadequate. A second archive was located but its collection of newspapers before May 1987 was incomplete. Adapting to this would have meant redefining the population and redrawing the sample, since some publications had been added and others closed in the interim. Eventually a 'full' 1986 archive was located in another city. A researcher travelled there only to find that the library's collection of daily newspapers was incomplete, lacking some titles from more distant areas, and copying had to be done by library staff with a knack for choosing something other than the requested material – invalid for a random sample. The gaps in the sample were ultimately filled by requesting the required issues and pages individually from the public library in each newspaper's place of publication. The sampling project took nearly two years to complete.

Broadcast news archives are more of a rarity than press archives. The Vanderbilt Television News Archive at Vanderbilt University, Nashville, Tennessee is notable for its 20 years of video recordings of television network news from CBS, NBC and ABC. Other archives of varying completeness exist in other countries, sometimes in unexpected places and with a surprising depth and breadth of coverage, but they are not always easy to locate. However, most archives are frustratingly elitist. In New Zealand the prestige British and American newspapers are all available, but despite their much greater circulations, none of the British 'popular' dailies are available either by purchase or in libraries. This is a pity, since the elite press tends to be linguistically conservative, and the popular press more innovative and in many ways more interesting to the sociolinguist. Similarly, broadcast archives have a tendency to record the prestige stations and ignore the popular stations which often draw most of the audience.

It is sometimes possible to draw on media data gathered by other researchers for different purposes. Unfortunately, such second hand samples seldom provide the material you really want and are rarely as easy to access or use as they seem. In the end, the amount of compromise needed and the little time saved tend to make it counterproductive. Another apparent shortcut which has cost researchers more time and trouble than it has saved is obtaining a newspaper's computer typesetting tapes. In theory this should provide a ready-keyed computer archive of all the newspaper's copy. In practice, the current state of software means the time spent acquiring tapes, stripping them of typesetting codes, translating them from the newspaper's computer format to your own, and checking them against the published copy may easily exceed the time that would be spent rekeying your own transcript direct into a computer.

Recording your own

In most countries, there are no copyright barriers to recording broadcast material for research purposes, but this needs checking out first. News organizations seem to be growing more wary of research uses, especially if there is a chance some of their material may end up being available to a wide group of researchers or publicly presented in some form. In the United States, I have had to seek permission to record certain televised news programmes, and that agreement was contingent on a guarantee to wipe the tapes after a certain number of months.

Recording broadcast material has its own problems not present in the face-to-face sociolinguistic interview. Excellent sound quality is possible by direct line between a good receiver and a good recorder. But broadcast schedules do not wait for researchers to set up their machinery, and it is easy to miss the start of a programme. The Auckland radio sample required extensive preliminary monitoring to make up a schedule of daily news bulletins on all stations (advertised schedules and actuality did not always coincide) and I had to familiarize myself with the kind of material which surrounded the news. On the five selected days, it required an operation of military precision from 6 a.m. to midnight recording simultaneous news bulletins sometimes at half-hourly intervals from up to six radio sets on to six tape recorders – plus a back-up running ready to be brought in if something failed. Despite all efforts, the start of a number of bulletins was missed. One whole bulletin went unrecorded for reasons which I never fathomed. The Glasgow University Media Group (1976: 48) fared worse. They lost over 5 per cent (some 16 hours) of the news scheduled for recording through operator error or equipment failure. In fact, they reduced their planned full-year sample of television news on the (then) three British channels to five months because the operation was too arduous and the amount of material too great.

Another false shortcut is to request recordings of broadcast material from the originating station. It is usually much less trouble to record it yourself. Stations normally do not make – let alone keep – recordings of their output. Attempting to assemble a sample of transmitted news on the basis of written scripts is also unsatisfactory. Although virtually all news in broadcast bulletins is scripted, these are hard to obtain, and what is read out *does* differ from what was scripted – sometimes in ways which are important to the analysis. It is far more efficient and less troublesome to record the material and then have it transcribed. In many places services exist which record news and sell the transcriptions to business and government clients. Such transcripts tend to be rather costly, and it is wise to verify their accuracy before basing a close analysis on them. Philo (1987) notes that there are important differences between the scripts of Britain's ITN for its own news broadcasts and what was actually said on air. He calls into question Harrison's critique (1985) of the Glasgow University Media Group's controversial analysis of ITN news (1976, 1980) because Harrison based his analysis on these discrepant transcripts.

On not drowning in data

In the course of sampling media language, researchers end up collecting a lot of material they do not want. With newspapers this does not matter much, since the unwanted material was easily collected and is easily culled. But with broadcasting, collecting and transcribing material is time-consuming. Even if one wants only a particular category of news such as industrial items, one has to record everything. In recording half an hour of a particular DJ' speech, you would probably find that she produces only a couple of minutes of speech per hour. Leaving a recorder running ensures not missing what was wanted, but it equally ensures there is a massive amount of material you don't want. The language has then to be edited out on to another tape, a process which is difficult and time-consuming without semi-professional facilities. At two minutes an hour, you record 15 hours of airtime to assemble a 30-minute sample, which will take another 30 to 40 hours to edit down. At that point the more risky alternative begins to look attractive: use the pause button and guess when the DJ is about to speak next.

Even when one collects only what was planned, it is easy to end up with a vast amount of data which never gets classified let alone analysed, and which was therefore a waste of time gathering in the first place. Careful advance planning based on familiarity with the output of the chosen outlets and a realistic assessment of time and resources is essential. The most pressing question is always how much language needs to be collected. The answer depends on what a project is trying to do. If you are wanting to draw general conclusions about, for example, the use of sexist language in a particular newspaper, your sample will need to be both large enough and representative enough to justify those conclusions. If you wish to make generalizations about features which might have occurred in your sample but did not, then you require a very large random sample which gave those features an adequate chance to show up. If you are interested in the way language reveals the media's values, close analysis of just a single text may be illuminating – but such concentration is not a shortcut. It presupposes that you are already familiar enough with a range of material to know that this one text is a particularly good and typical example. I needed six months of coverage (400 stories) about climate change for a sample on which to base generalizations about the accuracy of news and public comprehension of it (Bell 1989). Three months proved to be too short a time to allow for fluctuations in coverage of a single topic.

To look at a particular language feature, the amount of language needed is governed by how often the feature occurs. In the Auckland radio study, I analysed the consonant cluster variable, on which much research has been done before and since (summarized in Guy 1980). The variable occurred every three seconds, so the amount of speech needed for an adequate N was only a few minutes per reader. I also looked at negative contractions, by which *not* is reduced to *n't*. This variable occurred only once every two minutes – that is about twice per news bulletin. I had to scan almost my entire 17-hour sample to get the number of tokens I wanted for all stations.

News language has the advantage of coming in identifiable chunks which are usually short even in print. Radio news items range from about 10 to 60 seconds long, and average about 20 seconds. Television news items average over 60 seconds each. The way news is structured into stories provides researchers with a ready-made classification system which makes time-consuming transcription less needful as a preliminary to language analysis. Broadcast news occurs as short bulletins broken into a series of items, so it is comparatively easy to find your way around a sample. A classification card noting topic and duration of items within bulletins is adequate, with transcription only necessary for specific analyses.

6 THE MEDIA REACT TO RESEARCH

There is one feature of researching the media which still manages to surprise even experienced practitioners: the porcupine reaction of media personnel. The situation described by one of the American pioneers of mass communication studies, Paul Lazarsfeld (1948: 115), has changed little:

> If there is any one institutional disease to which the media of mass communication seem particularly subject, it is a nervous reaction to criticism. As a student of the mass media I have been continually struck and occasionally puzzled by this reaction, for it is the media themselves which so vigorously defend principles guaranteeing the right to criticize.

The irony of the professional social critics' inability to accept investigation and criticism themselves does not diminish its reality. Findings which I had thought were innocuous academic observations on language styles in New Zealand broadcast news have provoked hostility. Sometimes the reaction can be extreme enough to jeopardize the conduct or publication of research. A project on domestic news services in the United States, sponsored by the prestigious Twentieth Century Fund, was aborted because the Associated Press refused access to its offices and files (Twentieth Century Fund 1981). The rationale behind this was unclear, because AP cooperated fully with the Fund's companion study of international news services (Fenby 1986). In another case, British sociologist Tom Burns saw the findings of his participant observation study in the BBC embargoed for eight years (eventually published as Burns 1977). Van Dijk (1988b) met with suspicion from editors (but not reporters) to his request to research the input materials journalists used to write stories.

The best-known case in the United Kingdom is probably the BBC's reaction to the *Bad News* studies of the Glasgow University Media Group (for example 1976: 56, 1980: 418). Now, one can enjoy the poetic justice of the Group's using methods associated with some news media – surreptitious observation in the newsroom and hasty, superficial analyses – against the media themselves. Nevertheless, it is hard to avoid the conclusion that the Group brought a good deal of this on itself through lack of diplomacy and research skills in its early days. ITN has had a much less publicly heated relationship with researchers. This is largely because whereas the BBC has often been prepared to host or debate with researchers, ITN has generally kept the door

locked. Schlesinger (1980: 341) notes that his approach to do participant observation work in ITN was 'rebuffed with sneers and insults',
but that the BBC's attitude was cooperative until cooled by a number
of factors (including the advent of the Glasgow Group). Despite this
pattern, I must record that a project of mine on the accuracy of news
reporting (Bell 1989) – research apparently predestined to wound the
sensitivities of the media under study – was given a mainly positive
reception.

The likelihood of reaction should not drive media language researchers away, but rather forewarn us on how to approach media
organizations and present our research to them with care. A good
starting point for this is direct, personal observation in a media
organization. But a second reaction encountered by researchers, even
those who have worked inside a media organization, is indifference
to the findings and their implications (Robinson and Levy 1986).

There are two considerations which help explain if not justify media
hostility to research. First, the best outcome the media can hope for
from most research is to be damned with the faint praise that they are
doing the job they claim to be doing. A more likely result is that
research will return a negative verdict on some aspect of their work.
Secondly, newsworkers and researchers operate on very different time
scales. In a working world dominated by daily and hourly deadlines,
the pace of research and the arcane interests of researchers appear
irrelevant, even frivolous. In my own experience, the constant
demands of working in a daily news service left me so far removed
from my research interests that I did not even retain examples of news
copy which I recognized at the time as having research importance.
To newsworkers, the results of even a small, rapid project seem to
arrive so long after the event that they must have been outdated by
change. Newsworkers see that the specifics of the news change by the
minute and feel that any study which covers things as they were years
or even months before is by definition obsolete and irrelevant. As the
editor of BBC television news said in introducing a researcher to staff:
'This is a philosopher [sic] who's writing a book on news. It'll be
finished in about a hundred years' (Schlesinger 1980: 345).

But usually such change is on the surface. The essential content of
media alters very little, even though precise names, programmes or
owners are constantly changing. Usually there is no need for undue
concern that a study will be invalidated by organizational change or
the passage of time. Media workers see their organizations as in a state
of continual flux, with staff turnover, programmes cancelled or com-
menced, new editorial directions set. And so they are – but that

change is largely superficial, and the underlying principles and operations shift remarkably little. It is the norm for large media organizations to be constantly undergoing change. A glance at nearly 70 years of BBC history shows it has always been in flux, the target of criticism by politicians, its shape and even existence threatened, stumbling from one crisis to the next (Burns 1977, Schlesinger 1987). But only the most significant technological changes or severe restructuring is likely to have major effects on standard media practices and products. That being said, just such a change is underway or imminent in the electronic media of many countries in the 1990s. Technological advances and legislative deregulation are leading to more outlets and more competition which may well reshape broadcast genres and styles.

3

The Production of News Language

The news is seldom a solo performance. In most face-to-face interaction, language is produced by a single individual, the speaker. We are accustomed to regard this as the norm – that the person who actually speaks an utterance is also responsible for the thoughts expressed and the form of words used. But there are many instances where production of a stretch of language involves a dozen or more people with different roles.

News media offer the classic case of language produced by multiple parties. Journalists, editors, printers, newsreaders, sound technicians and camera operators are just some of the people who contribute to publication or broadcast of a news story. Specifying what distinct roles may be involved in language production has exercised scholars in a number of communication-related fields – ethnography (Hymes 1974), sociology (Goffman 1981), sociolinguistics (Platt and Platt 1975), pragmatics (Thomas 1986) and discourse analysis (Tannen 1988). Most have recognized media as a particularly illuminating site for analysis. The roles we require to describe media language production will probably suffice both to describe the production of other kinds of language and to distinguish the functions which in other circumstances may be united in one individual. Here we will bring together ethnographic and mass communication interests, and examine these roles in their own right as well as their significance in shaping media language.

The reception of media language is as fragmented as its production. Media audiences are large and multilayered, ranging from the interviewer whom a newsmaker addresses face to face, to the absentee mass audience, which itself consists of different segments. Further, some participants are both producers of and audience for media language. Camera operators simultaneously form part of the live audience to a television programme and function as producers essential to its broadcast.

The traditional model of communication involves a speaker/sender, a message and a hearer/receiver. Many theorists from different disciplines (for example, Hymes 1974, McQuail 1987) have rightly elaborated on that simple, two-person, one-directional model. To describe the complexities of what really happens in any communication, the roles of sender and receiver must be further subdivided and made more precise (for example, Goffman 1981). Communication also involves feedback and is thus a cyclical rather than purely linear process (Westley and MacLean 1957). But no matter how strenuously we modify the simple model, the roles of speaker and hearer remain basic to any description (Hymes 1974: 54, Goffman 1981: 129). I find it convenient, as have most people who theorize about communication, to focus on each in turn while recognizing their interdependence. These two chapters deal with the producers of media language, and in chapter 5 I turn to examine the audience.

1 MANY HANDS MAKE TIGHT WORK

Even in a small newsroom, copy – that is, the actual written news story – is handled by a number of individuals and may follow a complex and often cyclical route. Figure 3.1 diagrams the path of a typical story through the newsroom of the daily system with which I am most familiar – the New Zealand primary industries news service, Medialink. Medialink is a computerized system, so all writing and editing occurs on screen not on paper.[1] But hard copy is printed out at each stage because it is easier to scan and to keep track of. The story's path through this system would be:

1   A document lands on the chief reporter's desk. It is a report from the fisheries control body, which says the squid season in New Zealand's 200-mile zone is proving poor. The 100 Japanese and Korean vessels licensed to fish in the zone are leaving for more plentiful fishing grounds around the Falklands/Malvinas Islands in the south Atlantic. Millions of dollars in revenue from licence fees may be lost.

2   A journalist is assigned to the story by the chief reporter. The journalist scans the written report and digs out earlier stories for

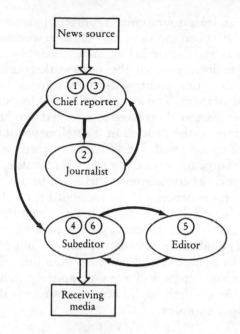

FIGURE 3.1   The path of a news story within a small newsroom: Medialink
primary industries news service, Wellington

background information. She telephones fisheries managers for
further detail and assessment, interviews industry sources for comment, then writes the story.
3 Chief reporter checks the story. If there are gaps, order problems
   or poor writing, he cycles it back to the journalist or makes minor
   changes himself.
4 Subeditor edits the copy – cutting, tightening, clarifying, reordering, and restyling writing which does not conform to Medialink
   style. Her close work on the actual copy may reveal further gaps
   or inconsistencies, which the subeditor refers back to journalist or
   chief reporter.
5 Editor gives story a final independent check, raising any questions
   with previous workers.
6 Subeditor transmits story from Medialink's computers to receiving
   teleprinters at media throughout New Zealand.

   The number of people who have handled the copy – and therefore
been in a position to modify the language – is by no means unusual.

Here we have at least four: chief reporter, journalist, subeditor, editor. While the subeditor does the main reworking, both chief reporter and editor regularly mark or make changes – usually minor, but sometimes major. Some of the newsworkers may make their inputs at more than one point, with copy moving back and forth between any two of them. The journalist handles her story up to four times if the other newsworkers have to refer back to her (steps 2–5). The cyclical nature of the process in a small newsroom where staff are constantly interacting makes it difficult to identify whose hand has produced which language forms. If a story is complex, requires more information, checking between newsworkers or back to sources, more parties come in on the process. If the journalist is careful and has the time, she may herself have gone through a number of versions, tightening and clarifying each time, before passing the copy to the chief reporter. The subeditor may do the same. While Medialink copy passes through more checks and balances than time allows in many daily news situations, steps 1–4 are a completely standard path for news to follow. As we shall see, in larger newsrooms the flow is correspondingly more complex.

2 PRODUCER ROLES IN NEWS LANGUAGE

The ethnographer/sociolinguist Dell Hymes (1974) distinguishes two roles played by the person we usually call *speaker*. There is the *sender*, who initiates, writes or modifies a stretch of language, and the *addressor* who actually speaks the words (table 3.1). This framework however proves too coarse for many situations particularly in the media, where a dozen individuals with quite different functions would be described as senders. The sociologist Erving Goffman (1974: 517) developed a finer distinction of roles as part of his 'frame analysis' of

TABLE 3.1: Roles in producing language

Hymes	Goffman	Bell
	⎧ Principal	Principal
Sender	⎨	
		⎧ Author
	⎩ Author	⎨ Editor
Addressor	Animator	Animator

interaction in everyday life. He eventually refined and defined three speaker roles, which effectively split Hymes's 'sender' into two (Goffman 1981: 144, cf. Levinson 1988):

- the *principal* or originator whose position or stance is expressed
- the *author* who generates the form in which the content is encoded
- the *animator*, the physical sounding box verbalizing the utterance.

Taken together, Goffman describes these as the *production format* of an utterance. The roles may be united in a single speaker in face-to-face conversation, but in other circumstances they may be divided (table 3.1). A government minister for instance may be the principal behind a public statement, her speech writer is author of the specific wording, and a spokesperson reading the text on her behalf is animator. In his paper on 'radio talk', Goffman (1981) turned his three-part division of roles to analysis of media communication and offers a more satisfactory description than Hymes.[2] Identifying the principal – the institutional voice – can be important to understanding the way in which newsworkers handle language (as we shall see in dealing with the ideological content of media, chapter 9).

Nevertheless, an adequate description of news language production requires us to divide Goffman's roles once more. Not all 'authors' play the same part. Most multiple-producer language is drafted in the first place by a single individual, who stands in a different relation to the text than those who modify this original draft. I therefore reserve 'author' for originators of a draft, and call those who modify it 'editors'. This gives us a basic four-part model, which should cover speaker (and more commonly, writer) roles in all situations, not just the media (table 3.1): principal, author, editor, animator.

Applied to the media, these roles are intended to identify the language function of newsworkers. They are not newsworkers' own labels for their jobs, or necessarily the best way to categorize them for other purposes, for instance as members of a complex organization or as 'gatekeepers' in the flow of news. However, media researchers have often identified a similar set of roles (for instance, Westley and MacLean 1957, Gans 1979: 83). This is not surprising, since decision-making about news content cannot be isolated from decisions about news language, or vice versa.

The number of language roles reflects the complex division of functions in news production which media researchers have long recognized. A number of excellent book-length studies in the United States and Britain have examined how news is generated, identified, gathered, selected and processed. The conclusion that news is not 'just the facts' but the product of organizational structures and professional practices is indicated in their titles: *News from Nowhere* (Epstein 1973), *Creating Reality* (Altheide 1974), *Making News* (Tuchman 1978), *Deciding What's News* (Gans 1979), *Manufacturing the News* (M. Fishman 1980), *Putting 'Reality' Together* (Schlesinger 1987).

My four-way division of roles above points to a division of responsibility for linguistic form as well as news content. Table 3.2 identifies roles and subroles in producing news (columns 1 and 2) – classifications which should be generally valid for other complex language production situations. The third column lists some of the job titles which the roles can carry in newsrooms, and column 4 indicates their language functions. Some titles are specific to press or broadcasting, either through usage or technology differences. Others are common to all media although the same title may denote different roles in different media. In general, I have used titles common in British and New Zealand rather than American practice. I use the overall term 'newsworkers' to describe all those who are regularly involved in overseeing, writing or editing news – centrally authors and editors, and on occasions professional principals (news executives) and animators. Table 3.2 presents only the roles as they operate within a single newsroom. We shall see below how these functions are duplicated at each step as stories pass from one news organization to another. The top-to-bottom ordering of table 3.2 also corresponds roughly to the hierarchy of command in news organizations (with the author/journalist as the main exception). In principle all the roles can be united in one person, in news production as in other situations. In large organizations the roles are in fact divided and subdivided, with titles multiplied to match.

Principals

The production of news presupposes two tiers of principals – the *business institution*, personified in proprietors and commercial managers, and the *news institution*, personified in professional news executives. Despite the convention of editorial independence from commercial interests, ultimate control lies not with news professionals but with owners whose interest is efficiency and profit.[3]

Of all producers, principals are the least directly involved in news language. In line with the conventional separation of commercial and editorial responsibility, proprietors in theory make no direct input to the specifics of news coverage or language. They do not see the copy,

TABLE 3.2 Roles in producing news language

Roles	Subroles	Newsroom position	Language function
Principal	Commercial: business institution	Proprietor Managers	No direct, overt language input
	Professional: news institution	Editorial executives	General language prescription, rare specific prescription
Author	Author	Journalist	Generates news language, responsible for original syntactic and discourse form
Editor	Overseer	Chief reporter (press) Chief subeditor (press) News editor (broadcast)	General and specific language prescription
	Copy editor	Subeditor Copy editor News editor (press)	Modifies language, responsible for its intermediate and final form
	Interpreter	News editor (press) Subeditor Duty editor (broadcast) Newsreader/newscaster	Responsible for prominence and presentation – order, headlines, links, visuals, graphological form, verbal interpretation
Animator	Transmitter	Newsreader Typesetter Proofreader Compositor	Responsible for accurate phonological/graphological transmission
	Technician	Printer Sound technician Camera operator	No language input Keeps channel open and noise-free

and have no stated role in prescribing their newsworkers' language. However, they do set the editorial policies which affect news language. A proprietor's definition of what will be treated as news and how it is to be reported has linguistic repercussions. Decisions on how certain individuals or groups should be labelled (for instance, references to the IRA in British media) may be made at the top levels of a news organization. More generally, the *Sun* and *The Times* of London have very different news styles although both are published by Rupert Murdoch's News International Group.

The second tier of control, news executives, go under a variety of titles such as editor, editor-in-chief, managing editor. They set general editorial policy but do not usually participate in the daily operation (although cf. Soloski 1989 on such editors' involvement). While they may not themselves regularly sight news copy before it is disseminated, they are nominally and legally responsible for the news output of their station or paper. Gans (1979: 94) discusses in detail the powerful but largely hands-off role of corporate and news executives in American national media.

News executives are the channel for implementing proprietors' policies, but also affect news language in two overt ways. Specifically, they may prescribe the ideological framing of news and its linguistic expression, such as who will be referred to as a 'terrorist' and who as a 'guerrilla' (Schlesinger 1987: 229). More generally, they also set routine guidelines for their journalists' language use. Leitner's research on the public broadcasting systems of the United Kingdom, Germany and Australia (1980, 1983e, 1984) is the leading account of language prescription by media.

Author

All news production focuses on an individual journalist writing copy. Journalists are the professionals whose daily occupation it is to produce news language. I distinguish this originating, usually sole author of a text from editors – those numerous others who operate on what an author has drafted. Authorship is seldom genuinely shared.

Journalists are authors, but they are not as original as may appear. Firstly, they are not the only people who generate news copy. In broadcasting, those who compile news bulletins may do much of the writing (Schlesinger 1987: 58). 'Star' television anchorpersons are normally entitled to write all or part of the copy they will read out (Gans 1979: 86). Material other than the 'body copy' (the continuous text of a news story) is usually generated by non-journalists: illustrations editors write captions to photographs, and subeditors write headlines. Nevertheless, the title 'journalist' labels those whose central job it is to write news. Others who undertake that task are at that time acting as author/journalist. Note also that, under pressure, the author and editor functions shown in table 3.2 are often redistributed. Late in the day at the Medialink news service, with copy piling up in the subeditor's tray, stories would regularly be subedited by the editor, chief reporter or even one of the journalists.

There is a second, more serious reservation about treating journalists as authors. My description of the journalist as sole originating author of stories is an extreme idealization. After all, the basic stuff of news is what people tell a reporter. Much of what a reporter writes is therefore paraphrased or quoted from what someone else said to him. That much is obvious, but journalists draw on written as well as spoken sources. Very few stories consist entirely of wording newly generated by the journalist from his own observation or verbal interview. Much news comprises updates and rewrites of previous stories. In some media *the* basic news-gathering practice is following up stories diaried ahead the last time they were covered. In addition, many stories contain material selected and reworked from documents generated by newsmakers or other media – reports, agendas, proceedings, transcripts, speech notes, news agency copy, newspaper clippings, press releases. Some stories are entirely cut-and-paste jobs from such sources.

The way in which journalists insert already existing text into their stories is only one example of a basic feature of media communication: embedding. Embedding incorporates one speech event into another (Goffman 1981). This happens most overtly in broadcasting, where recording technology enables actual strips of a newsmaker's speech to be embedded into a newscaster's or reporter's script instead of being quoted at second hand. Another layer of roles is needed to describe the part which newsmakers play in media communication, embedded within the format I am discussing here. There are even different layers of receivers – studio audiences as well as the mass broadcast audience. Such embedding has a profound effect on the nature of media discourse, which we will explore below.

The journalist is therefore as much a compiler as a creator of language, and a lot of the news consists of previously composed text reworked into new texts. This is, of course, a main means by which journalists meet the productivity demands of their employing media. A standard quota of stories ranges between four and ten per day. Generating that amount of fresh text is impossible, so generous adoption of old text is required. The smooth, unified surface of most news stories thus conceals a motley of origins. This complicates our approach to news language. It is not possible to treat any story as the solo, first hand product of the ostensible source journalist unless we have proven this by eye witness observation of the journalist at work. A newspaper byline is no guarantee of authorship in our sense. As a journalist distributing press releases to New Zealand newspapers, I regularly see stories which are 90 per cent my writing, bylined to a paper's own journalists.

When all that is said, however, the individual journalist remains the main channel where diverse sources converge into a single flow of copy. To mix the metaphor, the journalist gathers up scattered strands of information and weaves them into one text. Editors hold journalists responsible for wording they re-use as well as for what they have generated themselves. A journalist sanctions the form of language culled from other sources just by adopting it.

Editors

I distinguish three kinds of editorial function: overseeing, copy editing, and interpreting (table 3.2). These functions are differently distributed and labelled in different newsrooms, hence the proliferation of titles in this level of the table. Large newsrooms divide the work among numerous positions, while in small news operations a single individual may perform several functions. For our purposes, we overlook positions which have little direct impact on news language, for example the 'copytaster' who selects and rejects stories but does not alter their form, or the 'producer' who oversees on-air transmission.

The *overseers* are the hands-on editorial staff who run the day-by-day news operation. They go under a variety of working titles, usually chief reporter on a newspaper and news editor in broadcasting. In many media these overseers do not sight reporters' copy before it is transmitted or published. Their language role is confined to specific but retrospective critique of a reporter's writing, or input to general language prescriptions such as the newspaper's stylebook. In more careful newsrooms, journalists' copy goes to the chief reporter before moving on down the production line. The chief reporter will normally deal only with major gaps, reorderings or content problems.

Every story passes through the hands of a *copy editor* before publication or broadcast. This practice – occasionally neglected by smaller media – allows an independent eye to assess content and style, and spot problems the journalist-author may have missed. In New Zealand and the United Kingdom the position is called 'subeditor' – or just 'sub'. The activity is 'subbing'. A number of the other roles in table 3.2 – chief reporter, news editor, newsreader/newscaster, even the editor – may also perform copy editing functions in the process of doing their main job of allocating stories to pages or checking factual accuracy.

Just as it is the journalist's occupation to generate news language, the copy editor's profession is cutting and modifying that language. Not surprisingly, a state of war commonly exists between the two groups. Severe editing may result in a form of words virtually unrecognizable from the original. Retrospective complaints by journalists that their copy – particularly when it appears over their byline – has been subedited into nonsense or inaccuracy are commonplace in the newsroom.

The third editor subrole is that of the *interpreter*, responsible for the prominence a story receives and how it is displayed. Reporters do not compose headlines, decide on type sizes or order stories on the page or in a bulletin. These tasks are performed by subeditors in the press (often after the main decisions have been made by a news editor), and in broadcasting by duty editors (under a variety of titles). These persons hold prime responsibility for the manner in which stories are presented.

Broadcast newsreaders have a similar interpretive function and may give a story a particular 'reading' through linking material, comments, intonation or nonverbal cues. The way in which a story is framed and presented, particularly through headlines or visuals, can radically affect how it is understood (see Davis and Walton 1983a). But interpreters do not generally interfere with the main news text, the 'body copy', apart from cutting to fit available space or time.

Animators

Animators play the physical and technical roles necessary to communicate authors' stories to their audience (table 3.2). In broadcasting, the primary animator is the newsreader/newscaster, the *transmitter* (remembering that journalists or even newsmakers may voice parts of their own story). The newsreader is responsible for phonological form. She can intentionally affect the meaning of a story through linguistic or paralinguistic cues, or intrude unintentionally on a story's content by committing 'bloopers' (Goffman 1981).

Typesetters are the press equivalent of the newsreader. The typesetter – a dying breed in Western news production as computer technology promotes direct input by journalists – has the task of accurately keying in the print journalist's copy, just as the news-reader's primary role is to voice the broadcast journalist's copy accurately. Typesetters' only obvious effect on the form of news language is again by mistake – 'typos', lines dropped, paragraphs out of order. Their work passes unnoticed if they are doing the job properly.

The secondary animators are the *technicians* who operate the communicating technology – printers, sound persons, camera operators and the like. Their work is a necessary condition for communication to take place.

3 THE NEWS ASSEMBLY LINE

The processing of news involves the complex and rapid movement of copy among individuals within a newsroom. I have attempted above to abstract from the welter of newsroom positions the standard roles played in news language production and processing. We now turn to track the path of a story first through a local newsroom, and from there to newspapers on the other side of the world.

The local newsroom

At the beginning of this chapter we looked at how a story moved through the small-scale Medialink copy system. Figure 3.2 shows how roles are split and the number of participants increased in the newsroom of a moderate-sized daily – *The Dominion*, Wellington's morning newspaper, circulation about 70,000.[4] A typical story would move through this system thus:

1 The Medialink story on the bad squid season is received at *The Dominion*. The chief reporter – the 'overseer' – assigns a journalist to follow it up.
2 The journalist/author gets additional information and fresh quotes and rewrites the story.
3 The chief reporter checks it, and may make copy editing changes.
4 The news editor accepts the story for publication. As 'interpreter', he decides on its length, prominence and presentation, and allocates it to a page. In a copy editing function, he too may mark major changes such as reordering.
5 At peak news times, a news executive – the editor or a deputy –

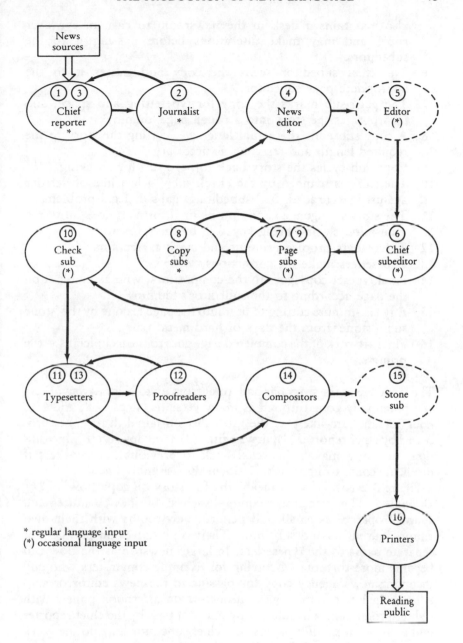

FIGURE 3.2   News processing on a local paper: *The Dominion*, Wellington's morning daily. Not all copy goes via editor or stone sub. Typesetters, readers and compositors now eliminated by journalists' direct inputting of copy

also maintains a desk in the newsroom to cast an eye over copy, and may make alterations before passing it to the subeditors.

6   The chief subeditor scans the copy and passes it to the appropriate page subeditor.

7   The page sub marks the copy for typesetting and space, and incorporates the story into a rough page 'dummy'.

8   A copy sub edits the actual language, cutting the story to the required length and restyling as necessary.

9   Copy sub cycles the story back to page sub for checking.

10 The story is scanned by the check sub – a last line of defence against inaccuracies, bad subediting, gaps or legal problems.

11 The story's language is now in its final form. It goes on to the 'transmitters', first being keyed in by the typesetters.

12 The readers proof a printout and mark corrections.

13 Typesetters make the corrections.

14 Final typeset copy goes to the compositors, who assemble it on the page according to the subeditor's 'dummy'.

15 Any last-minute cutting to fit it into the page is done by the 'stone sub' ('stone' from the days of hard metal type).

16 Final artwork of the completed page goes to the technicians – the printers.

The language in the story has had input from up to eight newsworkers and potentially gone through as many versions (steps 2–8, and 10). Four versions are likely as the journalist's original draft (2) is processed by chief reporter (3), news editor (4) and copy sub (8). In addition, the copy may be recycled back to previous newsworkers if problems come to light further down the assembly line.

Figure 3.2 is still by no means the full story on copy flow at *The Dominion*. The specialist sections – such as business, features and sports – operate as small, independent newsrooms with their own editor, journalists and subeditor. Their copy moves on parallel but separate paths to the typesetters. In larger newsrooms the flow can become more tortuous, involving for example copytasters who cull incoming news agency copy for passing to the news editor or subeditors. In less careful organizations, or on afternoon papers with tighter production schedules, copy may not pass by the chief reporter and editor. On smaller papers, the chief subeditor may do the work of the news editor, and other subeditor roles are combined.

International news flows

We have seen how a story is processed within two typical local newsrooms, the small Medialink system and the larger *Dominion* operation. While copy movement within a newsroom may seem complex enough, most news in fact weaves a much more intricate way to its consumers. News outlets publish more copy which has been generated by other, external news agencies than by their own in-house journalists. Each agency has its own copy handling system, at least as complex as Medialink's. The squid season story already mentioned has followed a typical path – first moving through the Medialink assembly line to finished product, then transmitted to *The Dominion* where it is treated as the raw material to be cycled through that paper's own complete news system. As source of the raw text on which *The Dominion* works, the Medialink production process is thus in a sense embedded within *The Dominion*'s own.

The news production system reveals its real complexities with international news. The average international news item published anywhere in the world has probably been through at least four separate newsrooms. It has passed across the desks (nowadays, through the computer terminals) of newsworkers at a news agency's regional bureau, the agency's central bureau, the national agency in the receiving country, and at the local news outlet itself. At each stage, copy is received, put through the newsroom's editing process and transmitted on to the next receiver, where the cycle is repeated. At each stage there are copy editors with the right to change the language.

The New Zealand Press Association is the national news agency through which news is exchanged among New Zealand's daily papers and fed out to the international agencies. Suppose NZPA receives the Medialink story about squid fisheries. It edits and transmits it to member newspapers throughout New Zealand and also judges that the Falklands/Malvinas angle will interest the United Kingdom and Argentina. The story sets out through the international wire system (figure 3.3):[5]

1 The Press Association receives the story in Wellington from the PA agent at *The Dominion*. The story is edited and transmitted to the Australian Associated Press-Reuter in Sydney, Australia, which serves as clearinghouse for both incoming international news and outgoing news of the region.

2 AAP Sydney selects, edits and transmits the story to the Reuters World Desk in London.

3   In London, the Reuters copytaster accepts it for local distribution. The copy is sent (untouched) to national press and broadcast media in London and to the United Kingdom Press Association, which edits for retransmission to British provincial dailies.
4   The copytaster also accepts the story for South America, and a copy editor reworks it for transmission.
5   In Buenos Aires, the copy is translated into Spanish and distributed throughout the continent.
6   *La Prensa*, the prestige Argentine daily, receives the story and processes it through the newsroom to publication.

The story has taken at least seven steps from its origin in Wellington to publication in Buenos Aires. At each step, two or more newsworkers have handled the copy, and the story has gone through between 10 and 20 versions. This is entirely typical of the path which copy follows through the national and international wire systems.

The wire systems are complex and difficult to get precise information on, so the detail of copy flow I have shown in figure 3.3 gets more speculative the further it moves from New Zealand, where I am writing. In my experience (Bell 1984a) newsworkers know only their own isolated sector of the system and offer quite misleading information about neighbouring sectors. Even the two main studies of the agencies and their operations (Boyd-Barrett 1980, Fenby 1986) did not attempt to trace the detailed flow of international news. Van Dijk's study (1988a) of global news coverage on a single day in 1982 examined how newspapers edited the Reuter wire story on the assassination of Lebanese President Amin Gemayel. However, he gained access only to the wire story and the final published copy, not the intermediate stages.

The flow of international news is massive as well as intricate. The Big Four news agencies – Reuters, Associated Press, United Press International, and Agence France Presse – provide a large majority of the world's news about itself. Their combined outputs are estimated at 33 million words a day (Righter 1978: 50). That figure, however, aggregates all the agencies' 'wires' (Reuters alone offers 30 different services), which provide different selections from the same pool of stories. About 2500 stories and half a million words per day is my own best guess of core international news volumes.

Despite the size of their operations and the importance of what they carry, the international news systems are operated by a handful of people at each point. Even at major gates in the system, copy is at

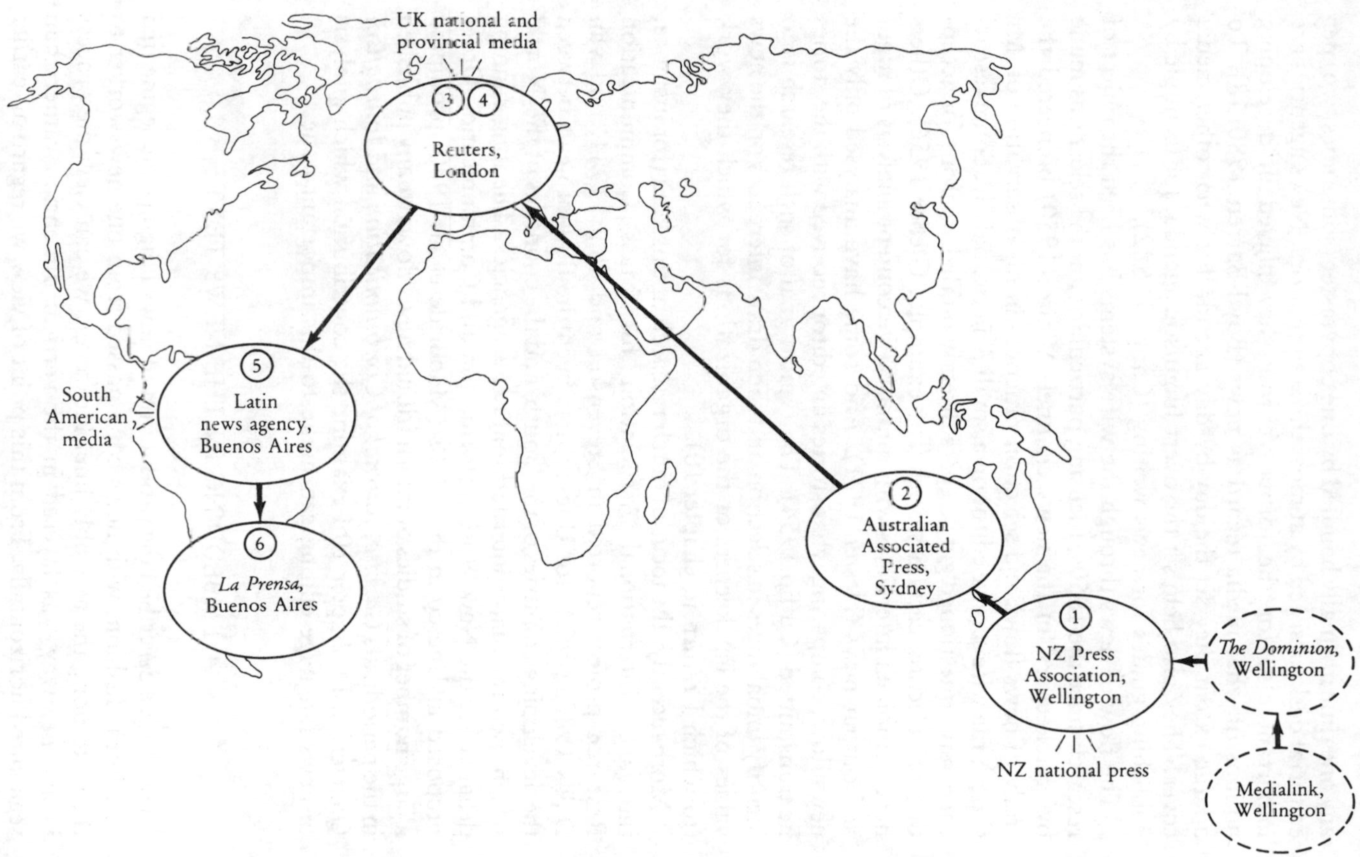
UK national and
provincial media
3
4
Reuters,
London
5
Latin
news agency,
Buenos Aires
South
American
media
6
La Prensa,
Buenos Aires
2
Australian
Associated
Press,
Sydney
1
NZ Press
Association,
Wellington
NZ national press
The Dominion,
Wellington
Medialink,
Wellington

FIGURE 3.3 International news flow: how a story gets from Wellington to Buenos Aires

any one time normally handled by one copytaster (sometimes two) per editorial desk, assisted by at most three subeditors. News agencies are important also for the formative role they played in developing notions of what media regard as news (Boyd-Barrett 1980: 18). To a large extent they set the day-by-day agenda for what other media cover. They also help set the overt linguistic agenda, for example by publishing guides for news writing (Cappon 1982).

The flow of news through the wire systems has been the object of research since the 1950s, focusing particularly on the selections made by 'gatekeepers' in the news channel. White (1950) pioneered the study of news flows and selection practices in his observation of 'Mr Gates', the wire service editor on a small American daily. Some researchers have questioned gatekeepers directly on their reasons for accepting or rejecting certain stories (for example, Gieber 1956). Others have combined interviews with quantitative content analysis of input and output news (Hester 1971). And some have analysed only the news flow, comparing what stories an editor received with the stories he transmitted (Cutlip 1954). The typical goal of such research is to identify imbalances in selection and then draw inferences on the news values of the gatekeepers or the organizations for which they work (to which I return in chapter 10).

More recently, the focus of much research of this kind (for instance, the large International Association for Mass Communication Research project reported in Stevenson and Shaw 1984, and van Dijk's 1988a project for Unesco) has been the flow of news between the developing countries of the 'South' and the countries of the 'North' which own the major international news agencies. The long-running debate over the New World Information and Communication Order proposed in Unesco in the 1970s (MacBride et al. 1980) prompted a large number of studies of international news flows (many published in the periodicals *Gazette*, *Journal of Communication* and *Journalism Quarterly*). In chapter 10 I examine the contribution which analysis of news language editing can make to this important issue.

4 EMBEDDING IN THE NEWS TEXT

So far I have described the production of news language as segmented in a linear fashion, with news copy passed from one newsworker to the next along the assembly line. However, we can view the process in another way – as layered in the vertical dimension rather than segmented horizontally. From this point of view we regard all earlier

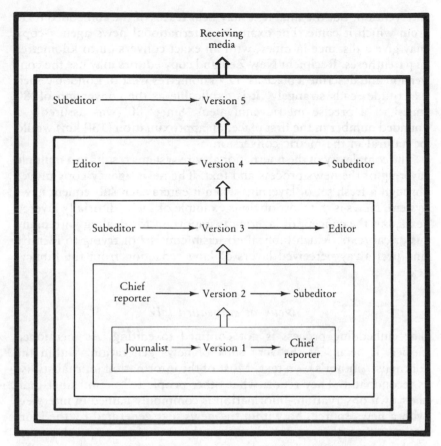

FIGURE 3.4   The embedding of each version of a story within the succeeding version as copy is edited at Medialink (versions 1–5 are the outputs of steps 2–6 in figure 3.1)

versions of a story as embedded within the final text. Each successive handling of the copy produces a potentially different text, which is input to the next stage of the process. Implied in each layer is not just the text and its content but the full speech event which generated it, including the participant sender and receiver, and the time and place it occurred. Figure 3.4 re-diagrams the Medialink news system as a layering of news process and text, rather than the linear flow of figure 3.1.

The many layers of editing are not generally evident in final news copy, since editors aim to produce a unified text which conceals their intervention. But the final text may bear traces of the embedded texts from which it came. For example, international news agency copy may give a distance in miles, with an exact conversion to kilometres in parentheses. Recipient New Zealand copy editors may use the conversion and describe a place as '129 kilometres west of London'. Such exactitude reads strangely. It is explicable as the conversion of '80 miles' to a precise metric equivalent. Since '80' was assuredly a rounded number in the first place, an approximation (130 km) would be natural in the metric conversion.

The complexity of the international wire systems results in a multiple layering of the news process and text. The news agency copy moves through a fresh set of layerings when it enters each subsequent news system. News is the most obvious example of such editorially layered texts, but the concept of layering is important for dealing with many historical texts. Much biblical criticism consists of trying to identify and peel away perceived layers of later redaction from the biblical text.

News as embedded talk

The embedding process is not confined to editing. As mentioned earlier, it begins at the very start of news generation, within the journalist/author's own text. Most of the information journalists use is secondhand. They report what other people tell them rather than their own observation. Information is commonly gained in interview with a news source. So within the news text generated by the journalist/author, there is embedded the substance of other speech events. Each has its own sender, receiver, and setting of time and place. We see this most obviously through the use of recording technology in broadcast news. Here the actual event through which the journalist acquired her information – an interview – can be replayed within the frame of the journalist's own story-telling. Longer stories on programmes such as BBC Radio 1's *Newsbeat* or Radio 4's *World at One* are often composed of a complex of several embedded interviews.

Broadcast technology makes overt the embedded speech events which are beneath the surface of all news copy. In printed media direct quotation is substituted for broadcasting's ability to carry the voice of the newsmaker. Figure 3.5 shows how an interview is embedded within the news story (cf. Burger 1984: 67). The story originates in a speech event which provides the journalist with information – an interview with a news source. The journalist transforms this information into a story, which is received and edited by a series of copy

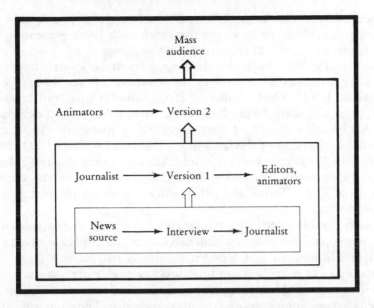

FIGURE 3.5   The embedding of the news-gathering interview in the final news story (all editorial steps collapsed together at middle level)

editors. Finally it is received by transmitters and technicians (in the terms of table 3.2) who channel the story to the mass audience.

The concept of embedding is extraordinarily important for understanding the language of news discourse. Journalists are rarely on the spot for unscheduled news events. Other people's accounts are the journalists' basic stock-in-trade for reporting on events. Further, news is what people say more than what people do. Much – maybe most – of what journalists report is talk not action: announcements, opinions, reactions, appeals, promises, criticisms. Most news copy is therefore reported speech – although it may not be overtly attributed as such.

Not surprisingly, we find that the same kind of formats needed to characterize news stories are used to describe other kinds of story-telling: in everyday conversation, fairy tales and literature. Goffman's *Forms of Talk* is concerned in large measure with the embedding of one kind of utterance within another as well as with the participation framework of speakers' utterances (1981: 3). Goffman writes: 'A speaker can quote himself or another directly or indirectly, thereby setting into an utterance with one production format another utterance with its own production format, albeit now merely an embedded one' (Goffman 1981:227). Clark (1987) calls this the 'layered dimension' of language use, with each layer presenting the content of the previous layer to a new audience.

Literary theorists have also developed frameworks to analyse the narrative structure of the novel (for example, Bruce 1981, Leech and Short 1981). Thus *Wuthering Heights* has at least four layers of narration, including Nellie Dean's narrative told to Mr Lockwood, Mr Lockwood's record of that narrative in his diary, and Emily Brontë's authorship of the book itself (Leech and Short 1981:263). Bruce (1981) diagrams – in a similar fashion to my figures 3.4 and 3.5 – the narrative structure of *Hansel and Gretel*, *Rip van Winkle*, *The Turn of the Screw* and other works, with up to six layers of embedded narration.

There are other art forms which approximate to the broadcasting of newsmakers' own voices within news stories. The play within a play used in Elizabethan and modern theatre is of just this kind. The technologies of recording and broadcasting enable mass communication to overcome the disjunction of place and of time which exists between the communicators and the mass audience. The communicators and their audience are located in different places, and broadcast technology bridges the gap between them. They are also usually separated in time, since most radio and television content is not broadcast live. Recording technology enables 'present-ation' to occur – the displaying of the past as if it were the present. It makes possible the showing of 'actuality' so that events recorded either visually or in sound are transmitted as if they were live. Hence the confusion which audiences can experience over genres that may contain both live and recorded material. Switching on a sports programme, it may not be immediately obvious whether what appears on screen is present or past action.

It is the whole speech event which is embedded within the story, not just the producer of news language but its audience and setting. Typically, the audience at one level of the text becomes the producer at the next level, as figures 3.4 and 3.5 show. In interview the journalist is audience to the newsmaker. But she then becomes producer of a news text for which her editor is audience. The technicians perform their function by being audience to the newscaster's performance. We will deal with the significance of the producer as audience and the audience as producer in chapter 5.

Finally, newsworkers and newsmakers themselves distinguish the embedded format of the interview from the higher format of actual news transmission shown in figure 3.5. A newsmaker who tells a journalist something 'off the record' defines it as belonging to the interview only. It is unavailable for reporting to a wider audience in the newsworker's eventual story. The newsmaker may deny ever having said it if the journalist does report it. Among the newsmaker's most difficult tasks is to accommodate speech to both the embedded and outer audiences (chapter 5).

Roles for newsmakers

Newsmakers are in a different position from a news outlet's own language producers, even when the two appear on camera together. They are on a different 'footing', in Goffman's terms, they have a different alignment to what they say. The newsmaker is not mandated by the news outlet and does not stand in the news organization's hierarchy. Within a news organization people's roles are meshed into the one authority structure. They are obligated to each other to fulfil their different functions from principal down to animator, dependent on each other to accomplish their shared business of communication. There is no such mandate between the reporter and the reported. A spokesperson is mandated by those whom she represents.

When reported speech from a newsmaker is embedded into the journalist's story, a separate, embedded set of roles is needed to describe the newsmaker's standing as a speaker. News sources can be described in terms of the same generalized speech roles we identified in table 3.2: principal, author, editor or animator. The news media in fact provide the main public stage for the playing of such distinct roles (as evidenced by the number of media examples cited by Goffman 1981 and Thomas 1986). Most newsmakers speak on behalf of a group or organization. As such, a newsmaker may be just an animator, a mouthpiece reading a statement on behalf of other principals or authors within an organization. He will refuse to answer questions because he lacks the authority to generate any new speech. Or the newsmaker may be an author – a spokesperson with a circumscribed mandate to give a form of words to policy set by others. Or she may in fact be a principal, the head of an organization, with power to make policy on-camera, to commit the organization to a course of action. In the next chapter, we see how journalists turn the range of newsmaker inputs available to them into a coherent story.

4

Authoring and Editing
the News Text

We have seen that journalists rely primarily on other people's accounts
of events in their authoring of stories. Fishman's study of the day-by-
day work of a journalist on a small California paper puts it like this:
'This fundamental principle of news fact can be stated like this:
something is so because somebody says it. Newsworkers take their
facts from other people's accounts' (M. Fishman 1980: 92). Further,
most of what journalists 'write' is actually a reprocessing of already
existing text. Van Dijk (1988b: 96) maintains that news production
should be seen largely as a matter of text processing, particularly
because 'most of the information *used* to write a news text comes in
discourse form'.

1 CONSTRUCTING THE NEWS TEXT

In this chapter I first scan briefly the kind of inputs journalists draw
on and how they embed those sources into a story. I use analyses
of stories culled from my work as a journalist and editor, together
with material from van Dijk's pioneer studies in the same field
(1988b: 110ff.). Then we turn to examine how and why news is edited
as it moves from the author/journalist along the editorial production
line described in the previous chapter.

Types of inputs

Journalists draw on both spoken and written inputs for their stories.
In a study of climate change news in New Zealand (Bell 1989), I asked
news sources what kind of contact they had had with the journalist

who wrote the story about them. Over half the 200 stories had arisen from interviews either face to face (18 per cent) or by telephone (37 per cent). At least a quarter drew on press releases (often more or less verbatim), with no direct contact between the newspaper's journalists and the source. Remaining stories were based on some other written document supplied by the source, for instance a research report, or on journalists' coverage of public addresses such as conference papers.

Van Dijk (1988b: 126) found he could class the input sources behind a sample of stories in Dutch newspapers into 12 categories. My own analyses and experience yield the following classification:

- interviews, either face to face or by telephone
- public addresses
- press conferences
- written text of spoken addresses
- organizationally produced documents of many kinds: reports, surveys, letters, findings, agendas, minutes, proceedings, research papers, etc.
- press releases
- prior stories on a topic, either from own or other media
- news agency copy
- the journalist's notes from all the above inputs, especially the spoken ones.

The journalist's main spoken source is the interview (and notes taken from it). Secondary are public addresses of all kinds, and press conferences, which are a combination of both address and interview. Journalistic wisdom holds that there is no substitute for talking to a newsmaker. Even when documentary sources are available, the journalist's instinct is to go direct to the author of a document for verbal explanation of its contents rather than simply culling information and quotations from the written text. This practice is based on the (quite true) premise that the story narrated verbally is likely to be more focused, more simply expressed, and offer the chance of more usable quotes than a written document.

Despite the emphasis on talking to newsmakers, documents play a large part in news reporting. I estimate that a majority of our stories at Medialink news service incorporated some material from documents, and a quarter were probably drawn completely from written sources. The documentary inputs are of two main kinds: those already written as news, and those not written as news. The second group consists mainly of official documents of some kind: reports, agendas, judgements and the like. Journalists covering technical areas – or 'rounds' – such as science and health will often draw their stories from journals of primary publication, translating the specialist academic paper for mass consumption (Dubois 1986, Adams-Smith 1987, 1989). Jones and Meadows (1978) found that science programmes on BBC radio drew on scientific journals and conferences for about 40 per cent of their items. Written texts of prepared speeches are also important.

Journalists favour written sources which are already prefabricated in an appropriate news style and therefore require the minimum of reworking. These are of three kinds: news agency copy, press releases and prior stories on the same topic. News agencies provide a majority of any newspaper's copy. Most agency stories will be run almost verbatim, but some will be assigned to a journalist to find a new or local angle using the agency story as a basis. I deal with agency copy in some detail later in the chapter.

The press release was invented in the United States at the beginning of the twentieth century (Nelkin 1987: 128). Now it is a staple of journalism, openly despised but heavily used by newsworkers. A well-written press release about something with news value has a high chance of being picked up and published largely untouched. Sachsman (1976) estimated that 20 per cent of environment stories are drawn from press releases rewritten without any fresh input from the journalist. A further 20 per cent of stories also drew on public relations material. The volume of press releases generated can be huge. Sachsman also found that media in the San Francisco Bay area received over 1300 press releases on environment issues in a two-month period.

Still more highly favoured are previous stories on the same topic. These may be from the journalist's own paper, but often come from other media. News media feed voraciously off each other's stories. While they always try to find something new to update and begin the story, an evening paper will often reproduce the bulk of a story published by its morning competitor. Even specialist media such as science programmes draw on other media for information (Jones and Meadows 1978). This means that news language is frequently recycled. Text from a continuing story may come round again and again in little-changed format. At Medialink perhaps half of all our stories were updates which incorporated sections of an earlier story on the same topic. Other media probably have similar proportions.

News selection and processing has often been described in terms of news values (Galtung and Ruge 1965) or news-gathering routines (Tuchman 1978). These factors are important, but they overlook the significant role which pre-existing text can play in newsworkers' judgements. Input texts which are already cast in news format and style stand a much better chance of selection than texts which are not appropriately packaged. The extent to which input materials can be reproduced rapidly and with little editing is a major factor in their being selected for publication. Working as an organizational press officer, I have often had journalists ignore suggestions of stories to follow up themselves. They will, however, reproduce the story faithfully when it is supplied as a ready-made press release a week or two later.

The three kinds of prepackaged news distinguished above have a head· start on other news inputs. A story which is marginal in news terms but written and available may be selected ahead of a much more newsworthy story which has to be researched and written from the ground up. So in relation to the first category, the press release, the advantage lies with those potential newsmakers who can afford to pay someone to write for them. Generally this means government ministers rather than their political opponents, government departments rather than individuals or pressure groups, and large businesses rather than consumer or citizens' groups. Secondly, the use of prior copy embedded into updated stories favours publication of something which has already been in the news. This is a paradox of news work, since it clashes with the ideal of news as new. Yet it remains true that the refurbished old story often has a better chance than the brand new. Thirdly, the news agencies' provision of ready-made copy strengthens their well-known agenda-setting function (Boyd-Barrett 1980). The use of these last two categories is now enhanced by technology. Prior stories are held in the computer and can be called up and embedded in an updated story rather than having to be retyped. News agency copy often inputs direct into a newspaper's typesetting computers. This gives it an advantage over all other copy, since the newspaper does not have to pay someone to key it in afresh. When a press release I distribute is picked up and carried by the NZ Press Association, most newspapers will publish this agency version received through the computer rather than the original which they receive direct but in hard copy. The proportion of stories which are picked up has been shown to rise when they are received in electronic form rather than hard copy (Neuwirth et al. 1988).

The situation of written inputs to news is further complicated because most source documents are themselves composite, with text from earlier documents embedded within them. The origin of a three-paragraph, routine hard-news story analysed in M. Fishman's (1980: 87) study is completely typical. Information on a man's death originated in accounts from those who witnessed it and from hospital staff. These accounts were written up by investigating police. The police account then formed the basis of the coroner's report. Finally, at three removes from the original eyewitnesses, the coroner's report formed the sole source for the journalist's story. Fishman describes this process in precisely the same terms of 'layering' as I have used. He concludes (1980: 141) that the basic raw material of staple hard news is the supply of documentary information produced in just this fashion by bureaucracies.

A large proportion of news is talk about talk, especially in political and diplomatic affairs. It consists entirely of what newsmakers have said by way of announcement, protest, plea, or some other speech act. Sometimes this becomes verbal tennis, as in the gist of this item, heard on New Zealand radio:

> The paper reports the Government's denunciation of Japan's rejection of South Pacific nations' demands for abandonment of gill net fishing.

Indeed the standard news-gathering response to a decision or announcement is to elicit and report reaction from affected parties. Even on television, which supposedly seeks to display action, the Glasgow University Media Group (1980) found nearly 20 per cent of the copy read out by newscasters and reporters was reported speech. A lot of this language is in fact pseudo-direct speech, composed by authors other than the principal to whom it is attributed. The direct quotes in a press release were almost certainly not verbalized by the named source. They were written by a press officer and merely approved by the source (sometimes not even that).[1]

Apart from stories published verbatim from press releases or agency copy, most stories are based on more than one input. Covering a speech by a government minister is a frequent news-gathering routine. In constructing a story from the speech the journalist will draw on sources such as:

- the written text of the minister's prepared speech
- (journalist's notes of) the minister's speech as actually delivered, which may diverge anywhere between 0 and 100 per cent from the prepared speech

- a press release containing those points of the speech the minister wants reported
- an interview after the speech with the minister herself.

To these four inputs may be added advance written briefing materials, prior verbal indications from the minister's press secretary on the content of the speech, an official report released at the time of the speech, subsequent telephone calls to interested groups for comment on the minister's statement, and so on. There is a three-stage process involved in much routine, preplanned news-gathering: *preparation* (invitation, announcement, agenda, etc.); *event* such as press conference, speech, meeting; *follow-up* through on-the-spot interview, telephone interviews with affected parties, telephone calls to check facts (van Dijk 1988b: 128).

Journalists' use of inputs

The record of an interview or spoken address is kept by the journalist. The record may be verbatim in the form of a tape recording, a selective but more or less verbatim shorthand transcript, or highly selective longhand notes. This material may appear in a story as direct quotes, indirect quotes, or unattributed information. It may be paraphrased or summarized. Direct quotation, enclosed between double "quote marks", is supposed to be verbatim. Much that appears as indirect quote is paraphrase, and much unattributed information draws heavily on what a newsmaker has said. Written documents may similarly be used either for quotation or to provide background information.

Researching how journalists work and what inputs they use is not easy, as van Dijk and his co-workers found (1988b: 125). I was able to take advantage of records of my own work. To illustrate, let us look at one story which I wrote concerning the introduction of the gorse mite into New Zealand to control gorse, a noxious weed which costs the country many millions of dollars annually. Analysing the story in retrospect (I had no thought of analysis at the time it was written) I found I had used no fewer than eight inputs:

1 Notes from a brief preliminary face-to-face interview with the leader of the group of scientists who had been researching the introduction of the mite. The interview largely pointed me to other sources I should interview and to written sources, and updated developments since the last of the documentary sources had appeared.

2   Notes from a later telephone interview with the same group leader.
3   The 350-page Environmental Impact Assessment (EIA) on the effects of introducing the gorse mite. This is itself a highly composite document, drawing heavily on earlier reports. In particular the EIA stresses that three previous impact assessment documents 'should be consulted before reading this EIA' – and it embeds these as appendices.
4   Draft press release written by the principal scientist involved.
5   Cover letter from this scientist accompanying the press release.
6   Copy of a press release (and published clips) issued the previous year at an earlier stage of the assessment.
7   Notes from my telephone interview with the scientist (and follow-up questions in subsequent phone calls).
8   Amendments to my draft story made by both scientist and group leader.[2]

Now, this was a press release issued by an organization rather than a story written direct for a newspaper. It therefore had more time spent on it than would be usual on a newspaper, especially in the follow-up phone calls and checking of copy. The use of the scientist's draft press release and cover letter would also be atypical although not unknown. Otherwise the kind and number of inputs are not unusual for a technically complex story of its type.

The story was 24 paragraphs long. Of these, nine were based mainly on the spoken inputs (interviews) and 15 on written inputs. It was notable that the spoken took the lead and the written provided background. That is, paragraphs 1–6 were largely from spoken sources, paragraphs 12–24 from written sources, and paragraphs 7–11 were of mixed origin. This confirms the importance of the spoken in focusing the main points of a story, and the written in providing detail. Figure 4.1 shows the first few paragraphs of this story as published (verbatim) in one newspaper, and how the eight inputs were used to build the text of the news item. The process is even more complex than shown, since the story's lead paragraph (sentence S1) effectively drew on all eight sources in summarizing the main point. This is a common tactic for presenting the opening punchline of a story, and supports van Dijk's finding (1988b: 133) that lead paragraphs tend to be constructed through summarization.

Detailed analysis of how information and wording from the different sources were used is beyond our scope here, but we can give an indication of the ways in which inputs are transformed into final text. Figure 4.2 shows how one paragraph of the story is derived from

INPUTS

1
Face-to-face
interview
with group leader

2
Telephone interview
with group leader

3
Environmental
Impact Assessment

4
Draft press release
from scientist

5
Cover letter
from scientist

6
1987 press release

7
Telephone interview
with scientist

8
Amendments by
group leader
and scientist

S1

S2

S3

S4

S5

S6

S7

S8

S9

S10

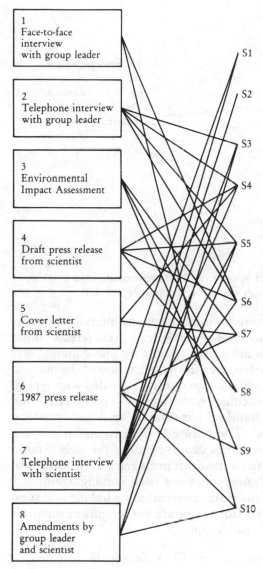

FINAL COPY

Mite leads gorse war

A TINY mite has arrived in New Zealand to lead the fight against the country's most costly weed, gorse.

A consignment of several hundred gorse spider mites was flown into Christchurch by the Department of Scientific and Industrial Research.

The mites were imported in sealed containers from the CABI Institute for Biological Control at Ascot near London.

They were taken to DSIR's maximum quarantine facility at Lincoln and will be released for multiplication in August and throughout the country in the spring.

The mites are a brick-red colour and measure less than a millimetre. They live in colonies of thousands inside webs spun on to gorse branches and feed heavily on the plant.

The importation follows issue of a permit by the Ministry of Agriculture and Fisheries.

DSIR Entomology Division director John Longworth said introduction of the mite culminates a decade of research, environmental assessment and public consultation.

"Because releasing bio logical control agents is an irreversible step, the impacts, costs and benefits have been carefully assessed over several years," he said.

Detailed tests carried out in England since 1980 had shown the mite would estabish only on gorse and not damage other native or economically important plants in New Zealand.

A 350-page environmental impact assessment circulated last November concluded there were no compelling economic or environmental reasons to prevent introduction.

FIGURE 4.1   Embedding of inputs to construct the text of a news story (*The Daily News*, New Plymouth, 4 August 1988)

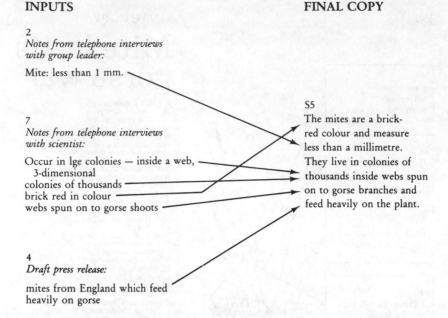

INPUTS   FINAL COPY

2
*Notes from telephone interviews
with group leader:*

Mite: less than 1 mm.

                                                    S5
                                                    The mites are a brick-
7   red colour and measure
*Notes from telephone interviews   less than a millimetre.
with scientist:*   They live in colonies of

Occur in lge colonies — inside a web,   thousands inside webs spun
   3-dimensional   on to gorse branches and
colonies of thousands   feed heavily on the plant.
brick red in colour
webs spun on to gorse shoots

4
Draft press release:

mites from England which feed
heavily on gorse

FIGURE 4.2   The embedding of spoken and written inputs into final news
              text: one paragraph from the story in figure 4.1

different inputs, principally my notes of telephone interviews (inputs
2 and 7), plus a phrase from the scientist's draft press release (input
4). The means by which this information is turned into a unified text
are of interest. The paragraph moves from description of the mite, to
its habitat, to how the mite actually operates. It is loaded with typical
journalistic detail, in particular with figures – 'millimetre' and
'thousands'. The scientist's standard phrasing of 'brick red *in* colour'
becomes 'a brick-red colour'. The phrase '3-dimensional' is omitted
– implied by the fact that the mites can live 'inside' the web. And in
picking up the final phrase from the draft press release, the pro-form
'the plant' is used because 'gorse' does not need naming again.

Other paragraphs in this story are constructed by linking and summarizing information derived from separate paragraphs in the press
release issued the previous year (input 6):

detailed tests carried out in   → S7 a decade of research,
   England since 1980   environmental   assessment
+ wide-ranging scientific and   and public consultation
   public   consultation   since
   1982

Van Dijk (1988b: 133) found that selection and deletion were the main strategies used in dealing with input texts, with some summarization. The processes I see at work in my own example include:

1 Selection among available inputs and corresponding rejection of most of the written material in order to handle the size of the EIA and the number of other inputs.
2 Reproduction of source material. I found that the later paragraphs which provided detail and background tended to reproduce wording from input texts rather than undergo the wholesale blending and rewriting evident in the early paragraphs.
3 Summarization in early paragraphs of information to be detailed later (compare S7 and S9 in figure 4.1). The degree of summarization is greater than van Dijk's studies found and may reflect the longer time I had available to write the story.
4 Generalization and particularization. In S7 of the above example we see a shift from particular to general, and from general to particular in the S5 description.
5 Restyling and translating were common. Typical of the translations (almost always resulting in abbreviation) which journalists perform on official or scientific prose are these from later paragraphs of the story:

The aim of biological control is not eradication of gorse but the slow gradual suppression of the weed. → It will not eradicate gorse but may suppress it gradually.

The amount of gorse in New Zealand would need to decline by well over 50% before significant losses were felt by the [beekeeping] industry. → The amount of gorse would have to fall by well over half before the industry noticed the loss.

These strategies serve the same goals which we shall see below for copy editing – reducing the amount of material, enhancing news value, restyling, clarifying and simplifying. It will be obvious that drawing together material from such a range of sources is demanding on the journalist's powers of comprehension and assimilation of information. Sometimes the resulting story shows that those demands were too great, as we shall see in chapter 10.

2 HOW NEWS IS EDITED

Editing is a common activity for language users. Most written language is edited, even if it is just the quick rescanning and minor alterations which one gives a personal letter. Editing is the process by which one text is transformed into another text which is different in form but congruent in meaning. 'Congruent' signifies having an equivalent and compatible meaning, although not necessarily containing all the information in the original. In mass communication, editing is institutionalized and professionalized, offering an ideal site to study the process.

In chapter 3 we saw the complexities of the process by which news is edited as it moves from one editor and news organization to another. The world's copy editors handle hundreds of millions of words daily in a highly structured system, but observations vary on the scale of language editing undertaken at various 'gates' in the news system. My own impression is formed from both research on editing in the New Zealand news system (Bell 1984a), and the experience of editing news copy and being edited. This indicates firstly that at some 'gates' in the system significant editing is normal, while at others the copy is just passed on with little or no change. But secondly, even at points where heavy editing is common, many stories pass scarcely touched, possibly on grounds of excellence but more probably through lack of time. According to Rosenblum's insider's view of international news gathering and processing (1979: 113), incoming stories may be 'rewritten completely for clarity and background' at the international agencies' central desks. The same source says the *Los Angeles Times* foreign desk spends at least an hour on even the smoothest dispatches. Few newspapers do that. Boyd-Barrett's information was that deadline pressures meant the agencies rarely indulged in major rewrites (1980: 77). Editing usually consisted of deleting sections of a story, adding basic explanatory material such as background or a person's position, and cleaning up spelling mistakes and stylistic problems. Van Dijk's study of how one wire story was handled in newspapers around the world (1988a: 116) found that editing was confined to deleting chunks of copy and minor restyling.

At this point we should recall that much of the world's news undergoes a process far more radical than editing within the same language. Translation between languages is a major language function of the international agencies. Because it is a time-consuming and expensive process, the need for translation reduces news flow by at least half (Boyd-Barrett 1980: 58). It is not clear how much of this reduction results from rejecting more stories and how much from shortening accepted stories. The major languages of international news are (in descending order) English, Spanish, French, German, Arabic and Portuguese. Most news for other-language countries originates in English and is translated either in the receiving nation or at the international agencies' central desks.

Editing analysis offers us the rare opportunity to stop the production line and analyse language in the making. It is a natural laboratory in which linguistic structure is put under the microscope in a way usually only possible with artificially generated examples. As an indication of the kind and scale of linguistic alterations which editors regularly perform, below (left) is the text of a sports story transmitted by Australian Associated Press-Reuter from Sydney. Beside it is the version edited by the NZ Press Association.

AAP/S1 The waterlogged conditions that ruled out play yesterday still prevailed at Bourda this morning, and it was not until mid-afternoon that the match restarted.

S2 Less than three hours' play remained, and with the West Indies still making their first innings reply to England's total of 448, there was no chance of a result.

S3 At tea the West Indies were two for 139.

PA/S1 Waterlogged conditions ruled out play this morning, but the match resumed with less than three hours' play remaining for the final day.

S2 The West Indies are making a first innings reply to England's total of 448.

S3 At tea the West Indies were 139 for two, but there's no chance of result.

The NZPA subeditor preserved most of the information of the original, but set about the syntax with a will. When we analyse in detail what has happened, no less than a dozen major changes have been made to produce just the first, 22-word paragraph of the PA version from AAP's original copy:

1 The place adverbial *at Bourda* has been deleted.
2 Time adverbials *yesterday* and *still* deleted.

3   Main verb *prevailed* deleted.
4   Relative clause *that ruled out play yesterday* raised to become main clause.
5   Relative pronoun *that* and definite article deleted.
6   Clefting reversed, so that *it was not until mid-afternoon that the match restarted* becomes *the match did not restart until mid-afternoon*.
7   Time adverbial *not until mid-afternoon* deleted.
8   Lexical substitution of *resume* for *restart*.
9   Coordinator *but* substituted for *and*.
10   Main clause of AAP/S2 *less than three hours' play remained* embedded into S1 under *with*.
11   Finite verb *remained* becomes non-finite *remaining* under *with*.
12   Time adverbial *for the final day* inserted from another version.

These are completely typical of the changes editors make – deleting words and phrases, replacing one word with another, and altering the actual structure of a sentence.

The study of news editing is rewarding but fraught with problems (see Bell 1984a). As data we need the input and output versions of a story – what a copy editor received, and what he sent on after he had finished with it. Getting access to such copy can be difficult, since obviously only the output version is actually published – and in the case of news agencies, not even that. Boyd-Barrett observes (1980: 103) that agency copy is hard to get hold of direct, particularly the version originally written by the source journalist. Agency stories are often difficult to identify in the press, and in any case may have been edited in unspecified ways. In my experience, some news organizations are willing to make old copy available. But it comes in huge volumes and is highly perishable, disappearing from the newsroom within hours or days of receipt.

The sheer volume of words is a deterrent, particularly the difficulties it creates for what is the first step in an editing analysis – identifying what is the input to a given output story. The complexity of copy flow within and between newsrooms described above makes it difficult to be sure exactly what version a particular newsworker or newsroom may have received. The only foolproof method is when input copy bears an editor's pencil markings. But editing is increasingly computerized, and in many newsrooms there are no printouts even at the end of the production line. My principal editing study was fortunately conducted when news copy in New Zealand was still

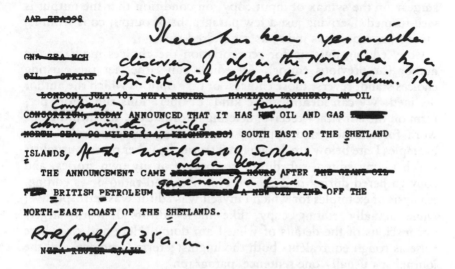

FIGURE 4.3   A page of wire copy with markings by recipient New Zealand editor

'hard', and I had access to the copy which had come off the teleprinter and bore the receiving editor's markings. When hard copy is lacking, one can sometimes identify an input through internal evidence such as idiosyncratic phrasing or information (for instance figures). In other cases, identification can be impossible, especially when a big story produces a flow of 10 or 20 updates from the wire services. Figure 4.3 reproduces a typical page of hand-edited hard copy.

The linguistics of copy editing

Once input and output versions have been matched, we move to the second step in editing analysis: describing the lexical and syntactic changes by which the output copy has been derived from the input. The editing process can be specified by rules similar to those conventionally used in linguistics. For example, the dozen editing changes in the cricket test match story above (p. 67) could be expressed as formalized linguistic as rules (although I will not do so here: see Bell 1977, 1984a). A set of editing rules rewrites the input copy as the output, in a manner similar to the standard rules of grammatical theory.

They cover all types of linguistic operations and can perform major surgery on the syntax of input copy, on condition that the output is well-formed. Deriving just a few paragraphs of output copy from its input may require as many as a hundred rules.

Copy editing puts up for renegotiation the choices made by the author (or previous editor). An editor can either let the existing choices stand, reverse those choices, or take options which the author declined. We can identify three kinds of operations subeditors perform on the copy they receive: deleting information, substituting one word for another, and applying or reversing syntactic rules. The examples I cite below are drawn from stories by other press journalists which I copy edited, subeditors' reworking of my own stories, and copy gathered during research on New Zealand radio news editing. Analysis of examples for which I myself was editor was retrospective: while actually editing copy, like most editors I work largely unconscious of the details of what I am doing. Here and elsewhere I use as rough equivalents both the linguist's term 'sentence' and the journalist's usually one-sentence 'paragraph'.

INFORMATION DELETIONS are very common and generally take out information which the copy editor apparently considers superfluous. Van Dijk (1988a, 1988b) found that deletion was the most common operation for news agency copy to undergo. In the 80-odd stories I analysed for the editing aspect of my Auckland radio news study (Bell 1977), it was rare for any sentence to pass the copy editor without some constituent being deleted. Place and time adverbials are often omitted, especially in the first paragraph (rules 1 and 2 in analysis of the cricket story above). Within a noun phrase, non-head items often go – adjectives, numerals, embedded prepositional phrases, relative clauses:

> his research into a new   → his research
> modelling technique
>
> a new oil find   → a find

Details of age, occupation and nationality are omitted, as are exact numbers of people or amounts of money. The name of a person, place or other entity may go if a story focuses on what happened rather than whom it happened to:

> a third girl, Josephine Kona   → a third girl aged 20
> Burton, 20, masseuse

Single words are deleted less often than one might expect. The loss of just one word does not achieve much abbreviation: taking out a whole phrase or longer sentence constituent is more effective. One particularly common deletion removes the attribution of a story to a news agency, and less frequently attribution of a statement to its source. In this example, datelined Tel Aviv, the copy editor deleted both:

| An Israeli military force has crossed the border, an Army spokesman announced here, Agence France Presse reported. | → | An Israeli military force has crossed the border. |

The above are the simplest deletions – those which can be cut straight out without requiring repairs to the sentence which remains. Many such deletions will leave the structure of the sentence unaltered apart from loss of the items which have been removed. The second kind of deletion performs radical structural changes while leaving the surface of the remaining sentence quite unruffled. We have already seen an example above:

| The waterlogged conditions that ruled out play yesterday still prevailed at Bourda this morning, and it was not until mid-afternoon that the match restarted. | → | Waterlogged conditions ruled out play this morning, but the match resumed . . . |

Skilful deletion has left behind a sentence with a very different syntactic structure, but still well formed and requiring no repairs at all (although the editor also makes a couple of lexical substitutions). This is a complex example of a common phenomenon. It is motivated by the desire to cut, but the physical form which the deletions take is influenced by the technology used. Editors working on hard copy favour changes which are easy to make and follow on the page, such as deletion which allows the surviving words to be rejoined without further ado. Large-scale reordering of sentences or of constituents within sentences is disfavoured as difficult to mark clearly on paper.

It also warns us against regarding these operations as representations of editors' conscious processes. It is the stringing together of surface words which the editor is conscious of, not the radical syntactic restructuring. The operations are rarely conscious, and editors are surprisingly unaware of what they are doing with language. Even for myself, as a journalist editing news copy and as a linguist analysing editing processes within the same day, I am largely unaware of the precise operations performed as I edit (and I imagine that becoming too aware could lead to paralysis!). In some cases, how we would describe an operation for linguistic purposes is demonstrably different from how the editor thinks of it.

The third type of deletion leaves behind an ungrammatical sentence which requires repair. The repairs needed may be quite minor, such as replacing definite with indefinite article:

> the West German newspaper   → a West German newspaper
> *Die Welt*

In other cases deletion leaves a sentence that is so badly wounded it can be saved only by major syntactic surgery. Subjects are executed, leaving truncated sentences behind. Headless phrases mourn the loss of their nouns. Main verbs disappear without trace. Transitive verbs have their objects amputated. Subordinate clauses stage successful coups and gain their independence as main clauses, while entire sentences are taken prisoner by marauding subjects from other sentences. The copy editor may apply various syntactic rules to rebuild the remains into a well-formed sentence again. This was done in the cricket example with a clause left lying around after the rest of the sentence had been incorporated elsewhere:

> . . . and with the West Indies   → The West Indies are
> still making their first   making a first innings reply
> innings reply to England's   to England's total of 448.
> total of 448 . . .

But more often the editor's solution is to transplant the surviving bits into another sentence, usually the preceding one:

> S1 He plans to gain experience   → He plans to gain experi-
> of a new separating tech-   ence of a new separating
> nique developed at the Insti-   technique . . .
> tute and introduce it to New
> Zealand.

S2 The technique is used to   . . . to extract protein from
extract protein from ani-   animal tissue.
mal tissue, for example in
recovering insulin from pigs'
pancreas.

LEXICAL SUBSTITUTIONS replace one or more words with alternative items. So *modify* is replaced by *change*, *leader* by *head*, *originated from* by *came from*, *increasing demand* by *increasing market*, *in the past 10 years* by *in the last decade*. Some substitutions shift away from full equivalence to the words they replace, but in the context of the whole story they remain acceptable glosses. In other instances, as we shall see in chapter 10, the substituted words mean something quite different from the input copy.

Another kind of change reduces information by substituting a specific reference with a more general one:

imported from the CABI Insti-   → imported from England
tute for Biological Control
at Ascot near London

SYNTACTIC EDITING RULES are the third kind of editing change. The rules we have seen used to repair ungrammatical structures after deletions are quite typical. Some rules become obligatory after certain deletions. If the antecedent of a pronoun is deleted, the pronoun must be de-pronominalized. Variations on coordination or de-coordination, relativization and de-relativization are particularly common. Attributions have different sentences embedded as their complements. A noun phrase in one sentence is embedded under a preposition in another sentence. Relative clauses are re-embedded into other sentences or raised to become main clauses – as in rule 4 of the cricket story (p. 68). This typical example of deleting and reordering uses the redundancy of *speech* and *talk about* to eliminate the relative clause:

The Annual General Meeting   → Former Lincoln College
will open with a keynote   principal Sir James Stewart
speech from Sir James   will address the Annual
Stewart, a former Lincoln   General Meeting on the
College principal, who will   direction of agricultural
talk about the direction of   policy.
agricultural policy.

The copy editor sacrifices the detail of 'opening keynote speech' in favour of the single strong word *address* and putting Sir James Stewart – the main news interest – at the start of the paragraph.

Copy editing renegotiates syntactic choices made in the input text. This gives a three-way classification of syntactic editing rules: applications, reversals or alternatives. If the original text did not apply a rule, the editor may reverse the choice and apply the rule. Typically, relative clauses are reduced, agents deleted from passives, *there* inserted, and prepositional phrases preposed and reduced.

Secondly, the editor may reverse choices previously made. Coordinated sentences are split again. Complementizer *that* is reinserted, *there* deleted again, and clefting reversed (cricket story, rule 6). Passives are returned to actives, deleted agents reinserted:

Several hundred gorse spider mites were imported from England by the Department of Scientific and Industrial Research.	→	The Department of Scientific and Industrial Research has imported several hundred gorse spider mites from England.

Thirdly, the editor may select an alternative output other than the one used in the input text. Such rules are among the copy editor's most common tools. One verb tense or aspect replaces another – simple past to present perfect is especially common, as in the example above. Alternative determiners, coordinators (cricket story, rule 9) or complementizers are used, all with little change in meaning.

The effects of technology on editing

The examples I have cited come from both editing by pencil on paper and electronic editing on video display units/terminals. But a change of technology may result in a change of editing practice. Technological change seems unlikely to create new kinds of editing rules, but it could alter the frequency with which some rules are applied. Some kinds of operation are easier on screen than on paper – and vice versa. We saw above that editors working on hard copy favour simple deletions which can be just crossed out without further reordering or rewording. On screen, however, sentences and sentence constituents can be shifted around much more easily. Although no one has yet researched the matter, I would expect that editors working on electronic copy perform more radical reordering than when they worked on paper.

On the other hand, viewing later pages of a long story is more difficult by computer. Pages cannot be spread out and scanned at a glance. Even with hard copy, editors already often used only the first page of longer stories and ignored the rest. Electronic editing may strengthen this tendency. However, it must be said that another aspect of the technology tends in the opposite direction. Although viewing the whole story may be more difficult, working on screen makes it easier to actually pick up and shift material from the end of the story to the beginning. However, the only research I know in the area (Neuwirth et al. 1988) indicates that the amount of editing drops with the introduction of electronic news processing. They hypothesize that this is because the story is harder for journalists to come to terms with on screen than on paper.

The few studies which have compared electronic and hard copy editing practices agree that electronic editing takes longer than pencil on paper (Shipley and Gentry 1981) but is more accurate. Garrison (1979) found that many editors liked to work from both hard and 'soft' copy, especially for substantial rewriting. This is certainly my own practice when editing anything but a very short story which is entirely visible on a single screen. I mark major reordering of sentences on hard copy, then make the changes on screen. But for rewriting within a sentence, I work only on screen because the whole stretch of copy I am operating on is displayed at once.

3 WHY EDIT?

Copy written by one newsworker is always edited by another. A main reason is that the time-span in which news is produced does not permit the original author enough distance to identify the gaps, confusions, wordiness and weaknesses in what she may have written. Only a fresh eye can catch those things in the time available. Copy editors must watch for problematic content of all kinds – gaps in the story, inaccurate information, confusion, contradictions, potentially libellous material, and the various kinds of nonsense which a reporter may commit to paper.

The interest of the editing changes outlined is not just that they happen but *why* they happen. What function is served by these dozens of changes which editors make in the copy they handle? The researcher's question is echoed by the cry of journalists everywhere to their copy editors: why – when I had written it perfectly in the first place – did you come along and mess it up? Rosenblum's wry definition (1979: 110) of the goal of the copy editor gives an indication: 'to add information to dispatches by shortening them and to provide a rounded picture of the world while throwing away most of the material available'.

The editor's aim is to improve copy – to turn out concise, clear, newsworthy stories from writing which may be far from that. I identify four functions for copy editing: to cut, to clarify, to maximize news value, and to standardize language. Of these, maximizing news value is the primary function, and much of the cutting and clarifying is done to serve a story's newsworthiness.

Cutting

The copy editor's first task is to reduce the volume of news to a level where it approaches what the outlet can use. In the BBC newsroom the copytaster rejects about 90 per cent of incoming news agency copy (Schlesinger 1987: 60), a typical ratio across the media. While the main means of reducing the flow is through acceptance and rejection of complete stories, abbreviating the stories which are accepted also serves to reduce. Some international agency stories reach 2000 words, several times the space most newspapers would devote to a foreign story. For broadcast news the disparity between input and output lengths is even greater. The average radio news item is three or four sentences long. An incoming agency story may run to many pages of copy, and the main cut is made by rejection of complete pages or paragraphs. The editor usually cuts 'from the bottom' by keeping the first page and dropping the rest into 'file 13' – the wastepaper basket.

Wholesale rejection of incoming stories, and cutting of complete paragraphs from many that are accepted, are the two main means of reducing the flow of news copy. But conciseness is a goal of news writing which guides how editors handle the paragraphs they do not cut altogether. Their cuts are of three kinds: those which delete real information, those which delete redundant information, and those where deletion results from a lexical or syntactic operation. The cricket story above was cut from 62 to 51 words by a combination of all those means.

Many of the information deletions cited remove information which the editor judges to be excessive. What constitutes 'excessive' depends on the editor's view of her particular audience. The issue becomes clearest with copy originally targeted at another audience – either a wider audience, such as a local paper receiving copy from a national news agency, or a narrower audience, when the paper supplies local news to the national agency. News which is the lead story locally may merit only six paragraphs for distribution to the rest of the country. So for national distribution on Medialink, I cut an enthusiastic local correspondent's blow-by-blow preview of a deer farming conference to under half its original 22 paragraphs by radical deletions and paraphrases such as:

Post-conference activities ~~on the Thursday~~ include ~~the Criffel deer~~ sales *on Mr Tim Wallis' property, near Wanaka*, ~~or a flight over Fiordland to see the original stamping ground of New Zealand wapiti-type deer.~~ ~~As well,~~ workshops ~~on management aspects of cross-breeding red deer with New Zealand and Canadian wapiti will be staged~~ *on Mr Alan Hamilton's deer farm, near Queenstown.*	→ Post-conference activities include sales and workshops at deer farms *in the region*.

Note the use of the pro-form *in the region* to paraphrase the two italicized locative phrases.

But not all cutting removes real information from a story. Much of it simply reduces redundancy by deleting content which is explicit or implied in what remains, as when *lax quality assurance procedures* becomes just *lax quality assurance*. Saying the same thing in fewer words also works:

The present survey *is being carried out on* at least six pig farms in Canterbury and *in the southern half of the North Island.*	→ *covers* at least six pig farms in Canterbury and *the southern North Island*.

That paragraph shrank from 24 to 16 words with no loss of information. Reworking to avoid subordinate clauses or prepositional phrases may typically halve the number of words:

it is important for farmers to   → farmers should consider
consider

nashi orchards in the Nelson   → Nelson nashi orchards
area

Such operations obviously serve to abbreviate, but they simultaneously perform the third (and primary) editing function – maximizing news value. They pack the maximum content into the minimum number of words, particularly in the story's first paragraph. They tighten the writing and so strengthen its impact.[3]

Clarifying

Journalists are professional writers, but they are still capable of producing confused, vague or ambiguous writing, particularly under the pressure of deadlines. It is the copy editor's task to clarify the confused and to ensure that the story contains enough background and explicit reference to be understood on its own.

To be certain that background or reference is adequate, the editor may have to add information. Clarification thus conflicts with the previous goal, abbreviation. However, the addition of background or explicit reference is one of the prime functions of international news agency editors (Rosenblum 1979: 111, Boyd-Barrett 1980: 77). Judgements on what constitutes too little information in incoming copy are based on the same criteria as judgements on what is too much: the editor's assessment of the audience's interest and knowledge. Again, local and national media differ in the degree of detail they require. A person's title may need expansion away from the local scene. *The Prime Minister* had unique reference within her own country for over a decade, so the British media did not need to name her. But there are dozens of prime ministers internationally, so for international usage *the British Prime Minister, Mrs Thatcher* had to be spelt out.

Besides ensuring the story is self-sufficient in information, copy editors are called on to clear up confusion. The cricket story illustrates:

The waterlogged conditions *that ruled out play yesterday* still prevailed at Bourda this morning, and *it was not until midafternoon that* the match restarted.

The relative clause, clefting and use of *not until* in the AAP copy are complex structures which impede understanding. So rules 4, 6 and 7 detailed in the earlier analysis (p. 68) reverse the relativization and clefting and delete *not until* to produce a much clearer Press Association version:

Waterlogged conditions ruled out play this morning, but the match resumed with less than three hours' play remaining for the final day.

Maximizing news value

Making the most of a story is the copy editor's prime function. Journalists do not always get the best out of their own stories. My working guidelines for Medialink reporters included a list of questions designed to get them to review critically the story they were writing:

1 Is this really a story?
2 Has the best lead been used?[4]
3 Is the story ordered in the best way?
4 Is each paragraph tightly written – especially the lead?

Cutting and clarifying can in fact be regarded as means to the end of newsworthiness. If a story is confused or inexplicit, if it is longer than its content warrants, then it loses news value. The journalist's idea of news value is a slippery one. Sociologists (for example, Tuchman 1978, M. Fishman 1980) have found newsworkers remarkably hazy over this basic concept of their profession. I will not try here to analyse or explain it (see chapter 8), but simply note that it includes values like negativity, proximity, recency, unambiguity.

Most copy editing is designed to maximize news value – to make the lead 'harder' and more striking, the source's credentials more authoritative, the writing more crisp, the appeal to the audience more compelling. An editor may believe that a journalist has in fact missed the main point of her own story, and that there is a better lead buried further down the copy. Such reworking, particularly without reference back to the journalist, is the cause of a great deal of newsroom heartache. And a copy editor's arrogance may bring him and his organization to grief if the journalist had valid reasons for the lead she used. But sometimes the editor is right. Much of what journalists have to write about is dull and routine, but even such stories offer better leads than the one on the left of the following example, the original and edited versions of a Medialink story.

S1 A group of nine English wool spinners have been impressed by the professionalism of the New Zealand wool industry.

S2 The group have been brought to this country by the New Zealand Wool Board for an intensive look at our industry, which supplies the United Kingdom with a large proportion of wool used in carpets.

S3 Mr Colin Lawton, of Fred Lawton and Sons, a Yorkshire spinning firm, said the demand for tufted wool carpets in the UK and Europe means an increasing demand for New Zealand wool.

S4 "New Zealand wool has the right characteristics for the latest trends in carpet manufacturing. It is strong, resilient, and holds dye well."

→

S1 European demand for tufted wool carpets is increasing the market for New Zealand wool, according to English spinning industry executives.

S2 "New Zealand wool has the right characteristics for the latest trends in carpet manufacturing," Mr Colin Lawton, Managing Director of the Yorkshire firm Fred Lawton and Sons, said today.

S3 "The fibre is strong, resilient, and holds dye well."

S4 Mr Lawton is with a party of nine industry executives brought to this country by the Wool Board.

S5 New Zealand supplies much of the wool for English made carpets.

Down in the third paragraph was something with claims to news interest, so I brought it up to the lead. The new lead begins with *what* not *who*, since the spinning executives are not of automatic news interest as persons. It also sources the opinions to the whole group, not just to Lawton.

Choosing an alternative lead is just the most obvious way in which a story can be reordered to maximize its news value. In the example, part of the original S3 became the lead, and the supposed substance of the original lead I deleted as banal. I moved part of S4 up to the second paragraph, added its attribution from the remains of S3, and followed with the rest of the old S4. Material from the original S1 and S2 combines to make the new fourth para. The rest of the original

S2 was background, so gets split off and inserted lower down the story as S5. I could have continued to rework the story, particularly to shorten S2 – and doubtless there are further improvements on my version above. This kind and scale of reordering is by no means unusual. With one long story of mine, the first six paragraphs of a NZ Press Association rewrite used paras 12, 6, 10, 2, 1, 28 and 29 from my version!

Lead and order are the most important aspects of getting the most out of a story. But note other changes in the wool story, particularly the close relationship between cutting and news value. *The demand for tufted wool carpets in the UK and Europe* became *European demand for tufted wool carpets*. That is five words shorter. It also carries more punch because most of the words are contentful adjectives and nouns, including the strong *demand*. Four of the five function words of the original are eliminated. This explains the newsworker's liking for preposing. It emphasizes at the same time as it shortens, simultaneously cutting length and maximizing news value. An operation which achieves both is the copy editor's dream, although the other goal of clarity can be endangered in the process. Eliminating redundancy or creating tight structures can jeopardize comprehension, particularly for broadcast news.

The news value of the wool story is also enhanced by rewriting the description of the visitors. It is in a story's interests for its sources to appear as authoritative as possible. *Wool spinners* sounds like a pedal-power cottage industry. The rewrite makes the most of the sources' credentials as managers and directors of large companies – information extracted by questioning the source journalist.

There are other changes. Substitution of *market* avoids the double use of *demand* from the original S3. In the original S2, the serious purpose of the visit can be taken as read from the rest of the story – and can a *look* be *intensive* anyway? First person *our* is unacceptable in news reporting (outside quotes) which emphasises third-person objectivity. *It* in the second sentence of the original fourth paragraph has become too separated from its referent in the new version. It must be de-pronominalized to *the fibre* in S3, avoiding yet another use of *wool*, which occurs in every other sentence. (Such de-pronominalization is one of the few tamperings I would permit with a direct quote: otherwise it should remain verbatim what the source said.) *New Zealand* is redundant for local publication with mention of the Wool Board.

And so we go on, tightening, clarifying, extracting maximum value from a typical low-interest story which could have been much better written in the first place. The result adds information but is 17 words shorter than the original 108 words. The rewrite is in fact so radical that the processes become similar to those used in assembling input texts during the original authoring of a story (discussed in section 1 of this chapter). Lastly, however, note there is a semantic price for these syntactic and discourse changes. My version has attributed Lawton's opinion to the whole group of executives – but it is possible that the rest would not agree with him. And I have let *European* stand for *the UK and Europe*.

Standardizing language

The fourth function of copy editing is to meet language standards. These are of three kinds: the wider speech community's rules of the language's syntax, lexicon, spelling, and pronunciation; general guidelines on writing news; and the 'house style' of the particular news outlet. These standards may be overtly prescribed, unwritten or unconscious.

It is the copy editor's job to correct linguistic forms which do not conform to the speech community's prescriptions. Texts on news writing often concern themselves with the minor, disputed points of language which are the focus of overt comment in the community – split infinitives, prepositions at the end of sentences, neologisms, American versus British spellings or pronunciations.

General advice on news writing is found in texts such as those issued either by elite news outlets such as *The Times* or by news agencies (for example, Cappon 1982). The standard British work – in five volumes – is by Harold Evans (1972), one-time editor of the *Sunday Times*. Not surprisingly, such texts focus on the goals of copy editing we have already looked at – the production of brief, clear, newsworthy stories. In fact, a *description* of copy editing could easily be drawn from or adapted to *prescriptions* of how newsworkers should write. The texts are attempts to define the notion of good news writing. Such a standard is acknowledged throughout the journalistic profession, although every specific means for achieving it will be the topic of hot debate in newsrooms.

Specific 'house style' is most obviously focused in a news outlet's stylebook. House style consists of the minor style choices by which one news outlet's finished product is different from another's. It includes spelling and punctuation policies, and small but salient points of syntax and lexicon. Stylebooks tend to deal with the detail of style, usually covering only salient or conspicuous points. And although copy editors are the custodians of house style, they rarely consult their manuals. One function of editing standardization is to eliminate undesired idiosyncrasies from journalists' copy. We return in chapter 10 to editing and its repercussions on the meaning of news stories, and in chapter 8 to more detailed analysis of the structure and function of journalists' stories.

5

The Audience for Media Language

The audience are arguably the most important and certainly the most researched component of mass communication. The overwhelming bulk of 'research' on audiences is carried out for media organizations themselves. Most industry-funded surveys are concerned simply to count heads and describe them on a few demographic parameters, principally age, gender and occupation. Media live by the size and composition of their audiences, and information on these vital statistics is of consuming interest to owners and managers. Advertising rates are controlled by the number or kind of people who will be exposed to an advertisement. The very nature of broadcasting is such that research is required to find out whether there is an audience at all, since at the time of communication the animator cannot know if anyone is actually listening.

Many disciplines have approached audiences from their own perspectives. Sociological research has gathered information on the size of audiences and their structure. Social psychology has examined how audiences are affected by media content, or how they use that content. Cultural studies has considered how different kinds of people get different meanings from media content. Much early media research concerned itself with the effects of mass communication on the audience – what do media do to people? After decades of contradictory and inconclusive studies (cf. Howitt 1982), the question was turned around – what do people do with media? This 'uses and gratifications' approach (for instance, Klapper 1960) waned in its turn, and interest in the power of mass communication has reasserted itself (McQuail 1987). Research into media effects is of little interest to us here. But another strand of audience-oriented research focuses on how audiences comprehend media content, and we shall examine this in chapter 11.

The audience dimension provides the main defining features of mass communication. In one formulation, six out of seven characteristics of mass communication focus on the audience (McQuail 1969a: 7):

- large audience relative to other communication situations
- public accessibility of mass media content
- heterogeneity of the audience
- simultaneous contact with widely separated individuals
- one-directional flow and impersonality of mass communication
- the mass audience as a creation of modern society.

The seventh characteristic McQuail singles out is the complex nature of media organizations, which we covered in chapter 3. The audience-related characteristics of mass media and their difference from face-to-face communication are the focus of this chapter. We shall look at several factors which influence the shape of media language: feedback and the lack of it, communicators' stereotyping of the audience, the segmenting and layering of the audience, and those occasions when communicators and audience exchange roles.

1 DISJUNCTION AND ISOLATION

Mass communication is structurally different from face-to-face communication. It involves a disjunction of place, and often also of time, between communicator and audience. Media are based on technology, and it is technology which prescribes their location. That location is separated from the audience which, with satellite links, may now be half a world away. Technology tends to be inflexible in its location. Printing presses and mainframe computers do not move. The equipment needed for television coverage of a major event is massive and not easily transported. Radio is the most adaptable medium, and it is radio which has been most successful in overcoming the divide between communicator and audience.

The structural divide in mass communication has radical effects, particularly on broadcast media. Broadcasters operate from moment to moment with no assurance that they even have an audience. This is despite the fact that the television presenter is seen to be looking straight into the viewer's eyes, simulating direct contact and personal relationship (Mancini 1988a). Their production is a continuing act of technological faith, since even without mechanical problems, the broadcaster may doubt that an audience exists. Witness the late-night

DJ whom I heard close down his show with the words 'Goodnight, you three'. Burger (1984: 30) puts it well: 'If it is difficult to say who the sender is in mass communication, it is much more difficult to say who the communicator is actually communicating with.'[1]

The same technology which confines the communicators gives the audience freedom of movement. Audience members can be anywhere that technology, physical conditions and social custom permit. Newspapers can physically be read almost anywhere – although courtesy prescribes that they may not be read in many situations, from the dinner table to the lecture hall. Television can be received anywhere, but for most of us is restricted to one or two rooms at home. Radio is the most available medium, with transistors and Walkman sets allowing listening in many otherwise inaccessible or inadmissible settings.

The fracturing of location in mass communication is not a single break but multiple. Audience members are separated not just from the communicator but from each other. They can no more communicate among themselves than they can reach back to the media sender. This contrasts with other, non-mass communication situations, where the audience is always physically in contact. Even at huge events such as a rock concert the audience is together. A concert before 50,000 people has a far bigger audience than many mass media, such as local newspapers or radio stations. But these events are not therefore more 'mass' than the media. The crowd at the concert can do two things which the media audience cannot do: they can influence the musicians' performance in real time, changing what happens on stage. And they can influence each other to act as a group. The members of the mass audience, however, remain isolated from the communicator and each other. There are, of course, means by which media receivers can know how their fellow receivers are responding, and we touch on these below. But these means are by and large cumbersome and after-the-event, rather than immediate as with a live-show audience.

As well as the disjunction of place, there is often a disjunction of time between communicator and audience. With the press, this is always so, by the nature of the technology. Broadcast technology closes the gap, but even so most broadcast content is recorded rather than live. This holds especially for television, where live performance is the exception rather than the rule. Even in programmes presented live, such as the news, the majority of content will be prerecorded. Technology enables past events to be replayed as if they were current, just as it enables the distant to be made present in location. Radio again proves the most flexible medium, with a large amount of its content presented live, although of course most music – which is the staple of radio – is recorded. The time disjunction militates against audience response, just as does place disjunction. The audience cannot affect the shape of what they receive prerecorded from the media. They can only make an all-or-nothing objection that something has been transmitted at all – which happens from time to time.

Feedback

The fracture in the communication process has significant consequences for language production. Speaking rights belong to the mass communicator alone. One-way communication is not an unusual feature of public gatherings, but in mass communication distance and time dictate it. The feedback which is an integral factor in individual spoken communication is delayed, impoverished or lacking altogether in mass communication. Audiences are deprived of the usual means of inducing communicators to modify their production. Mass communicators are deprived of the usual access to recipients' reactions. The lack of two-way communication is pointed up by a device used occasionally in television advertisements selling television sets. These picture a viewer being able to converse with the people appearing on her screen. The viewer is surprised – and we are amused in turn as we view her – by the impossibility of the situation.

Although feedback is not absent from the mass communication process, in few cases is the audience member on equal terms with the communicators. These cases are audience participation programmes, especially the phone-in radio programme. Otherwise, direct feedback by the audience is subject either to delay – influencing subsequent but not immediate production – or to reduction: the audience member's response remains under the editorial control of the communicators. While media organizations do tend to pay disproportionate attention to letters or telephone calls from audience members, actual working communicators dismiss such respondents as 'cranks' (Schlesinger 1987: 107). However, this means of feedback does have the advantage of being far more immediate and forceful than retrospective circulation or audience figures. Complaints cannot turn back the clock and get something un-published again. But they can prevent the same thing being broadcast in the next news bulletin, or elicit an apology in tomorrow's paper.

The first form of feedback is direct audience response. The second is audience or circulation figures. The audience exercise their main influence on the media just through being the audience – or by deciding to be someone else's audience. Media managers are riveted by audience ratings or paid circulations. However, such figures generally come to hand somewhat after the time they refer to. Both types of feedback, therefore, are available only as input to future not present communication.

Even these limited sources are often ignored by mass communicators, and the more directly a person is involved in production, the less notice he or she takes of figures produced by audience research. Broadcasters follow their programme's ratings – the numbers in the audience – especially where this is a factor in the continuation of their output and employment. But they take little note of even the gross demographic data offered by an ordinary audience survey. The focus of ratings or circulations is audience size not audience kind. While they may give communicators some idea of how many are in their audience, they offer little information on the sort of person to whom communicators should be attuning their production.

Finally, audiences do provide something which could be regarded as feedback, although 'commentary' might be a more appropriate label. Matthewson (1989) examined how viewers talked back to the television while viewing popular programmes. The kinds of utterances responding to a game show and the soap *Days of Our Lives* included insults – 'Tony you creep', 'oh you patronizing bastard' – and advice such as 'go with your instincts Marie', 'Melissa don't do it'. Matthewson concluded that such utterances were aimed at other viewers present rather than the television set. Addressing the box in the corner conveys to companions one's attitudes on the television content. Viewers also assume the roles of characters they are watching, speaking 'with' the television, for example in adopting a character's accent.

Communicators' image of the audience

Mass communicators have only the haziest concept of what kind of people make up their audience. Isolation from the audience is a characteristic of mass communicators. Ironically, the more 'mass' the medium, the greater the isolation, so that one (radio) broadcaster speaks of 'the degree of self-absorption, amounting almost to autism, which is one of the most pronounced traits of television' (McIntyre 1988). This is promoted by physical and social isolation from those who are not fellow professionals. The staff of any media outlet tend to work from the site where their technology operates. Almost all those in the newsworker roles presented in table 3.2 (p. 39 above) work exclusively from their organization's location. Principals, editors and animators are largely housebound. The technology and operational systems are centralized, and newsworkers are largely the servants of the technology and logistics of their trade. The authors – journalists – go out more, but much of their voluntary socializing is with other journalists.

The stay-at-home nature of most newsworkers' jobs keeps them out of contact with the audiences with whom they are communicating. Burns' study of the BBC (1977) reflects this phenomenon in its title, *Public Institution and Private World*. His finding has been echoed by others (for example, Donsbach 1983, Schlesinger 1987): communicators are not just ignorant of the nature of their audience, they are uninterested. Their attitude ranges between 'a cultivated indifference and contemptuous dismissal' (Burns 1977: 133).

But regardless of how inadequately based their conceptions may be, communicators do work with an idea of the audience they are speaking to and what they want. Pool and Shulman (1959) questioned journalists on who they had in mind while writing a particular news story. The journalists claimed to think of 'imaginary interlocutors', but those images were formulated only in the most general terms. Television production staff show considerable fixation on the audience as a factor in choices which have to be made. Espinosa's study (1982) of production conferences on the *Lou Grant* show concluded that the audience is 'embedded' in producers' and writers' discussions as they construct the script. In deciding story lines for the show, producers followed four guidelines – engaging the audience, considering the audience's knowledge of the world, meeting the audience's expectations of the show, and not dividing the audience.

Professionalism and stereotyping

Communicators need the audience, whose approval must be won. But the audience is at the same time denigrated precisely for being thus persuaded. Although mass communicators do not usually volunteer descriptions of their target audience, they will respond with (often derogatory) stereotypes of audience members: 'Mum sitting in the best armchair drinking cocoa with a teenage son on the sofa trying to get his hand up his girl's skirts' (quoted in Burns 1977: 133). Such stereotypes are evoked as reasons for specific editorial choices, while some journalists speak of writing for family members or friends. Similar paradoxical attitudes occur among stage performers and service personnel such as waiters and salespeople. Burns (1977: 133) notes the 'countervailing, and ordinarily concealed, posture of invidious hostility' which such occupations show when the served public is absent. The hostility of the servers to the served is at the core of the comedy in John Cleese's classic television series, *Fawlty Towers*.

Such conclusions are surprising to the researcher and repellent to the media consumer. One begins to wonder on what basis mass communicators manage to operate. The 'missing link' between media producers and consumers is professionalism (Schlesinger 1987: 106). Mass communicators are interested in their peers not their public. Fellow communicators and co-professionals are their salient audience. Donsbach (1983) found that British and German journalists held a very low opinion of their readers, which legitimated journalists' serving as their own imaginary audience, despite the fact that they were clearly unrepresentative of the public (cf. also Robinson and Levy 1986). But although communicators in a real sense talk *for* other communicators, this does not mean they are talking *to* each other. Professionalism (cf. Soloski 1989) involves a consensus among communicators about how they should address different kinds of audiences.

Ignorance of the audience is no barrier to formation of a stereotyped image. We may suppose that it is even an aid. The mass audience is so large and diverse that conscious attempts to cater to it could be counter-productive. McQuail writes (1969b: 79): 'No "imaginary interlocutor" is likely to approximate to the realities of the undifferentiated mass audience, and whatever assumptions the communicator makes are bound to be of an imprecise and limited kind.'

Beliefs and stereotypes about recipients and their speech patterns are the sole practical input to mass communicators' linguistic output. Mass communicators can cater only to a stereotype of the audience's own language. In so doing they are aware of social groups rather than individuals. The inter-group dynamics of a society – how one group regards another – are therefore primary influences on how mass communicators talk.

2 MULTIPLE ROLES IN THE AUDIENCE

I discussed in chapter 3 how the production of media language involves many people in many roles. We described these roles first in a linear fashion, with news language moving from one to the next along a production line (figures 3.1–3). Then they were pictured vertically, as an embedding of one set of roles within another in the pro-

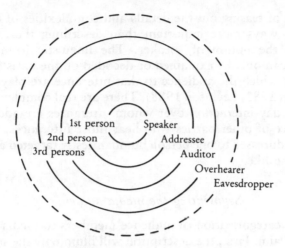

FIGURE 5.1   Persons and roles in the speech situation

duction process (figures 3.4–5). The result of this process, presented in chapter 4, is a news text which is multilayered, containing within itself the output of the previous stages of text generation. The same need to recognize a succession of roles and multiple layering arises in describing the media audience.

Scholars from a variety of approaches have given thought to the differing roles played by different audience members in face-to-face communication (for example, Goffman 1981, Clark 1987). Several of those who have worked in this area have drawn heavily on the media for examples (Levinson 1988). My own analysis (Bell 1984b) views the roles as concentric rings, like the skins of an onion (figure 5.1). These roles are ranked according to whether the persons are known, ratified and/or addressed by the speaker, the grammatical first person:

1   The main party in the audience is the *addressee*, the second person, who is known, ratified and addressed by the speaker.
2   There may also be others, third persons, present but not directly addressed. I use the term *auditors* to describe parties in the group who are known and ratified but not addressed.
3   Third parties whom the speaker knows to be there, but who are not ratified participants, are *overhearers*
4   Finally, the peripheral participants are other parties whose presence is not even known let alone ratified – the *eavesdroppers*.

The task of teasing out the details and complexities of these roles is in many ways more important than describing the roles incorporated in the notion of speaker. The linguistic form of many utterances can only be explained or decoded on the basis of analysis of the roles which the audience to that utterance are playing (Clark and Carlson 1982, Levinson 1988). There are real complexities possible in everyday interaction over whom utterances are addressed to, the influence of other parties who hear those utterances, utterances which are addressed to one person but manifestly targeted at someone else, and the like.

Segmenting the media audience

I apply the categorization of audience members to media language, with a dual aim. First, the description will illuminate the structure of the mass audience, and secondly, the categories needed to describe the media audience will illuminate the situation of everyday speech.

The media audience obviously has more in common with the audience present at a public event such as a political meeting than with those in face-to-face conversation for which the figure 5.1 description was designed. In order to apply this framework to mass communication, we need to modify it in two ways. In mass media the category of *known* is inappropriate (Bell 1984b: 200). Mass communicators never know whether they have an audience, let alone who is in it. Because their audience is remote from them, the communicator cannot access them directly at the moment of speaking in the way the face-to-face speaker does. So envisaging or *expectation* replaces knowledge as the communicator's input to monitoring his own speech. These expectations work to stereotype the nature of the audience, as noted above.

Audience roles have to be distinguished in terms of the communicators' expectations: the target audience who is addressed, the auditors who are expected but not targeted, the overhearers who are not expected to be present in the audience, and the eavesdroppers who are expected to be absent from the audience. The four-way division is not entirely satisfactory for public gatherings or for media communication. At the inner and outer edges of the public or media audience, we can undoubtedly identify addressees and eavesdroppers. But in between the extremes we do not have the clearcut distinction, which face-to-face conversation offers, between the ratified auditor and the unratified overhearer. Instead there is a continuum running from the targeted addressees to the excluded eavesdroppers, with different segments of the population falling at different points on the continuum.

The addressees are the target audience of a particular mass media outlet. They may not be just a single kind of person, but a number of different groups – although media do tend to think in terms of a typical reader or listener who can be described as a bundle of characteristics. The distinction between addressees and the rest of the audience is clearest in advertising. Commercials tend to be implicitly or explicitly addressed to a specific section of the population (Leech 1966: 63): youth, parents, surfers, shoppers. The addressees are therefore those to whom the communicator is addressing herself. But we should note here the difference between known and envisaged addressees. In face-to-face communication, we can see who was addressed by a speaker and describe that addressee's characteristics. But in mass communication it is impossible to locate specific addressees (Bell 1984b: 201). There is no one of whom we can say 'the communicator addressed that person.' The communicator doubtless has a particular kind of receiver in mind. Audience surveys can estimate who the actual receivers are. But because mass communication is a fractured interaction, we can identify actual addressees only *post hoc* by reference back to the people the communicators intended to address.

The other clearcut role is the eavesdroppers. Mass communication is for the mass. One of its defining characteristics is that it is available to everyone, but there are limits to this availability. The most obvious is legal: some magazines may not be sold to people under a certain age. A similar but softer stricture recommends that television programmes after 9 p.m. may not be suitable for children. There are geographical or technological limits on reception, but generally everything which is published or broadcast in mass-audience daily media is in some sense held to be suitable for the whole population to receive (whether this is really the case is another matter). When one moves towards the more specialist media such as magazines or cable television, audiences become exclusive, and eavesdroppers are possible. Those beyond the limits, usually the young, are eavesdroppers in the classic sense if they do read or view the forbidden material: they may become embarrassed on discovery.

Between the addressee and the eavesdropper is a finely graded continuum of audience segments. Take the audience for a rock music station of the kind found in most Western cities (figure 5.2). Its addressees – target audience – are in the 15 to 24 year old age group, and it draws 67 per cent of its listenership from them. As we move

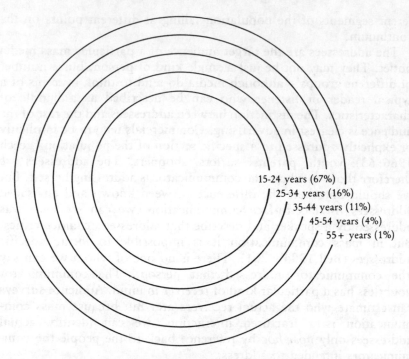

15-24 years (67%)
25-34 years (16%)
35-44 years (11%)
45-54 years (4%)
55+ years (1%)

FIGURE 5.2   From addressees to eavesdroppers: audience segments for a rock music station, ZM Auckland (Bell 1982a)

out from the target age group, we pass through the station's auditors to the periphery of its audience. Some 16 per cent are aged between 25 and 34, 11 per cent 35–44, 4 per cent 45–54, and 1 per cent are over 54 years old. (It will, of course, also have an audience segment younger than 15, omitted here for simplicity's sake.)

With each year of additional age, it becomes less likely that a person listens to this station. But there is no point on the continuum at which we can say some of the audience are ratified and others not: we are dealing merely with degrees of envisaged audience membership. At the outer edge of the audience, however, we would in fact be very surprised if any 80-year-olds chose to listen to ZM. So strong is the age-grading effect of the music that any such could be legitimately described as eavesdroppers. Indeed, the most likely way the elderly would hear the station is if they could not get out of earshot of a grandchild's transistor. The problem with such a person being in the audience is less the actual music than the standards which are acceptable on such a station. The elderly will probably find not acceptable the DJs' occasional expletives or obscenities – unthinkable on stations targeted to older addressees.

Media attempts to define certain kinds of people as eavesdroppers are always liable to shipwreck. Because broadcast media in particular are universally available within a given area, it is very difficult to maintain that any individual is not a legitimate member of their audience. Eavesdropping is an ever-present possibility. New Zealand's prime minister in the mid-1970s, Norman Kirk, on one occasion telephoned – on-air and unannounced – a phone-in radio station in the capital city, Wellington, when something had been said to upset him. Until that point, Radio Windy could have reasonably designated the prime minister as beyond the limits of its audience. But Kirk eavesdropped. (Note, however, that it was the radio station which was embarrassed by the eavesdropping not the prime minister.) Despite the generally vague concept which mass communicators have of their audience, they are capable of adjusting to identifiable and influential audience segments such as their own managers, owners, pressure groups and politicians. Norman Kirk had to ring Radio Windy only once to be catered to thereafter as a potential audience member.

3 AUDIENCE EMBEDDING

However, even a fine grading of audience roles is insufficient to cater for the mass communication situation. Here we have not just circles of the present audience. We have layers of communication embedded one into the other, each of them containing its own potential set of the roles outlined in the previous section. This concept is less well developed in linguistic research than in literary or narrative analysis (for instance, Bruce 1981, Leech and Short 1981, Clark 1987).

Mass communication is not alone in needing a dual set of roles. Any interaction which takes place for presentation before a live audience is potentially best described as dual-layered. The obvious case is the performance of a play. Within the play we require all the ordinary face-to-face roles. It is, in fact, theatrical examples which often best illustrate roles such as auditor and eavesdropper. The play takes place before the public audience. It is embedded, setting and roles, within the outer format created by the presence of the paying public. That public itself is described by the same roles. There are the addressees of the play, its target market. The auditors and overhearers, here as in mass communication, are graded from fully expected to highly unexpected attenders rather than two distinct groups. Finally come the eavesdroppers, those who sneaked in the back without paying. Even in live performance, the complications need not end there. The Jacobean theatre device of the play within a play can embed a complete new set of roles into the play itself.

'Recorded before a live audience'

Mass communication is very similar to this, differentiated by the characteristics of technology and distance. A television drama is performed for the cameras in similar fashion to the live theatre performance. The mass audience who view it are segmented like the live audience, but separated from the actual performance by place and usually time. Quite commonly the formats of the live and mass performances are combined. We see in the credits that a TV comedy was 'recorded before a live audience'. This creates a triple layering of play, live audience and mass audience (figure 5.3).

What is most obvious in television drama also occurs in other genres. Even the 'simple' radio or television news interview involves an embedded situation in which the journalist talks to the newsmaker, and the record of that is then presented to the listeners or viewers. A studio panel of interviewer and interviewees plays out the normal face-to-face roles of speaker, addressee and auditors. The panel may be recorded before an invited live audience, as well as broadcast to the absent mass audience.

In such formats, layer boundaries may be deliberately crossed. The live audience to a panel discussion may at some point be invited to

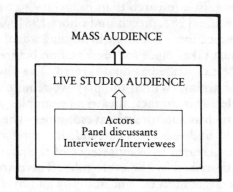

FIGURE 5.3   Audience layering in mass communication

ask questions or state viewpoints. They are then to some degree incorporated in the core situation of the panel debate, but they remain on an unequal footing with the panel members, who retain their priority speaking rights. A politician being interviewed before a live audience may address that audience directly rather than the interviewer. Such a technique is powerful precisely because it breaks through from one layer of the interaction to another (cf. the example in Levinson 1988: 213). The Shakespearean soliloquy achieves its impact by similar means.

Burger (1984: 44) uses a different but compatible image to describe mass audience roles. He pictures mass communication as consisting of two circles. There is the primary, inner circle of the communicators, for example in a studio discussion or drama. Their communication is 'refracted' on to the secondary, outer circle of the mass audience. If a studio audience is present, they are represented by a third, intermediate circle.

Designing talk for the mass audience

Two characteristics of mass communication – its accessibility and the heterogeneity of the audience – make the production of media talk a demanding business. Goffman's rich essay on radio talk (1981: 234ff.) explores the complexities of communicators' changes in footing as they shift from direct announcing at the microphone, to interviewing a studio guest, to addressing a live audience, to talking off-air to their technicians. Playing to two or three layers of audience, each containing diverse segments, is clearly a difficult language skill. It is precisely this kind of complex linguistic manoeuvring which public figures undertake constantly in the media. Interviewers orient their talk to the mass audience, not just the immediate audience, by their manner of questioning and by re-presenting prior talk in order to clarify points for the wider audience (Goffman 1981, Heritage 1985).

The difficulties are well illustrated in the classic case of former US President Jimmy Carter's interview with *Playboy* magazine.[2] During the 1976 presidential campaign Carter gave an interview to *Playboy* journalist Robert Scheer. As an addendum, while leaving after the interview, Carter departed from his deliberate interview style to make remarks on lustfulness, using terms such as *screw* and *shack up with*. The remarks upset many of his supporters. Solomon (1978) analysed the interview and concluded that the change in Carter's style was acceptable in the immediate context of the interview with Scheer, but violated his relationship to the public audience. Our recognition of audience roles and layers locates the site of the conflict. Carter had trouble with both the layering and segmenting of his audience. His words were appropriate for his addressee in the immediate interview. But they were inappropriate to be transmitted, by means of the *Playboy* feature, to the next layer, the mass audience. It seems likely the mass addressees, the magazine's core readership, may not have been offended by the article. But a high-circulation magazine will always fall into the wrong hands, if only those of other journalists. So the entire nation became auditors to Carter's remarks. Still more deeply offended were a group we might justifiably call eavesdroppers on *Playboy*: conservative religious supporters of Carter. These would assuredly not normally sight such a magazine. But the accessibility of the media, and their openness to being picked up in other media, makes their eavesdropping legitimate.

Carter was doubtless also subjected to what Davison (1983: 3) has called the third-person effect: 'People will tend to over-estimate the influence that mass communications have on the attitudes and behaviour of others.' Many would have regarded his remarks as unseemly for a future president in their potential to offend unspecified other citizens although not themselves. By this means different mass audience segments are influenced by their presumptions about other segments. Goffman captures it well: 'The issue, then, is not what *offends* the listener, but what a listener assumes *might* offend *some* listener or other' (1981: 244). Skilled politicians can use this presumption to influence not the actions of their ostensible addressees in a televised political speech but of such auditors as business decision makers.

Fill (1986) uses the apt term 'divided illocution' for public statements catering to a diversity of audiences. He notes the complex manoeuvres which politicians may have to accomplish in a single media speech in order to satisfy diverse constituents. A speech delivered in an international forum when a politician is abroad may in fact be primarily directed to the absent audience of the politician's constituency back home.

4 COMMUNICATORS AS AUDIENCE

One group in the audience for mass communication stands in a special relationship to the communicator and the message: those who are co-responsible for production of the message. The role of the editors, producers, technicians and others introduced in chapter 3 is not to make their own verbal contribution but to facilitate communication of others' contributions to the distant mass audience. These people function simultaneously as both audience and communicators. To a large extent they exercise their professional roles through being members of the live audience to media content. In this they are not unique. Studio audiences are both audience to the central event of an interview or play, and communicators in so far as their reactions are themselves transmitted. But the production staff are employed specifically to monitor the quality of the communication, to ensure that it meets professional standards of production, and to communicate it properly.

While they function as audience at the embedded level of communication, they are themselves simultaneously communicators to the mass audience. Their presence in the audience for mass communication is in fact required for the communication to take place at all. This is not surprising since mass communication requires technology, and technology requires technicians. The presence of technicians can combine with the quirks of technology to make trouble for the on-air communicator. Microphones are not always switched off at the moment the broadcaster thinks they are. Goffman (1981: 267) shows how the mass audience can be made eavesdroppers on remarks which were addressed as off-air asides to the technicians. He cites 'Uncle Don', after closing his children's programme and wrongly assuming the microphone was off: 'I guess that will hold the little bastards.'

The technicians are just the most obvious example of the communicator as audience. Every person involved in the news process is producing a text for consideration by the next person on the production line. The broadcast journalist produces for the copy editor, and the copy editor for the newsreader. An editor is at the same time both audience and producer – audience to the extent of receiving and reading an existing text, and producer to the extent that she intervenes in the form of that text and it is her version which passes to the next producer in the chain. The communicators play to many communicator audiences: editors, owners, managers, technicians, animators, absent fellow professionals, newsmakers, and their own selves.

The editor roles such as news editor or chief reporter are journalists' closest, and arguably most important, audience. While a few programmes have studio audiences, in most cases it is other media professionals who form the only live audience to broadcast production such as a newscast. They include the superiors for whom journalists and other authors are writing. In many cases these will check specific story content and style when it emerges from the other end. Especially in public service broadcasting the practice of upward referral of important editorial decisions may be required: 'The wrath of the Corporation in its varied human manifestations is particularly reserved for those who fail to refer' (Huw Wheldon, then managing director of BBC Television, quoted in Kumar 1975: 76).

The animators are an important audience. Authors and editors are required to maintain technical standards – for instance, of sound quality – which will be of professionally acceptable quality for transmission. Similarly, broadcast journalists must produce text appropriate for newsreaders to read aloud, avoiding locutions which will be hard to pronounce. The news outlet's principals are a significant audience/producer group. Owners and news executives are rarely active regular participants in the production process. But they are able to interfere with the process when things are not to their liking. Their producer role is therefore exercised largely through membership in the audience. They are *post hoc* consumers with special rights of feedback on something which has been published, and consequent prescriptive rights on how such things will be handled in future.

Authors are also audiences of their own production. Spontaneous conversation does not allow speakers the capability to alter their speech during the act of production except in retrospect by correction, self-repair, etc. But when the role of animator is separated from that of author, and particularly when the message is recorded, the language can be altered in production without the public audience perceiving it.

There remain two other groups of producers-as-audience, beyond the immediate fellow workers. First are the producers' absent fellow professionals. As noted above, newsworkers produce for their professional peers rather than for the ostensible main audience, the mass public (Burns 1977, Schlesinger 1987). The other individuals actually involved in the production chain are the frontline representatives of the fellow professionals. But it extends much wider than that. Newsworkers in parallel positions in rival media are a significant and conscious audience for producers – probably the most salient audience of all, with the news world's value placed on getting a story first, before the rivals. The parties most salient in my mind during actual copy handling are the principals, fellow journalists and rival professionals in other competing organizations.

The final group are the newsmakers themselves. During the news production process, after their involvement in providing information, they may be contacted again for further information. On occasion they may check either specific facts or the copy as written for accuracy (a rare procedure in journalism). In any case, asked or unasked, the newsmakers also act as *post hoc* audience, in much the same way as do principals. And they often exercise their right to complain about the way they have been presented.

The audience as communicators

Media try to break out of their isolation and lack of feedback and to overcome the usual limits of media communication. Radio offers by far the best examples of such formats. As a medium it is the most flexible in its lesser technological and personnel requirements. A local radio station can be run with comparatively little equipment and few staff. It is also the most flexible for innovative audience involvement. Phone-in or talkback programmes have attracted the attention of a number of linguists. This is partly because they offer the possibility of easy recording of conversation. Provided the differences between the format of such publicly displayed conversations and ordinary face-to-face conversation is remembered, this does not cause a problem.

Several linguists have studied such programmes precisely because of the interesting nature of speaker and audience roles. Troesser (1983) and Selting (1985) have both researched – apparently unaware of each other's work – a weekly audience-participation programme in the Ruhr region of West Germany, *Hallo-Ü-Wagen*. The programme operates from an outside broadcast vehicle, parked each time in a different town in the region. The moderator, Carmen Thomas, chooses a theme from listeners' suggestions and invites expert guests to join her to talk about it. The vehicle front stands open so that the public acts as a live audience to the programme, which is carried on loudspeakers as well as transmitted for broadcast. Members of the public can queue up to make their own contribution at the microphone.

Aside from the programme's greater accessibility to public participation in the localities it visits, the structure of the audience here is little different from that pictured in figure 5.3. The core group is the moderator and invited experts. The live audience are on the street rather than in a studio. The broadcast audience are remote as ever. During the programme members of the live audience can be briefly incorporated into the core group around the microphone. The difference lies not in the structure of the audience but in the setting.

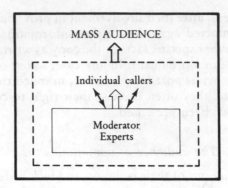

FIGURE 5.4 Breaking down the barriers: participation format of radio phone-in programme

Taking the programme on to the streets makes it more accessible to public participation than requiring the audience to come in to the studio. Otherwise the programme is conducted in a similar fashion to a studio discussion before a live audience.

This programme is unusual in its willingness to go out to people rather than expecting them to come in to the broadcasters. This itself is a considerable revolution in overcoming the remoteness engendered by the usual media situation. In radio the usual way of incorporating the audience is through the telephone. This enables people to participate easily, by linking the technologies of telephone and broadcasting. The format, as Crisell (1986) notes, is 'highly radiogenic'. You do not have to be part of a live audience to participate: individuals from the mass audience are briefly incorporated into the actual production of the media content to which they are listening. This direct link to the mass audience, in real time as opposed to delayed response, is practically unique in mass communication (figure 5.4). However, the disjunction between the media communicators and the mass audience remains, even though one member of the mass is temporarily plucked from obscurity to join the inner circle of communicators. Leitner (1983a) provides a detailed analysis of two pioneering phone-in programmes in the United Kingdom in the mid-1970s, the BBC's *It's your Line* and Independent Radio London's *Open Line*. He examines the consequences of the format for the linguistic and communicative style of the participants.

A final way in which the audience become communicators is through generating at the planning and production stage the themes which media will cover. This is a very rare phenomenon in the media and tends to be regarded with suspicion by both media and social authorities. In New Zealand, and doubtless in other countries, 'access' radio stations operate which enable interest groups to present their own programmes, with technical expertise provided.

Attempts to unite communicators and audience are usually motivated by a belief in the worthwhile contribution which audiences have to make to their own communication. Mody (1986) describes an experimental radio station set up in Jamaica under a United States agricultural aid programme. The station was designed to make the audience the source of the programming they would receive. Community researchers were employed to convey locals' needs, and villagers were trained in news collection. The innovative format was accompanied by linguistic originality. Instead of scripting standard news bulletins, the station presented its information in an 'on-air simulation of the casual everyday exchange of news' (Mody 1986: 156). And it used creole rather than standard English, which was the accepted norm for broadcast speech. The use of creole was eventually diluted after government pressure. In due course the international funding came to an end and the station returned to standard formats.

There is a paradox evident throughout this chapter which lies at the heart of all mass communication: the simultaneous omnipotence and helplessness of the audience. Communicators are in a sense slaves to their audience. This becomes overt when a music star is required to replay, at concert after concert, popular songs that the audience *will* hear live as well as on record but which the musician wants to leave behind. Or when the TV star is forced into an on-screen role or stereotype in other contexts. Members of the audience have the power to switch off, to refuse to buy, to reject a media outlet. On the other hand, they are helpless. Audience power becomes effective only if exercised *en masse*, which is beyond the influence of the individual media consumer. In the following two chapters we see how media language is affected by both the power and powerlessness of the audience.

6

Stylin' the News: Audience Design

As news consumers, we are very aware that different media regard
different things as news. A mass circulation tabloid such as the British
Sun covers different stories from those in elite readership papers like
The Times or *Independent*. Still more obvious are the contrast in
presentation. The 'popular' and 'quality' British dailies look entirely
different from each other – in design, typography, use of photographs
and other visual techniques.

The differences in content and visual styles are paralleled in the
language used. This chapter deals with the linguistic styles of different
news media and offers an explanation for why they differ. In so doing
we shall see how the mass communication situation heightens factors
operating in everyday communication between people. The processes
which mould language style in mass communication are similar in
kind – but often greater in degree – to those which operate in face-to-
face interaction.

1 STYLE IN LANGUAGE

Style shift is variation within the speech of an individual speaking a
single language. That intra-speaker variation can occur on many
linguistic levels, from the 'micro-variables' studied by sociolinguists
to larger scale manifestations such as turn-taking and politeness strategies, which are not so amenable to quantitative research. The
audience design framework proposed in Bell (1984b, cf. Milroy
1987: 171ff.) was developed in an attempt to account for this intra-
speaker variation. Specifically, it accounted for the range of variation
I had found in news styles, variation which did not fit the commonly
advanced explanations.

The foundational research on style shift was Labov's pioneering sociolinguistic study on the stratification of English in New York City (1966, 1972a). Since then sociolinguists have been accustomed to differentiate the inter-speaker and intra-speaker dimensions of language variation. The inter-speaker or 'social' dimension has been correlated with differences in the measurable social characteristics (such as age, gender or social class) of a person – the speaker. Audience design proposes that the intra-speaker or stylistic dimension of language variation can be primarily correlated with the attributes of the hearers. That is, speakers design their talk for their hearers (the term 'design' is not meant to imply detailed awareness of individual language choices.)

Audience design

Audience design informs all levels of a speaker's linguistic choices – the switch from one complete language to another in bilingual situations (Gal 1979, Dorian 1981), choice of personal pronouns or address terms (R. Brown and Gilman 1960, Ervin-Tripp 1972), politeness strategies (P. Brown and Levinson 1987), use of pragmatic particles (Holmes 1986), and quantitative style shift (Coupland 1980, 1984). The data I present below are drawn from studies of radio and press news styles in United Kingdom and New Zealand (Bell 1982a, 1988, 1991a), demonstrating how newsreading styles largely correlate with their audiences.

I believe the essence of style is that speakers are responding to their audience. It is typically manifested in a speaker shifting her style to be more like that of the person she is talking to. The basic dimension on which we can examine a speaker's style is therefore a responsive one.[1] A second dimension of audience design suggests that communicators' strategies will sometimes be responsive and sometimes 'initiative' (Bell 1984b). That is, speakers are often primarily responding to their audience in the language they produce. But they also on occasion take more initiative and use language to redefine their relationship to their audience.

Within the media, some genres are more prone to response and others to initiative. We shall see in this chapter how the more formal genres such as newscasting are towards the responsive end of the scale. National newscasts still retain the depersonalized, status-oriented flavour advocated in a 1936 BBC memorandum: 'The BBC . . . has many voices but one month . . . It is a commonplace that "announcers sound all alike". That is a tribute to their training' (quoted in Kumar

1975: 77). Other formats such as advertising, DJ patter and on-air discussions are more prone to communicator initiative, as chapter 7 shows. This 'hierarchy' of programme types has more often been assumed than demonstrated. There is, however, supporting evidence in Lipski's (1985) collation of data from Spanish-language radio in the Americas. It shows a clear grading in all countries from news, the most 'responsive' format with the lowest frequencies of local phonological variants, through DJ patter, to sports commentary with the most local, 'initiative' variants.

The accommodation model

While audience design came from a disciplinary background in socio-linguistics, a parallel approach arose in social psychology: accom-modation theory. Crudely characterized, speech accommodation theory proposes that speakers accommodate their speech style to their hearers (Giles and Powesland 1975). In the past decade the theory has been extensively developed, expanded and revised (for instance, Thakerar et al. 1982, Giles et al. 1987, Coupland et al. 1988). The proliferation of complexities is at times in danger of obscuring the framework's principal insight. Nevertheless the main findings in this field make it clear that speakers respond primarily to their audience in designing their talk.

Mass communication research can both learn from and offer something to the study of speech accommodation (cf. Bell 1991a). The theory was largely developed to analyse and account for how speakers modify their speech in the complex dynamics of interper-sonal encounters where one moment's speaker becomes hearer the next moment. We have seen that mass communication is very dif-ferent, with a largely one-way traffic. Nevertheless, as the data presented below will show, accommodative strategies of convergence and divergence, of shift towards national or local norms, or in relation to actual and stereotyped audiences are all operative.

Accommodation theory also attempts to specify the motivations which lie behind use of particular accommodative strategies. Approval seeking has been recognized as a prime motive in accom-modation. This is very powerful in mass communication, where we assume that communicators are always in some sense trying to win the approval of their audience (McQuail 1969b). More recently accommodation theory has taken account of the simple factor of com-municative efficiency – the need to be heard and understood, to allow for recipients' physical situation and abilities (for example, Coupland et al. 1988). Such concern for receipt of a clear signal has always been a prime motivation in mass communication. Aside from keeping the channel open and noise-free, the communicator must take account of the range of situations in which the message will be received. The broadcaster repeats certain information on a regular cycle in the knowledge that radio is rarely the sole object of a listener's attention, that the audience comes and goes.

The audience accommodates

Mass communication also offers an intriguing, reverse form of accommodation which is impossible in one-to-one interaction but can also operate in public speaking situations. A speaker's belief about an interlocutor's style may not coincide with reality. In face-to-face communication, direct feedback from a recipient may persuade the speaker to modify an unsuitable style. In extreme cases, failure to adjust may lead the audience to break off the interaction. But in mass communication the weight of the two types of feedback is reversed. The audience has the power of choice. The second, supposedly extreme method becomes the norm − dissatisfied audience members switch off or tune in elsewhere. And the usual means of feedback face to face becomes the extreme − only a small minority of the mass audience ever directly contact the media with complaints or suggestions.

Assuming that audience membership usually signifies approval of communicator style, it follows the media attract the audiences which suit them. If the communicator is unsuccessful in accommodating to the audience, the audience will do the accommodating. If the style does not shift to suit the audience, the audience will shift to a style that does suit. The communicator will then have an audience which was unintended but whose composition in fact suits the style − or conceivably no audience at all.

2 STYLE AND AUDIENCE STATUS IN THE BRITISH PRESS

We can initially examine how style suits a news outlet's audience by means of just one linguistic variable. A rule characteristic of news language deletes the determiner in appositional naming expressions of the form:

[the] Australian entrepreneur Alan Bond
[a] Spanish tourist Josefa Morelli
[his] fellow left-winger Bob Cryer

The data are some 4000 tokens of noun phrases which meet the structural description of the determiner deletion rule. These were collected in the United States, United Kingdom and New Zealand at several periods between 1974 and 1990 (Bell 1977, 1985, 1988). The structure and development of the expression is an interesting study in its own right (chapter 9), but we will focus here solely on the relative frequency of the rule's application by different media.

Figure 6.1 displays the percentage of determiner deletion in seven of Britain's national daily newspapers in 1980. It graphs the number of times the determiner was actually deleted over the number of times it could have been deleted. The three 'quality' newspapers, *The Times*, *Guardian* and *Daily Telegraph*, delete very few determiners. The *Telegraph* shows the highest deletion at 12 per cent. The four 'popular' papers delete most of the determiners, between 73 per cent for the *Daily Mail* and 89 per cent for the *Sun*. This is more than a cut between two kinds of newspaper. We find that papers are grouped according to their readership profiles. What is more, they are graded and their rankings in figure 6.1 correspond almost exactly to the social status of their readerships. Only the *Guardian* breaks the perfect correlation between social group and determiner deletion, and then by

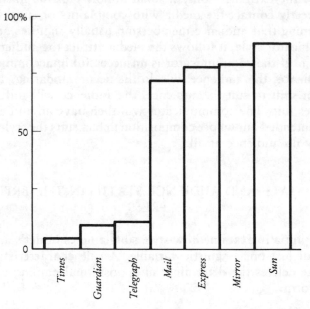

FIGURE 6.1 Percentage of determiner deletion in seven British daily newspapers

just one percentage point. This is shown in the National Readership Surveys conducted in Britain during 1980 (JICNARS 1980) which give us the different newspapers' rankings by the social grade of their readership. The surveys distinguish six socioeconomic classes (A, B. C1, C2, D and E). The first three categories represent the middle classes, and the last three the working classes. No matter how one manipulates the figures, the 'quality' and 'popular' dailies have quite distinct readership profiles. *The Times* has the highest-grade readership, followed by the *Telegraph* and *Guardian*. These three papers – as well as the *Financial Times* and the newer *Independent* – draw over 80 per cent of their readership from the upper-middle, middle-middle and lower-middle classes (grades A, B, C1). Then there is a considerable drop to the *Daily Mail* and *Daily Express* (and the more recent tabloid, *Today*). These are followed by the *Mirror, Sun* and *Star*, all of which draw about 80 per cent of readers from the working classes (C1, D, E).

The close reflection of audience status in linguistic style is no accident of this particular sample. Rydén (1975) studied the same variable in the British press ten years before my research, and found a similar correspondence. A large 1987 sample by Jucker (1989) gave strong confirmation to the pattern.[2] He divides the British press more finely into three groups, upmarket, midmarket and downmarket:

Upmarket:	*The Times, Financial Times, Guardian, Independent, Daily Telegraph*
Midmarket:	*Daily Mail, Daily Express, Today*
Downmarket:	*Daily Mirror, Star, Sun.*

Working in an audience design framework, he found that the upmarket papers deleted between 2 and 33 per cent of determiners in name appositions. The midmarket group ranged from 87 to 99 per cent, and the downmarket group showed 99 or 100 per cent deletion. The structure of determiner deletion reflects the social structure of the papers' readerships in some detail. There is a much greater social distance between the readership of upmarket papers and that of midmarket papers than between the midmarket and downmarket readers. The relative distance is mirrored in the relative amounts of determiner deletion. Jucker concludes that 'it is remarkable how perfectly the three types of papers are differentiated by their use of this construction' (1989: 211).

The papers' readership profiles are very stable over time, as other surveys show (for instance, Sparks 1987). Although individual papers lose or gain reader numbers, the kind of readers they have changes very little. In addition, new papers tend to fit into the existing categories and have similar readership profiles to existing papers. Thus, the *Independent* and *Today* have slotted in to the readership patterns of the established groups of papers. Their behaviour for the determiner deletion variable also fits the existing moulds, as Jucker's study shows.

The determiner deletion variable is diagnostic of the social stratification of a news outlet's audience. In another country and another medium, the same patterns reappear. Data from several samples between 1974 and 1984 on New Zealand radio stations show a similar good correlation between determiner deletion and audience status. Similar stratification patterns according to audience status are shown for a number of linguistic variables in several studies in different countries and languages. I found that negative contraction is stratified according to audience status in New Zealand radio news (Bell 1982a, 1991a). Brunel (1970) studied the styles of French-speaking radio stations in Montreal. For affrication of /t/ and /d/ (to [ts] and [dz] respectively), the elite CBF station used the lowest frequency (48 per cent). The teenage station CJMS used by far the most affrication (90 per cent), while the three middle-audience stations used intermediate values (53–4 per cent). Yaeger-Dror's (1988) analysis of the use of Hebrew dialects on Israeli radio again shows a similar pattern. Apical /r/ in the news language of five stations increases in accordance with their audience status.

3 AUDIENCE DESIGN IN NEW ZEALAND RADIO

I will present in some detail aspects of my own early studies on news styles of Auckland radio (Bell 1977, 1982a). Although I have updated aspects of this data from time to time since (Bell 1990, 1991a), the original research remains the clearest evidence of audience design in media language (cf. Milroy 1987: 81). The period at which I first studied Auckland radio proved to be optimal for an examination of language style. The five stations provided enough differentiation to be interesting stylistically. Two or three stations would not have given sufficient variety, and the present ten stations are more than can offer consistent stratification among audiences and language styles. It also provides a more detailed case study in the sociolinguistic analysis of media communication.

I describe here the situation as it was at the time of the main language sample used in this research, 1974, while updating some labels which have changed in the interim. Much of the basic programming and character of the stations remains remarkably unchanged despite several reorganizations of public broadcasting and the addition of several more stations (mostly FM). News programming, formats, sources and networking have altered more (particularly since station 1ZB went to a 'Newstalk' format), yet the audience design patterns are largely constant. The tendency for media outlets to maintain their audience profiles is strong despite outlets' attempts to attract new or different audiences. While stations have lost audience *numbers* to new stations, the *composition* of the audience they retain remains notably stable. Several resamplings of specific linguistic variables at intervals since the original sample also indicate that the basic patterns to be described here have remained very steady.

Radio in Auckland

Five radio stations broadcast news in Auckland city at the time of this sample (referred to by their call signs, as in table 6.1). Three were operated by the public corporation, Radio New Zealand, which networked much of its news from the capital, Wellington, for retransmission by local stations. Private radio was legalized in New Zealand in 1968, which permitted the pirate station Radio Hauraki (1XA) to set up on shore after several years of broadcasting to the youth of Auckland from a barge of doubtful seaworthiness anchored beyond the 12-mile territorial limit.

The five stations were differentiated by both programme content and audience membership. Table 6.1 charts a number of characteristics of the stations. Although it was the focus of this study, news is only one ingredient of broadcast programming. 1YA was (and still is) the Auckland repeater station of Radio New Zealand's National Radio network originating in Wellington. National Radio is the corporation's flagship, the prestige station of public radio, carrying much solid news, current affairs programmes, in-depth interviews, and other talk programmes. Its audience is among older people and the higher education and professional levels. 1ZB was Radio NZ's general-audience commercial station in Auckland. It is the city's chief service and information station, carried a lot of advertising, cultivating a homely relationship with its audience. The audience was middle New Zealand, in age and class, and their families. Station 1ZM was Radio NZ's rock music station, with a young, largely male audience to match. The private rock station, 1XA, was similar in tone

TABLE 6.1 Characteristics of five radio stations in Auckland, 1974

Radio station	Ownership	Audience	Community involvement	Programming	Music	Advertising	Announcer style	News 'station'
1YA carries National Radio network from Wellington	New Zealand (public corporation)	Older, with higher education, professionals	Nil	Highly scheduled: news, current affairs, concerts, drama	'Light' often from 1940s and 1950s	Nil	Detached, measured: prestige radio, prestige speech	YA: National Radio news, live from Wellington YAR: Regional news from 1YA Auckland BBC: Overseas Service relayed live from London
1ZB local Community Network station	Radio NZ	Age 30–50, family, mid status	Very high. Main local service and information station. Local sponsorships, interviews, advertising	Community information, sport, horse racing news, shopping tips, household advice, local news	Popular, 'middle of the road', established hits	A lot of advertising, much read in chatty fashion by announcer	Homely, familiar: programme 'hosts' – especially breakfast session – are local notables	ZB: Community Network news relayed live from Wellington ZBR: Regional news from Auckland (coded jointly as ZB/R for audience survey)

1ZM	Radio NZ	Young, largely male	Low	Continuous music	Rock: recent and often specialist	Some advertising, often music related	Archetypal disc jockey: dramatic, suave, frequent talk over music	ZM: Own news
1XA Radio Hauraki	Private	Young, low status, largely male	Some community information and sponsorship	Music	Rock: softer than ZM	Much advertising, aimed at teenage and twenties audience	A little quieter than ZM	XA: Own news
1XI Radio i	Private	Mid age and status, largely female	High involvement especially through talkback, interviews	Telephone talkback (especially daytime), interviews, music	Popular, some rock	Household oriented	Familiar	XI: Own news

Note: Here, as elsewhere in tables and lists, the stations are given in the order of their medium wave frequencies.

and appeal, but with a larger audience. Finally, the other private station, Radio i (1XI), at the time offered mainly telephone talkback programming to a middle audience similar in composition to 1ZB's, but with more women listeners. All stations except 1YA carried advertising.

The five stations broadcast eight distinct sets of news (table 6.1). National Radio broadcast a dozen bulletins daily from Wellington (coded *YA*). The local Auckland repeater station broke out of the network once daily for a bulletin of regional news (*YAR*). And in addition, three to four bulletins daily (coded *BBC*) were carried live from the BBC Overseas Service in London (now transmitted on the FM Concert Network). Station 1ZB carried news networked from Radio NZ in Wellington to the 20-odd local community stations throughout New Zealand (coded *ZB*). 1ZB itself also produced bulletins of local news (coded *ZBR*), broadcast immediately after many network bulletins. These five sets of news (YA, YAR, BBC, ZB, ZBR) were treated as separate and distinct for the language analysis. The situation on the other three stations was much more straightforward. ZM, XA and XI each compiled and presented its own news bulletins.

The multiple stations of New Zealand public broadcasting make possible a controlled comparison of news styles, which I present below. YA and ZB news originate in the same suite of studios in Wellington, with the same individual newsreaders heard on both networks. Similarly, YAR, ZBR and ZM also share a common pool of announcers reading the news in Auckland. This enables a comparison of the different styles used by a single newsreader when recorded on more than one station.

The random language sample consisted of about 17 hours of newsreader speech from the eight news outlets (chapter 2 covered much of the design and methodology I used in this sample). It yielded 80–200 tokens of the desired phonological variables for between four and nine newsreaders each on all stations except YAR. An additional non-random sample was collected during the months following the main sample period. This focused on gathering more speech by those newsreaders who were heard on two or three different stations.

This study argues that differences which may be identified between the news styles of Auckland's radio stations are the result of differences in audiences and their values. It assumes that membership in a station's audience evinces general approval of that medium, its content and its communicators' style. Random surveys of the Auckland urban area at the time of the language sample provided the main characterization of the audience. This audience survey parallels the random surveys of speakers which were at the base of the early socio-linguistic studies in speech communities (for example, Labov 1966, Trudgill 1974). Each Auckland survey questioned 586 respondents over the age of 15 in two areas of interest: media reception habits and demographic characteristics (gender, age, education, occupation). The survey distinguished five age groups, and five divisions of the education variable. The occupation scale had four ranked groups, plus a residual category for non-workers (omitted from rankings for social status).

These surveys enable us to construct a demographic profile of each station's audience, focusing on the proportion of that audience which comes from each age, education or occupation level. For the age variable the five stations divided clearly into three groups, as one would expect from the outline of their programming presented above. ZM and XA were very similar, with two-thirds of their audiences in the 15–24 age bracket and a mean age of 25.6 and 26.6 years respectively. (Doubtless these mean ages would have been lower if those under 15 years old had been included in the population.) ZB and ZBR (coded ZB/R) with a mean age of 43.1 years and XI (41.5 years) have the middle age audiences. YA's audience has very few in the youngest age group, a large proportion of the respondents over 55 years old, and a mean age of 47.4 years.

Education differences between stations' audiences were not strongly marked. The stratification for occupation is more evident (figure 6.2), as we might expect from the usefulness of occupation rather than education as a measure of social stratification in New Zealand (Pitt 1977). YA is clearly the highest status station on the measure. It has 50 per cent 'professionals' in its working audience, and the lowest proportion of manual workers. ZM and XA share similar occupation profiles to each other, weighted to the low-status end of the audience. And ZB/R and XI also have similar-occupation audiences, with profiles close to that of the general population. That is, they are the mid-status stations.

These survey findings reveal three distinct groupings of stations. We have YA with the older listeners and highest education and occupation levels, ZB/R and XI in the middle rank for occupation and age, and ZM and XA with the young male audience and low occupation levels. We will expect that if news styles are related to audience characteristics, the stations will rank in the same order.

A second axis of audience characterization intersects with the above. These two dimensions have been identified under a range of labels, including power and solidarity (R. Brown and Gilman 1960),

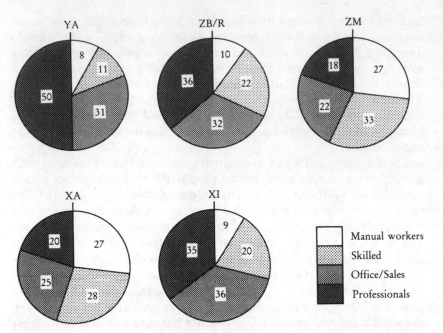

FIGURE 6.2   Occupation profiles of audiences for Auckland radio stations
(percentage of station's audience)

overt and covert prestige (Trudgill 1972), standard and local prestige
(Bell 1982a), and status and solidarity (Milroy 1980, Coupland
1985). The former terms in each pair are associated with overtly and
often nationally acknowledged speech norms, used by groups whose
social status is evidenced in high occupations, education levels and
incomes. These correspond to P. Brown and Levinson's notion of
'politeness' or 'deference' (1987). The latter terms (solidarity and
covert/local prestige) are associated with more covert norms, oriented
to family, peer group, local community and often working-class
values. Many studies have shown how such values influence language,
modifying or displacing linguistic variants widely regarded as
prestigious with variants which mark local, ingroup solidarity.

The local solidarity dimension was not directly surveyed for this
research. Programme content was used to infer the degree to which
stations and their audiences are locally oriented. The description in
table 6.1 indicates the relative strength of local commitment on the
different stations. The national stations YA and ZB clearly can have
little or no local identity. ZM and XA show a little, and ZBR is the

most locally oriented station, followed by XI (then YAR). The pull of the local factor could thus be reflected in some linguistic patterns on ZBR and XI.

Audience solidarity: consonant cluster reduction

One phonological / syntactic variable is examined here from the many which could have been analysed. In general, detail of linguistic environments is here kept to the minimum necessary to reveal the nature of the audience design. I have illustrated above with determiner deletion in the British press how audience status is reflected in linguistic variation. There is no need to duplicate the pattern here although it could equally well have been demonstrated for the Auckland radio data with a variable such as negative contraction (Bell 1990). Probably the most studied sociolinguistic variable in English is the rule which simplifies word-final consonant clusters by deleting the stop which is the last member of the cluster (Guy 1980). In this way *West Coast coal* may be pronounced *Wes' Coas' coal*. The reduction (often known as /t,d/ deletion) is an apparently universal marker of less formal speech styles, and also registers solidarity within some social groups.

Two linguistic factors were found to influence rule application here (Bell 1991a): the following phonetic environment, and whether the cluster occurs in the coordinator *and* or not. Following vowel, glide or pause disfavour reduction, while following consonant or liquid favour it. With a following alveolar stop, cluster reduction is especially high. In monitoring BBC radio, G. Brown (1977) never heard a [t] (as a released stop) in *West Germany*. Figure 6.3 graphs the percentage of consonant cluster reduction for all stations in the four environments of a following segment by *and* cross-classification. The pattern is very consistent, with a regular rise from the least favoured following vowel/non-*and* environment [– C, – &], to the most favoured consonant/*and* environment [+ C, + &]. Equally striking is the regularity of the station ordering. YA reduces least clusters, and ZB slightly more. Then come ZM and XA in a central grouping, and ZBR and XI together with the highest cluster reduction, approaching 100 per cent in the most favoured environment.

This ordering reflects the intersection of a local, solidarity factor with a status-oriented ordering. On the grounds of audience status, the stations should be ordered YA-ZB/R-XI-ZM-XA (as they had been for the negative contraction variable). But for cluster reduction, the strongly local news station ZBR has shifted well beyond XA and ZM, followed by the slightly less locally oriented XI.

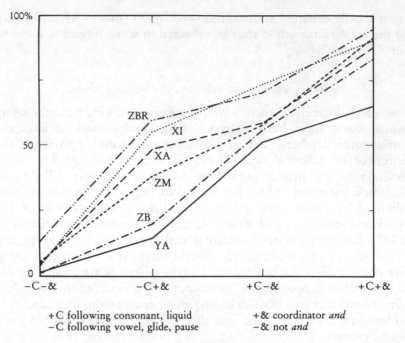

+C following consonant, liquid   +& coordinator *and*
−C following vowel, glide, pause   −& not *and*

FIGURE 6.3 Percentage of consonant cluster reduction on six Auckland radio news stations in four linguistic environments

The orderings are disturbed only by minor crossovers in the [− C, − &] and [+ C, + &] environments. Such deviations are not uncommon in environments where rule application is below 10 per cent or above 90 per cent. The major crossovers are predictable – ZM with XA, and ZBR with XI, the two station pairs with similar audiences. The rankings are remarkably consistent, the more so because the spread between stations is in most environments not great. The large N(= 3317) has here minimized the effect of fluctuations often caused by insufficient tokens. The presence of the local factor intersecting with status and modifying the rankings we would expect from status alone is confirmed by the distance between ZB and ZBR, the national and local news bulletins broadcast on the single station, 1ZB.

The finding of a local solidarity factor working against status is paralleled by other research on broadcast language. Lipski's (1985) quantitative data from Latin American broadcasting in Spanish shows that use of local phonological variants, especially aspiration and deletion of syllable- and word-final /s/, is stigmatized and minimal in news broadcasts, but increases in DJ speech and in sports commentary. Lipski notes the strenuous and affected avoidance of local and regional phonology by newcasters in the dozen Spanish-speaking countries he surveyed. Variants which are almost absent from everyday speech are restored in newscasting. Latin American newscasters apply /s/ reduction at generally less than 10 per cent, although application is 90 per cent in everyday speech.

Coupland (1985) shows how status and solidarity linguistic markers mix in the speech of a radio presenter in Cardiff. He identifies a blend of solidarity and status variants, which are often triggered by different kinds of content. Selting's analysis (1983) of an audience-participation radio programme adeptly shows these processes at work. The programme's moderator uses colloquial German, thus defining this media situation as informal. From this base, she converges down into strong dialect to address a local lad, and up towards High German to argue with an invited expert. The style shifts are accomplished at crucial points of an interaction, such as disagreement or hesitation by an interlocutor.

One newscaster, two audiences

The strongest evidence for audience design looks not at different newscasters on the one station, but at one newscaster on different stations. Several individual Radio NZ newscasters were recorded on both YA and ZB, and others on YAR and ZBR. These are in effect natural matched guises (Lambert 1967). Listeners record their approval of one of these by their presence in the audience of the station that broadcasts it rather than of the other station. The prestige of the guise then ranks according to the prestige of the audience who received it.

Figure 6.4 graphs the performance of three newscasters PB, SD and OJ, each of whom was recorded on both YA and ZB, and two, TA and AF, recorded on both YAR and ZBR. Here we see in miniature the same relationships graphed for the stations in figure 6.3.[3] The five newscasters shift in a consistent direction between their two stations, with the ZB or ZBR line always above the YA or YAR line. There is only one deviation in the twenty speaker-by-environment cells of the comparison. Newscasters SD and TA in particular shift by 20–30 per cent in some environments.

Such style shifts by single newscasters are not unique to this variable. Another variable – the voicing of intervocalic /t/ which makes words such as *writer* sound like *rider* – showed even more

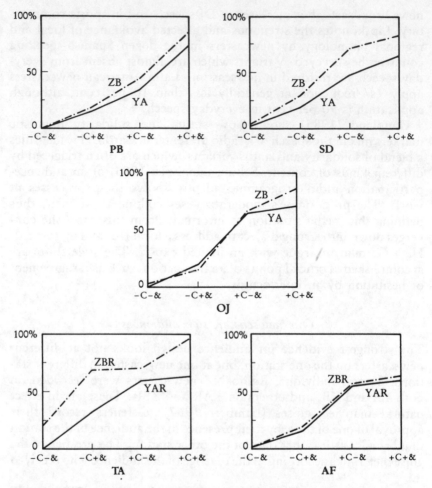

FIGURE 6.4 Percentage of consonant cluster reduction for three YA/ZB newscasters (PB, SD, OJ) and two YAR/ZBR newscasters (TA, AF) in four linguistic environments (key — figure 6.3)

marked shifts. For /t/ voicing six newscasters shift on average 20 per cent in each environment between YA and ZB, or YAR and ZBR (Bell 1991a).

Audience design is the only tenable explanation for the individual speaker shifts shown in figure 6.4. Single newscasters heard on two different stations show a remarkable and consistent ability to make considerable style shifts to suit the audience. These switches between stations are at times very rapid: at off-peak hours a single newscaster may alternate between YA and ZB news with as little as ten minutes between bulletins on the different stations. And not only do stations with different audiences differ systematically in their styles, those with similar audiences (ZM/XA and ZBR/XI) share consistently similar styles.

Sociolinguistic and ethnographic research has over the years suggested a variety of factors which can produce such differences within an individual's speech, including topic, setting and attention to speech. The evidence of newscaster shifts between stations leaves little place for such factors. It would be quite implausible to offer the original sociolinguistic explanation (Labov 1972a, cf. Bell 1984b) that newscasters are paying systematically different amounts of attention to their speech on the different stations. The physical setting of the communicator in the studio, and the audience anywhere at all, is the same regardless of the station. The topics of the news are broadly similar across the stations. News thus clearly falls on the responsive dimension posited by audience design.

Converging on a station style

The extent to which newscasters are designing their speech for their audience can be seen in their individual linguistic data (Bell 1991a). We can rank individual newscasters in implicational order from the least to the greatest overall degree of cluster reduction. The order of speakers coincides strikingly with the station order of figure 6.3, to the extent that it is in most cases possible to predict which station a newscaster is on according to his place in the ranking. The speakers fall into three linguistic groups: YA and ZB newscasters at the top, plus one from ZM. The bottom group contains all ZBR newscasters, all but one from XI, plus one each from ZM and XA. In the middle are three ZM and XA newscasters plus one from XI.

What is happening here is that individual newscasters are converging towards a common style of speech targeted at their audience. This is evidenced in the notably narrow scatter of newscasters from each station. As part of the audience design process, there is a consensus at work among a station's newscasters over what is a suitable style for their particular audience. Individual differences are minimized, and speakers tend to cluster around the station mean frequency for the variable, giving content to the notion of a 'station style' which is designed for its audience.

Whether we take the social or the linguistic variables as independent, therefore, the same relationships show up. The natural grouping of newscasters on stations, and of stations according to audience, undeniably stratifies news language styles. On the other hand, linguistically based groups of speakers apparently bear only the roughest resemblance to groupings according to the speakers' individual characteristics. Demographic data were obtained on a sample of Radio NZ newscasters to examine the place of the individual communicator. The three top-status speakers were grouped together, as were the three lowest-status speakers. Their pattern for this variable was quite equivocal. In the four cluster reduction environments, the top- and bottom-status groups crossed over twice. In no environment were they separated by more than 8 per cent, and the higher-status group in fact used *more* cluster reduction than the lower.

4 EDITING COPY FOR STYLE

Newscasters share a professional consensus about how their audience should be addressed, which is reflected in very similar values of linguistic variables and common styles for different audiences. In the absence of any direct audience feedback which provides a language model, communicators become more reliant on monitoring their own production. In the media this involves more than just critiques by individuals of their own output. It is yet another reason for the multiple handling of mass media copy. Many professional communicators – editors, producers, technicians – are employed for the exact task of monitoring and modifying other communicators' production.

The professional consensus becomes overt in the editing of the lexical and syntactic form of news. In chapter 4 I dealt with news copy editing as a qualitative process, focusing on the kinds of operations which copy editors perform. We saw that one function of copy editing is language standardization. This has a qualitative aspect, in that media may require or forbid the use of certain linguistic forms. Thus, some newspapers may always refer to newsmakers with the honorific *Ms*, *Mr*, etc., while others always use first names only.

More commonly, news outlets apply rules such as determiner deletion to varying degrees. This brings another aspect of the copy editor's competence into play. As part of the 1974 sample, I collected – as well as the finished news product – the news agency copy from which many stories were derived. It was then a straightforward analysis to compare the frequency of certain linguistic rules in the input copy with those in the output copy, and thus deduce what copy editors had done with those rules.

Copy editors can handle determiner deletion in three ways. They may leave the copy exactly as they found it. That is, if the determiner is present in the copy, leave it in; if it is absent (having already been deleted by a previous editor) then leave it absent. As active alternatives, a copy editor may delete a determiner which was retained in the input copy, or reinsert a determiner previously deleted. We can formalize this process through two editing rules. The editing rule of determiner deletion is formally identical to the ordinary linguistic rule of determiner deletion. The editing rule of determiner reinsertion reverses the deletion rule. Such editing rules are not simply optional. They are variable sociolinguistic rules (cf. Cedergren and Sankoff 1974).

Table 6.2 presents data on determiner deletion for two New Zealand radio stations, the Australian Associated Press-Reuter news agency from which they received their international news, and the NZ Press Association agency which edited AAP news for the private station XA. In news originating within New Zealand, both stations had low determiner deletion. Station YA, the prestigious National Radio (cf. table 6.1 above) permitted no determiner deletion at all. XA, the rock music station, had a level of 14 per cent deletion.

TABLE 6.2: Determiner deletion in two news agencies and two radio stations in New Zealand (per cent)

	Local news	International news
AAP-Reuter news agency	–	59.7
Station YA	0	4.5
NZPA news agency	–	53.5
Station XA	14.0	40.0

But in international news the picture is different. AAP – the source of international news for the other three – has 60 per cent deletion. That is unacceptable to the recipient stations, which start putting the determiners back in, shifting the style of the international copy (figure 6.5). YA reinserts almost all the deleted determiners to reach a level of 4.5 per cent in the international news it broadcasts. NZPA brings the AAP level down slightly to 53.5 per cent in the copy it transmits to receiving media. That frequency is then the input level to station XA, which reinserts more determiners to reduce the level further to 40 per cent.

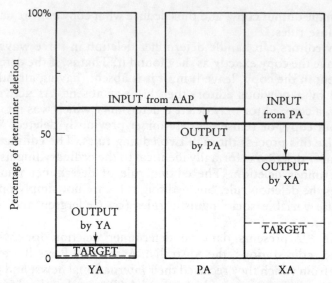

FIGURE 6.5   Determiner reinsertion in international news agency copy (AAP) by New Zealand copy editors in three news media: radio stations YA and XA, and the NZ Press Association news agency

The frequency of determiner deletion in a station's own internal copy clearly represents a target level. Copy editors in some sense 'know' the target level in their own station's copy, 'know' the frequency of deletion in external input copy, and apply editing rules to shift the input towards that target. The further a station's target level is from that in the input copy received, the higher will be the level of application of the editing rule needed to adjust that frequency. As a corollary to this, copy editors never apply a rule to delete determiners from incoming copy. Their move is always to reinsert the determiners, and never to delete more, because their target is a lower level of overall deletion. There is thus no *editing* rule of determiner deletion here at all. This does not mean that copy editors are any more conscious of their variable-rule function than they are of other editing operations. They work in this as in other operations largely by unexamined intuition, with only a very general notion of their news outlet's style.

The editor does not reinsert all the deleted determiners so that, even after editing, the style of external copy is not identical to internally originated copy. Editors are prepared to sanction in external copy forms which they would not accept from their own journalists. The more remote the point of origin of copy is, the less likely its style is to be like that of a recipient news outlet's. External news is written for a wider and potentially different audience from that of any one of its recipient news outlets.

Variable editing rules thus function to shift the style of the input text closer to the style which the station deems suitable for its kind of audience. This shows how a number of divergent styles can be derived from a single text. The same set of international news analysed here was received and edited by two internal news agencies and six different radio news stations in New Zealand. These diverse outlets have widely differing audiences, and language styles to match. They take a common input and apply variable editing rules to shape the style towards their own audience.

It is by such means that different media outlets achieve different linguistic styles. The kinds of style differences I have detailed for Auckland radio undoubtedly exist elsewhere. The differences between the BBC's Radio 1 *Newsbeat* programme and Radio 4's *World at One* parallel the New Zealand situation, and for the same reason – their different audiences. In the next chapter we shall see how another, still more highly planned form of media language – advertising – is styled to serve the persuasive purposes of the advertiser.

7

Talking Strange: Referee Design in Media Language

In Japan car manufacturers use English or French to advertise a new model to the Japanese consumer. The spoken soundtrack for one New Zealand commercial is entirely in German – although the car is not a German make. The actor in a New Zealand television commercial for dishwashing liquid speaks a London working-class accent. In the United States, French is used to advertise perfume, and a television commercial features a butler with a British Received Pronunciation accent.

We recognize these uses of foreign languages and dialects as common on our screens. But what is it that motivates advertisers to adopt linguistic codes which their target audience seldom hear outside the media, let alone speak themselves?

1 TAKING THE INITIATIVE

I showed in the previous chapter how style can vary within media language according to a number of factors such as the audience of the particular medium. This is the 'responsive' dimension of style, which I have characterized as audience design. But there is another dimension which I term the 'initiative' dimension (Bell 1984b). Here the style shift itself initiates a change in the situation rather than resulting from such a change. In responsive style shift, there is a regular association between language and social situation. The entry of outsiders to a local group, for example, triggers a switch from local dialect to standard speech. Initiative style trades on such regular associations, infusing the flavour of one setting into another, alien context.

Initiative style shift is essentially a redefinition, by the speaker, of the relationship between speaker and audience. The baseline from which initiative shifts operate is the style normally designed for a particular kind of addressee. So, speakers can persuade or convince someone intimate to them by shifting to the style or language one would normally address to strangers. With strangers the reverse tactic achieves the same effect: speakers can persuade a stranger by shifting to the style normally reserved for intimates. Such shifts appear to be powerful just because they treat addressees as if they were someone else.

2 THE REFEREES

This someone else I term the 'referee' (Bell 1984b). In referee design, speakers diverge away from the style appropriate to their addressee and towards that of a third party, a reference group or model. Referees are third persons not physically present at an interaction but possessing such salience for a speaker that they influence language choice even in their absence.

Referee design arises in a range of media genres. While most of my focus in this book is on the news, here we find that other genres come to the fore. Referee design does occur in some features of news language, but the news is mostly audience designed. As Montgomery (1988) notes, news tries to eliminate the personal and the interpersonal. In other genres, referee design of some kind is very common. Especially in radio, there is a conscious attempt to 'foreground the interpersonal', to build the relationship between presenter and audience. Montgomery's study shows how a British DJ projects an individual relationship with his audience and its members, for example using second person pronouns and vocatives – 'hi to Bob Sproat.' The DJ constantly counterfeits the physical co-presence of his distant and separated listeners, and simulates dialogue in what is in fact his monologue.

Referee design

Referee design is a rhetorical strategy by which speakers use the resources available to them from their speech community (Bell 1990). It is especially common in forms such as narratives, anecdotes or jokes. Referee strategies may be limited to creative use of the linguistic repertoire of styles or languages which a speaker herself normally employs. Or the strategies may draw on a wider speech

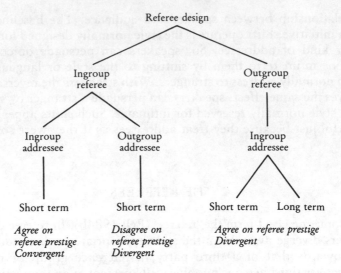

FIGURE 7.1   Categories and characteristics of referee design

community – socially, in adopting features from the speech of other socioeconomic, ethnic or age groups; geographically in the dialects of other regions or continents; or historically, in the forms of the language spoken (or supposed to have been spoken) at an earlier period.

We can categorize and characterize referee design in several ways (figure 7.1). All of these apply equally to media communication and face-to-face conversation:

- The speaker may be a member of the referee group (ingroup referee design), producing for an occasion heightened use of her usual speech patterns. Or she may be not a member of the referee group (outgroup referee design). The addressee may, likewise, be a member of the ingroup or outgroup
- Referee shift is basically a short term phenomenon, occurring for very short stretches of speech. But it may in certain circumstances be long term. Referee design may occur in isolated situations, or more widely across a group and its interactions with another group
- Referee design is generally linguistically divergent, with the language shifted away from the addressee's own speech patterns. But it may in some situations converge towards the addressee's speech.

- The speaker's linguistic repertoire may be monolingual, diglossic or bilingual, and accordingly be affected in different ways by referee design
- The shift towards the referee's language code may be accurate, correctly reproducing the referee's own linguistic patterns. Or it may be inaccurate, missing the target variety in a range of ways.

Ingroup referees

The division into ingroup and outgroup referees is fundamental (Bell 1990). Ingroup referee design sees you as speaker shifting to an extreme level of the style of your own ingroup. This may occur when the addressee is either also a member of your ingroup, or a member of an outgroup (figure 7.1). With an outgroup addressee, a speaker is reacting to that addressee by shifting towards an enhanced style of the speaker's own (absent) ingroup. Such a speaker is taking the initiative to reject identification with the immediate addressee, in order to identify instead with a referee not actually present. If a Welsh bilingual speaks Welsh to an English monolingual, that is ingroup referee design to an outgroup addressee.

The second type of ingroup referee design is where the addressee is from your own ingroup. With the outgroup addressee, you as a speaker are appealing to the identity of your absent ingroup in the face of an outgroup challenge. With an addressee from your own ingroup, you appeal to your solidarity with the addressee, to the common ground which you have as speakers of a language or dialect which is not shared with the outgroup. Radio presenters who wish to establish their solidarity with local listeners commonly use local linguistic features in this way. Coupland (1985: 158) shows how a record-request show in Cardiff is 'no less than a celebration of in-group solidarity, both symbolically (through dialect) and directly, through the show's content and design'. The show's presenter makes full and deliberate use of a range of linguistic variants of Cardiff dialect. In particular the fronted [æ:] – a stereotype of Cardiff English – is displayed in the presenter's repeated catch-phrases and in the show's own jingle: 'Hark, hark the lark in Cardiff Arms Park.'

In another country, another language and another genre, we find a similar pattern. Selting (1983, 1985) analysed the speech of the 'moderator' in an open-air audience-participation radio programme in the Ruhr. The moderator uses as her baseline style a colloquial German sprinkled with local dialect forms and very different from standard broadcast speech. At important points of the conversation, she adopts even more marked local dialect forms in syntax, phonology and lexicon. In some cases this is audience design, a response to the dialect of her immediate conversational addressee. But Selting found that these forms were used even with addressees who spoke other dialects. This is ingroup referee design – adopting stereotypical local dialect forms in order to signal to the mass audience her solidarity with them.

Outgroup referee design

Outgroup referee design (figure 7.1) is similar to ingroup in its socio-psychological processes: it too represents the claiming of an identity. But it differs in its social structure (the speaker's relation to the target group) and linguistic effects. Here speakers lay claim to a speech and identity which is not their own but which holds prestige for them. They diverge from the language code of their ingroup – and thus from their own usual speech – towards an outgroup with whom they wish to identify. Thus, in an otherwise standard-language conversation, local dialect forms can be introduced to provide anecdotal colour. Conversely, standard-language features may surface as a claim to intellectual authority during a conversation conducted in local dialect (Blom and Gumperz 1972). As with ingroup design to an ingroup addressee, both speaker and addressee agree on the prestige of the outgroup language for the purpose. That fact makes its use powerful. But in conversation such a switch is essentially short term. Continued use of that code would violate the norm of conversation between intimates, or in the extreme case redefine the relationship as no longer intimate.

However, while all other classes of initiative shift are by nature brief, outgroup referee design can be long term, even institutionalized. Diglossia is the classic case. In Ferguson's original definition (1959), the prestige or 'High' form in diglossia is not native to any group in the speech community. Rather, it is the dialect of an external referee, distanced either by space or time.[1] The common factor in all such situations is an orientation which regards the referee society and culture as superior, either generally or on some particular dimension. We see this reflected in media usage. In Switzerland (one of Ferguson's cases), High German – which is native to Germany not Switzerland – is used for formal media genres, and Swiss German for less formal genres (Burger 1984: 215). On private stations, everything is in local dialect except the news. Because both speakers and addressees share the same reference point, the shift to the referee code can be widespread and prolonged, but it may also be confined to certain genres, settings or topics.

The rule of determiner deletion discussed in the previous chapter provides an example of long-term outgroup referee design in a single linguistic feature. We saw in figure 6.1 how a media outlet's degree of determiner deletion corresponds closely to the social status of its audience. But just as striking in that graph is another factor: the polarization between the British quality and popular papers. The three national prestige papers – *The Times*, *Guardian* and *Telegraph* – delete at low levels, no more than 12 per cent. The four popular dailies have high deletion rates, at least 73 per cent.

There is clearly some other factor operating here – referee design. Figure 7.2 presents the degree of determiner deletion found in American and British prestige media in sampling from 1980 to 1982. The dichotomy between them is absolute. The four British media delete a maximum of 10 per cent of determiners. That is, they hold to semi-categorical retention of the determiner. The American media delete 75 per cent or more of the determiners, with all except the

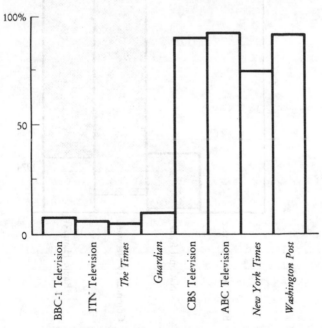

FIGURE 7.2 Percentage of determiner deletion in four British and four American prestige media, 1980–1982

New York Times deleting at least 90 per cent. For the American media, semi-categorical deletion is the norm. The British mass press has gone over to what it sees as the less formal, more popular American style of high determiner deletion. The prestige papers remain with the older retention of the determiner, which is now regarded (obviously with only partial justification) as characteristic of British versus American news style.

With such polarization between the two main international varieties of English, it becomes possible that different media within other countries may adopt one or other model as their target – their 'referee'. This has happened for New Zealand media (figure 7.3). We see in the 1984 data that the more prestigious National Radio retains most of the determiners, while the local Community Network station and the rock music station Radio Hauraki delete most of theirs. The division

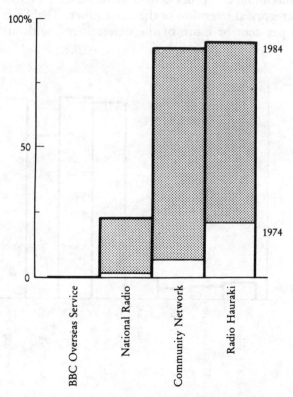

FIGURE 7.3 Percentage of determiner deletion on four New Zealand radio stations, 1974 and 1984 (BBC is rebroadcast on Radio NZ)

between the radio stations reflects very accurately their orientation towards British versus American linguistic (and cultural) norms, as shown in figure 7.2. The rule of determiner deletion is diagnostic of New Zealand media orientations.

In addition we can see how media change their orientation to referee models over the years. Ten years earlier in 1974, all New Zealand radio stations had a rather low level of determiner deletion (figure 7.3). Radio Hauraki – the rock station for a young audience – was predictably the highest, but still reached only 21 per cent. But the 1984 resampling showed that all stations had shifted upwards. In the case of the Community Network and Radio Hauraki, the shift is 70 or 80 per cent in just a decade. That is a rapid and massive leap in the normally slow timetable of linguistic change. They have in fact *switched* their orientation from low to high deletion, rather than just shifting gradually. Even National Radio has edged up to an appreciable number of deletions – 23 per cent – and away from its traditional model, the BBC Overseas Service news. In 1984 the BBC (still rebroadcast on Radio NZ's Concert Programme) remained as committed to absolute non-deletion as in 1974.

Such referee-designed changes for this particular variable are by no means unique to New Zealand media. The British popular press's shift

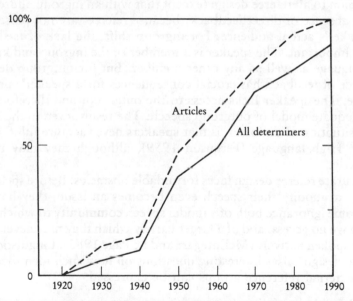

FIGURE 7.4 Percentage of determiner deletion in the British newspaper the *Daily Mirror*, 1920–1990, plus percentage deletion of articles only

to the high-deleting American model has occurred during the course of the twentieth century. The preservation of a precisely dated, accessible and high-quality archive allows us to study the development of media language in a way impossible in almost any other variety. Figure 7.4 shows the spread of determiner deletion from 1920 to 1990 in the *Daily Mirror*. From categorical non-deletion in 1920, the rule has risen in 1990 to 90 per cent. Application of the rule has increased each decade, sometimes by only a few per cent, at others by well over 20 per cent. By 1990 it is only the possessive determiners (in news language: *our, her, his, its, their*) which resist deletion. All definite and indefinite articles are deleted categorically from these appositional naming expressions.

Although the shift is much slower than for New Zealand radio, from nil to 100 per cent application in 70 years is still rapid for language change. Both are evidence of referee design as the precursor of audience design. That is, the synchronic social stratification of determiner deletion has resulted from the diachronic process, by which certain media have adopted external referee models to differing degrees at any given point in time.

The linguistic consequences

Common to all referee design (except that with an ingroup addressee) is the absence of direct feedback, because referees are not present in a speaker's actual audience. For ingroup shift, the lack of feedback is not important. The speaker is a member of the ingroup and knows its language as well as any other member. But for outgroup design, absence of feedback has crucial consequences for a speaker's performance. The speaker lacks access to the outgroup, and therefore has no adequate model of outgroup speech. The result, even in the long-term situation of diglossia, is that speakers never acquire full fluency in the High language (Ferguson 1959), although they may use it regularly.

Accurate referee design faces formidable obstacles. Before speakers' ability to modify their speech even becomes an issue, they have to overcome ignorance both of a model speech community to which they may have no access, and of a target variety which they may never have heard spoken natively (McEntegart and Le Page 1982). Linguistically, referee design raises interesting questions on how such identification with external reference groups can be expressed:

- What kinds of linguistic entities are used to represent referee design?

- What levels of language do they come from – discourse, phonology, syntax, lexicon?
- What is the minimum necessary shift for successful referee design?
- Is there a maximum allowable shift?
- And what in fact constitutes successful referee design? Is it native-like competence in the target code, or something less than that, or even something more or something different?

3 TELEVISION ADVERTISEMENTS AS REFEREE DESIGN

Initiative style shift is much harder to research than the responsive dimension. In face-to-face interaction, such shifts are by nature brief, sporadic and unpredictable, and have therefore not been much studied. But there is a more readily available data source in mass communication, where the forces of initiative shift are also operating. The structure of broadcast advertising provides a laboratory-like simulation of referee design conditions. Like face-to-face referee shifts, advertisements are very short (average 30 seconds). Their function is an initiative one – to persuade, challenge, seize the audience's attention, tell an anecdote. The language in them is used to simulate distance or intimacy of relationship.

Advertising is, together with news, the principal genre common to all daily media. As well as providing a good case study, it is an important genre in its own right. Its use of language is highly creative. While people may denigrate advertising as a cultural phenomenon, the well-made advertisement appeals to sophisticated linguistic skills (cf. Pateman 1983, Vestergaard and Schrøder 1985). The television commercial is as carefully crafted as a sonnet, and its linguistic forms are often poetic in nature. There is a two-way traffic of catchphrases between advertising and everyday language (Moeran 1984). Cars, cigarettes, alcohol and travel products lead the way in such creativity:

I thought St Tropez was a Spanish monk . . . until I discovered
   Smirnoff (vodka)

San Antonio, sans delay (American Airlines)

Born in Denmark. Raised in Britain (Carlsberg lager)

We've poured through the Reign (Guinness)

Put a tiger in your tank (Esso)

We may decry the commercial intent of such linguistic play, but the skill and impact are undeniable. To quote an American commentator (Collum 1989: 32): 'Advertising forms the aesthetic of American life. It is by far the strongest, most concentrated, and most conscious form of meaning-making to which most Americans are exposed . . . It fills our time and our heads with well-turned phrases and powerful images.' Advertising also receives resources far beyond those any other media genre can command. A commercial can easily cost many thousands of dollars per second to produce.

Foreign languages in advertising

Perhaps the most striking employment of linguistic resources in advertising is the use of a language which is not understood by the advertisement's target audience. This occurs in a minor way in all countries. French or English names or words are used in order to associate a product with values such as elegance or progress. Mass media multilingualism spreads far more widely in a country such as Japan. Haarman (1984, 1986) has researched the use of languages other than Japanese in television commercials there. A manufacturer will give a car an English name (for instance, Skyline, Lancer) to evoke quality, reliability and practicality. If elegance, taste, sophistication or charm is the desired association, French is used (Mirage), and Italian (Leone) for speed. Other languages used in naming products or as background to an advertisement include Spanish (for sex appeal), Portuguese, Greek and Finnish.

Haarman analysed over a thousand commercials (1986: 209ff.) videotaped from Tokyo television channels in 1984. Although he does not present this in his own figures, it seems that up to 40 per cent contain some foreign language (although this includes use of isolated foreign words, for example in product names). Commercials about cars, fashion goods, drinks and cosmetics use the most foreign elements. Foreigners – mostly Americans or Europeans – appeared in a quarter of the commercials, but mostly in non-speaking parts. Background songs are frequently monolingual in a foreign language, usually English. Very few advertisements use a foreign language by itself, most also use Japanese.

English and French both function as 'content' languages in Japanese commercials. That is, they are scripted into the copy of advertisements along with Japanese. The end result is many advertisements with scripts which most Japanese do not understand. English is the language of primary prestige. *New* – the most frequent adjective in

British advertising (Leech 1966) – is taken over into Japanese advertising in place of its Japanese equivalent. Other individual words, phrases or even whole sentences are produced in the foreign language.

Yet this does not alienate the Japanese consumer. They agree with the advertisers on the prestige of other languages on certain dimensions and are influenced by the general impact of the advertisements. Nor does it threaten Japanese identity. Haarman sees the use of foreign models and languages as consistent with Japanese stereotypes of foreigners. Despite the apparently massive influence of American culture on Japan, the stereotypes continue to exist in such a 'pure and stable form as hardly to be found in any other modern industrialized society' (1986: 216). Media multilingualism is an interesting phenomenon to occur in one of the world's most monolingual countries. It seems plausible that the monolingualism of Japan may be a factor contributing to advertisers' reaching for languages external to the country. In the same way, we shall see how New Zealand advertisers, in a country without great dialect diversity, make use of external dialects of English.

Non-native dialects

The data for this study (drawn from Bell 1986, 1990) is a sample of advertisements screened on New Zealand television, mostly in 1986. At the time New Zealand had two channels, both operated by the public corporation, Television New Zealand.[2] Both channels carry advertising, often a total of ten or more minutes per hour. Estimates vary on where the mix of programmes screened on New Zealand television come from (Lealand 1988). My own best guess is that probably only some 25 per cent of programming is genuinely locally made and therefore uses speakers of NZ English. About another 25 per cent is imported from Britain, mostly with speakers of Received Pronunciation (RP), but also with other urban and rural British dialects. About 45 per cent of programming is imported from the United States, and the remaining 5 per cent comes mainly from Australia and Europe. New Zealanders are therefore exposed in the principal mass medium to nearly double the amount of American English as of New Zealand English, and to about the same amount of British as NZ English.

The use of language in this sample illustrates three of the four categories of referee design:

1 As ingroup referee design to the ingroup audience, there are a number of advertisements which adopt strong New Zealand local

dialect in order to associate their product with ingroup values.

2   Short-term outgroup referee design occurs in a large proportion of advertisements which use non-native dialects such as British or American varieties.

3   Long-term outgroup shift occurs in one specific genre: all singing has traces of American accent.

4   The fourth category, ingroup design to outgroup addressees, is logically impossible here because the audience for New Zealand television is by definition a NZ English ingroup.

The principal data are some 150 television advertisements. Of these, 42 per cent used an audience-designed style, what I would class as mainstream New Zealand media speech – labelled 'Middle New Zealand' (MNZ) in figure 7.5.[3] 'Upper New Zealand' (UNZ) is the traditional speech of national newsreaders on television and National Radio, and of a handful of other media personalities. This is an accent intermediate between RP and NZ English. It is really a collection of different idiolects. Its speakers differ in how they realize its vowels, but share the common factor of intermediacy between RP and NZ English. Some vowels receive pure RP realizations, others pure NZ realizations. Certain speakers use either in different contexts. Still

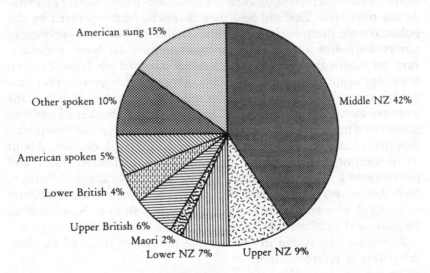

FIGURE 7.5   Dialects used in New Zealand television commercials, as percentage of total number of advertisements in which different dialects occurred (N=125)

other vowels are realized with values phonetically intermediate between RP and NZ. I am frankly undecided whether it should be treated as a normal New Zealand variety (like MNZ) or as an outgroup referee dialect. It falls between the two and shares features of both. My indecision reflects the real linguistic and cultural ambiguity of this variety.

About half of the 150 advertisements contained referee designed speech (figure 7.5). Ingroup referee design is heard in the 7 per cent which used markedly local ingroup speech. These I term 'Lower New Zealand' (LNZ). A few use the ethnically marked variety distinctive to some Maori speakers. The products these two varieties advertise are linked to the two kinds of values usually associated with strongly ingroup dialect – solidarity, home and friendship, for example in an advertisement for long-distance telephone calls; and macho male values, used to advertise home building products and four-wheel drive vehicles.

Short-term outgroup referee design is represented by a number of dialects not native to New Zealand. Upper British (UB: 6 per cent of advertisements) is associated with gracious, upper-class living. The advertisements tend to contain stereotype visuals of people getting into Rolls Royces or being waited on by butlers. Both Upper British and Upper NZ are used in advertisements to make authoritative statements, particularly voiceovers. (A brief monitoring of British commercial television suggests that RP is the favoured accent for voiceovers there also.) Most of the 'Lower British' category (LB: 4 per cent) were marked as lower-class British, especially London dialects. Five per cent of the spoken outgroup dialects were American. All these appeared to be produced by native speakers, many of them American media personalities. There is an assortment of other overseas dialects – Scottish, Australian, Singaporean – and a number of second-language accents such as Spanish- and French-accented English.

All the above are spoken language. Long-term outgroup referee design is evidenced (apart from the indeterminate UNZ class) only in the use of American forms in singing. This provides the largest single category of referee designed language in television advertisements – 15 per cent. American features appear in all singing in advertisements, just as they do in New Zealand music generally, reflecting the American origins and continuing dominance of most popular music styles (Lealand 1988).

The linguistics of referee design

Referee design can be manifested at any level of linguistic structure. Phonological, lexical, syntactic and discourse features are all used, but these resources are not employed equally. Distinctive discourse and syntactic markers were rare. Notable was the tag *eh?*. This is stereotypical of Maori English, and embedded in one of a series of advertisements in which (Maori) entertainer Billy T. James speaks in a caricatured Maori juvenile accent:

> Gee, can't wait till the school holidays. Not long to go now, eh?
> We're flying Air New Zealand to see the cuzzies at Whakatane.
>   Uhuh, give 'em heaps!
> So if you're going away, you better call Air New Zealand and make
>   a booking now.
> Flying's choice!

The infrequent use of syntactic markers is not surprising. Dialects differ less in their syntax than their phonology, and syntactic variation often involves non-standard features which will generally be avoided in such scripted speech.

The lexicon is the most obvious source of referee markers. In the UB advertisements we hear expressions which New Zealanders associate with the stereotype of the upper class Britisher – *positively terrific, absolutely super, truly spiffing*. These are even more obviously in the realm of stereotype than most referee designed speech, as are the visuals which tend to accompany them. The other main group of advertisements using lexical strategies is those with LNZ and Maori dialect. Here we hear the greeting *G'day*, the solidarity term *mate*, abbreviations such as *beaut* and *cuzzies* (for cousins), and *decent, choice* and *neat* as adjectives meaning 'good'. These lexical items are used to claim ingroup identity and establish solidarity. Other dialects which offer distinctive but comprehensible lexical alternatives are exploited, especially Scots – *bairns, wee, canny*.

The most common referee design strategy is to use phonological marking. Since the phonology is the major area of inter-dialectal difference, this is not surprising. Further, it is the vowel systems where most dialect differences are manifest rather than the consonants. But at this point the strategies of referee design are skewed: the consonants do much more than their share of the work. For example, most of the

LB advertisements seem to have working-class London dialects as their target variety. They concentrate on four features stereotypically associated with 'Cockney':

- /h/-dropping
- glottalized intervocalic /t/
- vocalized final /l/
- labiodental [f] for dental /th/.

This list of features is, unsurprisingly, similar to the one which Trudgill (1983a) made of markers of British working-class identity in pop songs. They are favoured as strategies in advertisements because the sounds themselves are already present in NZ English, although not necessarily in the same environment, and certainly at lower frequencies. In one ten-second advertisement, the speakers succeeded in producing three [f] for /th/, three vocalized /l/, and one glottalized intervocalic /t/. Those seven tokens are more than enough to mark the speech as LB (V = voiceover; A, B, etc. = characters):

A: Oh, I really don't think you should.
B: But it's a Cheezel, mate. Oh, it's worth a crack.
V: Cheezels – taste the cheese and listen for the crunch.
A: It was worth a crack, Nigel. Nigel?

Moreover, the advertisement shows signs of being scripted just so as to maximize the occurrence of these features. It chooses, for example, the name *Nigel* – pronounced with vocalized /l/ – for one of its characters (two mice!). The product name – *Cheezel* – is also highlighted through pronunciation with vocalized /l/. The scripting thus deliberately displays the dialect at its points of obvious difference to NZ English. The voiceover, by contrast, uses an unmarked New Zealand accent.

The vowels are, as I said, on first consideration the obvious resource for someone trying to imitate an outgroup dialect. But the salience of vowels as markers of another dialect is counterbalanced by the difficulty of achieving native-like control of an alien vowel system (Payne 1980, Trudgill 1981). The New Zealand advertising profession is obviously aware of this problem, and for some target dialects genuine native speakers are usually used. This recognizes that the risk of inaccurately imitating spoken American and UB is too great, given New

Zealanders' exposure to these varieties through other television programming.

In one instance we have long-term referee design. New Zealanders do not attempt to speak American even in advertising American cultural products such as country music. But in song American must always be attempted (cf. Trudgill 1983a). A New Zealand singer of country music appearing in a television commercial speaks throughout in straight New Zealand dialect, but shifts towards American features when he breaks into song. In the genre of singing, a new norm has been established, quite different from speaking norms. Every one of the 30 sung advertisements in this sample has American features – [a:] for the New Zealand diphthong in *time*, marked use of *lovin'* for *loving*, and voicing of intervocalic /t/ more consistently and frequently than in NZ English. Notable for its absence was any realization of postvocalic /r/ as in *card*, which Trudgill found as a marker in his study of British pop songs.

The stability of the norm is highlighted by the fact that even advertisements which appeal to New Zealand nationalism always have traces of American accent in their singing. A number of high-profile, patriotic songs have shown this. Most striking was a 1988 official recording of the New Zealand national anthem which used marked American phonological features. This can extend to the import of American cultural symbols, which contrasts with the awkwardness New Zealand songwriters feel about using their own local place-names or cultural phenomena (Lealand 1988). A patriotically toned advertisement for the high-circulation magazine, the *NZ Woman's Weekly*, used the expression 'from coast to coast' to convey its nationwide appeal. This reflects the geography of the United States, but in New Zealand's long, narrow islands the normal expression to encompass the whole country is 'north to south':

> There isn't a week goes by
>> that someone doesn't try
>> to get a little extra out of life.
> You may be surprised to know,
>> New Zealand, you're on show
>> each and every week of your life.
> From coast to coast and home sweet home,
>> everybody, everybody reads New Zealand's own.
> The Weekly puts the life in your week . . .
>> There isn't a week goes by
> The Weekly puts the life in your week . . .
>> Home sweet home

The Weekly puts the life in your week . . .
New Zealand's own
The Weekly . . .

Referee design is more a matter of individual occurrences of salient variants than of quantitative summings and relative frequencies. It is more important that a marked variant occurred once out of ten possible occurrences than that the unmarked variant occurred nine times. One of the strategies of successful referee design is to focus on few variants (even one) to the exclusion of others and keep on repeating them. In one 30-second UB advertisement, the vowel /i:/ is repeated 13 times:

If you want to clean your teeth fifty-one per cent better than the leading American toothbrush, you can either get a flip-top head, or get a Reach toothbrush.
Proven in clinical studies to clean teeth better, Reach has an angled neck to get right into the back teeth, and unique, long, soft outer bristles to massage and clean along gums.
So, to clean your teeth fifty-one per cent better, either get a flip-top head, or get Reach from Johnson and Johnson.

Three of those occurrences are in the product name. Another four each occur in *clean* and *teeth*, setting up a quasi-poetic assonance between product and function. The other two uses are for loaded words of approval: *leading* and *unique*.

In certain conditions, as little as one dialect-marked variant could be enough for successful referee design. In a three-second, ten-word stretch of speech, two occurrences of the RP /ou/ vowel in the words *motor show* were enough to establish the accent as UB. In other cases, three marked variants (two intervocalic glottal stops and a lexical item) were enough to claim a London identity. This enables advertisers to suggest associations in just two or three seconds of airtime, with visuals and soundtrack working together. One commercial used five native and non-native accents in quick succession:

V: The spirit Gran Turismo lives on at Cable Price Toyota:
A: Ze British have done it again in this 1929 limo . . .
B: . . . truly spiffing roadster . . .
C: . . . I remember once . . .
D: . . . a classic new look for the Forties brings you tonight's . . .
E: . . . 1954 New York motor show with the gull-wing Mercedes . . .

V: From this proud heritage Cable Price Toyota present their
unique range of Gran Turismo Toyota vehicles.

For longer stretches of speech, marked variants need to keep on occurring at regular intervals for referee design to be convincing.

Accuracy versus success

Assessing accuracy in the execution of referee strategies means
measuring the speaker's performance against the standard of native
speakers. But the essence of referee design is not the accuracy of the
speaker's production but the audience's perception of that production.
Success depends on who your audience is and whether your speech
puts them in mind of the intended reference group. Apart from the
American and UB varieties produced by native speakers, all of the
foreign varieties in this sample of advertisements were more or less
badly imitated. The advertisements included Scottish, Australian,
Singaporean, and various LB accents. Not one was reproduced with
anything like native accuracy. The most inaccurate in the sample were
the attempts at LB. There is even one advertisement where I have been
quite unable to decide what target accent the advertisers were aiming
at.

A television advertisement provides optimal conditions for accurate
referee design – resources to hire the best speakers, maximum rehear-
sal time for minimum finished speaking time, and a product which
can be re-recorded till perfect. Even so, the vowel systems of the target
accents are not achieved. It is unlikely, then, that referee design in ad
lib conversation will be any more accurate. The limits on consistent
production of an alien dialect seem to be quite severe. Two speakers
successfully maintained a ten-second LB dialogue, but a 20-second
monologue produced an indeterminate mixture of London and NZ
speech. Although London dialects are often heard on New Zealand
television, the crucial prerequisite is lacking: these varieties are not
present in the New Zealand speech community (cf. Trudgill 1986).
No amount of passive media reception compensates for the fact
that NZ English speakers rarely have the chance to interact with
addressees who speak these dialects natively.

Even Australian dialect is inaccurately reproduced, in spite of the
fact that the two countries are close neighbours, there is a lot of
exchange in travel and migration, and the accents are so similar that
usually only native speakers can tell them apart. The most salient difference between the two is /I/: centralized in NZ, close front in

Australian. An advertisement for Australian 'Riverland' oranges produced the first vowel of the name with [i:] – qualitatively accurate, but inaccurately lengthened. This hypercorrection might be a reflection of the actor's inability to produce the Australian variant (which is phonetically very similar to the close New Zealand realization of /e/). Or it may well function as a deliberate part of the referee design, exaggerating one of the most salient differences between Australian and NZ English.

The exact condition which obstructs accurate referee design – an absent target variety – also restricts the goal and mitigates the cost of failure. The more distant the referee outgroup, the less a NZ speaker may know their code. But, happily, the audience knows the outgroup code just as imperfectly, and may therefore be in no position to question the performance. Testing accuracy requires evaluation of speech by native speakers of the referee dialect. But testing success requires evaluation by fellow members of the speaker's own community.

The cultural implications

The preponderance of foreign dialect advertisements in New Zealand broadcasting is initially surprising. But it reflects a small nation's focus on the prestige of other culturally powerful nations such as the United States and Britain (Bell 1982b). Linguistically, it reflects the comparative lack of diversity within NZ English, which has less regional, social and ethnic dialect variation than many other countries. New Zealand advertisers therefore reach beyond the linguistic resources available in their own immediate speech community and draw language strategies from the vast array of English dialects world wide.

Such behaviour is widespread throughout the world. It is often the fruit of a colonial past, reflected in a linguistic colonialism which has frozen the momentary phenomenon of initiative shift into a norm in which the speech community acknowledges the status of the external, referee code. It affects attitudes to language, so that the external language or dialect is held in high prestige, and the local is denigrated. Such language attitudes and choices are reflected and embodied in the media (Bell 1982b examines these issues in more detail). This is both in explicit commentary, where media comment on language, and also in usage, where media adopt a certain dialect or language in preference to another. As a consequence it has taken New Zealand broadcasting many years to start realizing that 'this isn't the BBC'. Until the 1980s most announcers on prestige radio and television programmes spoke something akin to RP, and many were in fact British born and bred.

The language attitudes were part of a more general New Zealand orientation, which looked back to Britain as its model in many fields. The orientation has tended to fade, especially refocusing towards the United States over recent decades, as we have seen above. But the phenomenon of referee design is not confined to such dependency situations. As several researchers have noted, a feature of advertising as a persuasive language form is its search for novelty of expression (for example, Schmidt and Kess 1986). The use of foreign languages or dialects examined above is part of this quest.

Referee design offers a rich field for social and cultural analysis. Vestergaard and Schrøder (1985) note how advertising serves as a sociopsychological mirror, a means of 'taking the ideological temperature' of society. In my study, for example, 75 per cent of the spoken American-dialect advertisements were associated with American products or spoken by American media stars. For British dialects, the figure was only 30 per cent associated with British products or personalities. The remaining 70 per cent of British dialects were freely chosen by the advertisers to associate with their product. This implies that a British image is the target of more deliberately selected associations, whereas the American associations are less intentionally chosen. That seems to reflect, perhaps surprisingly, continued high prestige for British rather than American cultural norms.

Finally, there is clearly a sense in which media language generally could be regarded as referee design. All media language shares several features with ingroup referee design. Because the media audience is always absent, there is no genuine feedback. The communicator must therefore design her talk for a stereotype, an image in the mind, as we saw in chapters 5 and 6. And her language does indeed create a relationship with the audience rather than responding to an existing relationship. But the crucial difference to referee design is that the mass audience does receive the communication. In referee design, the reference group is by definition not only absent but out of touch. The peculiar nature of mass communication gives the media situation some referee-like features, but the abiding common ground with audience design remains paramount.

8

Telling Stories

Journalists do not write articles. They write stories. A story has structure, direction, point, viewpoint. An article may lack these. Stories come in many kinds and are known in all cultures of the world. They include fairy tales, fables, parables, gospels, legends, epics, and sagas. Stories are embedded in all sorts of language use, from face-to-face conversation to public addresses. The role of the story-teller is a significant one both in language behaviour and in society at large. Much of humanity's most important experience has been embodied in stories.

Journalists are professional story-tellers of our age. The fairy tale starts: 'Once upon a time.' The news story begins: 'Fifteen people were injured today when a bus plunged . . .' The journalist's work is focused on the getting and writing of stories. This is reflected in the snatches of phrases in which newsroom business is conducted. A good journalist 'gets good stories' or 'knows a good story'. A critical news editor asks: 'Is this really a story?' 'Where's the story in this?'

The remainder of the book is concerned with the nature of news stories, where they can go wrong, and how audiences understand them. Stories can be divided into hard news and soft, as we saw in chapter 2. The features are soft news, licensed to deviate from the structures of hard news (Cappon 1982: 111). Hard news is news as we all recognize it, and at its core is spot news – tales of accidents, disasters, crimes, the 'coups and earthquakes' of Rosenblum's title (1979). Journalists recognize the common threads in these kinds of stories, and may label any spot news 'a fire story' (Tuchman 1978: 102). A second major category of hard news covers politics or diplomacy: news of elections, government announcements, international negotiations, party politics. These two central kinds of hard news, as written by the international news agencies, provide our main examples as we analyse the structures of news in these two chapters.

1 NEWS STORIES AND PERSONAL NARRATIVES

As a first approach to the nature of the news story, I will compare news with another kind of story which has been researched in recent decades: narratives of personal experience told in face-to-face conversation. The similarities and differences between these two kinds of stories will illuminate what news has in common with other storytelling, and where it differs. Labov and Waletzky (1967) and Labov (1972b) have analysed the structure of such narratives into six elements:

1 The Abstract summarizes the central action and main point of the narrative. A story-teller uses it at the outset to pre-empt the questions, what is this about, why is this story being told?
2 The Orientation sets the scene: the who, when, where, and initial situation or activity of the story.
3 The Complicating Action is the central part of the story proper, answering the question, what happened (then)?
4 The Evaluation addresses the question, so what? A directionless sequence of clauses is not a narrative. Narrative has point, and it is narrators' prime intention to justify the value of the story they are telling, to demonstrate why these events are reportable.
5 The Resolution is what finally happened to conclude the sequence of events.
6 Finally, many narratives end with a Coda – 'and that was that.' This wraps up the action, and returns the conversation from the time of the narrative to the present.

These six elements occur in the above order, although evaluation can be dispersed throughout the other elements. Only the complicating action, and some degree of evaluation, are obligatory components of the personal narrative. To what extent do news stories follow this pattern, and where do they depart from it? In applying this framework, we will see how it needs modification to cope with news and the ways in which news stories differ from personal narratives.

Most of the examples I use in this and the following chapter are from the press. Because press stories are generally longer and carry much more detail than broadcast news, the structure of press stories is more complex. A framework which handles press news is likely to be adequate for the text of broadcast stories. Even long broadcast stories such as those carried by Britain's *Channel Four News* or *World at One*, with their multiple inputs, are shorter and less complex than many press stories. The use of the newsmaker's actual voice in broadcast news is in principle no different from direct quotation in printed news. For television news one would require additional apparatus to relate voiceover commentary to the visuals. This is less of a problem than it seems. The Glasgow University Media Group's analysis (see, for instance, 1976: 125) indicates that despite television newsworkers' efforts and beliefs to the contrary, the written text remains paramount and the visual subsidiary. In practice, news pictures are often tangential to the spoken text of a story, because it is impossible for cameras to be regularly in the right place at the right time. There are differences between printed and broadcast news styles, which we will touch on below, but the differences are less than the similarities.

Figure 8.1 displays a hard news story typical of those which appear daily on the international pages of any newspaper. The international news agencies (see chapter 3) are the chief suppliers of hard news and custodians of its style (as, for example, in Cappon's *Associated Press Guide to Good News Writing*, 1982). We can expect such stories to embody the core components of news discourse. Our example story contains some but not all of the elements of the personal narrative, and their order and importance are different.

Abstract

The importance of the lead or first paragraph in establishing the main point of a news story is clear from our analysis of editing in chapter 4. The lead has precisely the same function in news as the abstract in personal narrative. It summarizes the central action and establishes the point of the story. For major news stories, the lead paragraph is often set off from the remainder of the story in larger type or across several columns of the body copy.

In figure 8.1, the first paragraph presents two main actions – the wounding of the US soldiers, and the consequent alert for US troops in Honduras. The story has a double abstract, a feature which can also occur in personal narratives. The consequence is treated as the prior point, with the violent incident second. The lead as summary or abstract is obligatory in hard news, where in personal narrative it remains optional. The lead is the device by which copy editor or audience can get the main point of a story from reading a single opening sentence, and on that basis decide whether to continue.

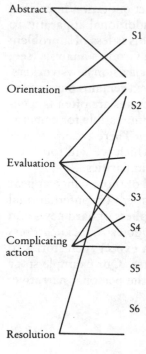

STORY STRUCTURE

Abstract

Orientation

Evaluation

Complicating action

Resolution

US troops ambushed in Honduras

TEGUCIGALPA

S1   UNITED STATES troops in Honduras were put on high alert after at least six American soldiers were wounded, two seriously, in a suspected leftist guerrilla ambush yesterday, United States officials said.

S2   Six or seven soldiers were wounded when at least three men, believed to be leftist guerrillas, used high-powered weapons in an ambush of a bus carrying 28 passengers 20 kilometres north of the capital Tegucigalpa, United States embassy spokesman Terry Kneebone said.

S3   The bus was carrying the soldiers from a pleasure trip at a beach on the Atlantic Coast.

S4   "It was a surprise attack," Southern Command spokesman Captain Art Haubold said in Panama City.

S5   "The US forces did not return fire. They kept going to get out of the area as quickly as possible."

S6   A Tegucigalpa radio station said an unidentified caller said the leftist group Morazanista Patriotic Liberation Front claimed responsibility for the attack. — NZPA-Reuter

TIME STRUCTURE

Time 7

Time 5

Time 5

Time 4
Time 3

Time 2

Time 8a

Time 6

Time 1, 8b

FIGURE 8.1   Narrative structure and time structure of international spot news story (*The Dominion*, Wellington, 2 April 1990)

Press news has headlines as well as lead paragraphs. The headline is an abstract of the abstract. The lead pares the story back to its essential point, and the headline abstracts the lead itself. In figure 8.1 the headline highlights the ambush, even though the lead begins with the consequent military alert. The lead paragraph is the journalist's primary abstract of a story. While to the reader the headline appears as first abstract in the printed story, in fact headlines are absent from broadcast news and even in press news are a last-minute addition. Broadcast news has no headlines, except in so far as stories are summarized at the beginning and/or end of a news bulletin. There are no headlines in news agency copy, from which most published news derives. Nor do journalists put headlines on their own stories: that is the work of subeditors. For journalists and news agencies, stories are identified by the ultimate in abstracts – a one-word catchline or slugline, unique to the story.

Orientation

In personal narrative, orientation sets the scene: who are the actors, where and when did the events take place, what is the initial situation? In news stories such orientation is obligatory. For journalists *who*, *what*, *when* and *where* are the basic facts which concentrate at the beginning of a story, but may be expanded further down. The lead in figure 8.1 crams in no less than five sets of people: United States troops in Honduras, the six wounded soldiers, the two seriously wounded, leftist guerrillas, and US officials.

International agency stories as received off the wire are 'datelined' at the top for time and place origin, with the deictics *here* and *today* used in the lead paragraph.[1] In this story the time of the ambush is given as *yesterday*. The time of the alert is unspecified (but in fact was also *yesterday* because this was published in a morning paper, and Honduras is some 18 hours behind New Zealand time). The dateline specifies the location from which the journalist 'filed' the story to the news agency. Here as in many newspapers, the dateline is carried below the headline and above the lead. The lead paragraph names Honduras, the second sentence (S2) specifies the exact site of the ambush and identifies the capital city, a necessary detail for news about a country whose geography will not be well known to the readers. Further detail of place is given in S3. In S4 there is a change of country with a regional command spokesperson outside Honduras quoted. This may indicate that the story has been combined by agency copy editors from separate despatches from both Tegucigalpa and Panama City.

Evaluation

Evaluation is the means by which the significance of a story is established. In personal narrative, evaluation is what distinguishes a directionless sequence of sentences from a story with point and meaning (Labov 1972b: 367). In the case of the fight stories studied by Labov, the point is often the self-aggrandizement of the narrator. Evaluation pre-empts the question, so what? It gives the reason why the narrator is claiming the floor and the audience's attention.

News stories also require evaluation, and in their case its function is identical to that in personal narrative: to establish the significance of what is being told, to focus the events, and to justify claiming the audience's attention. The story in figure 8.1 stresses repeatedly the importance of what has happened. *High alert, at least six* wounded, *two seriously* in the lead paragraph all stake claims on the reader to take these events, quite literally, seriously. The claims continue in the remaining paragraphs, but with diminishing frequency and force: *at least three men*, *high-powered weapons* (S2), *surprise attack* (S4), *as quickly as possible* (S5).

The lead paragraph is a nucleus of evaluation, because the function of the lead is not merely to summarize the main action. The lead focuses the story in a particular direction. It forms the lens through which the remainder of the story is viewed. This function is even more obvious for the headline, especially when it appears to pick up on a minor point of the story. Focusing a story is a prime preoccupation of the journalist. Until a journalist finds what to lead a story with, the story remains unfocused. It is an article but not a story, and may be rejected or rewritten by editors on those grounds. On the other hand, once the journalist decides what the lead is, the rest of the story often falls into place below it. If no good lead can be found, the material may be rejected altogether as a non-story.

In personal narrative, evaluative devices may occur throughout the narrative but are typically concentrated near the end, just before the resolution of the events. In the news story, evaluation focuses in the lead. Its function is to make the contents of the story sound *as X as possible*, where X is big, recent, important, unusual, new; in a word – newsworthy. The events and news actors will be given the maximum status for the sake of the story. In the same fashion, narrators of fight stories are at pains to enhance the scale of their adversary – 'the baddest girl in the neighborhood' – and hence the magnitude of their own eventual victory (Labov 1972b: 364).

Action

At the heart of a personal narrative is the sequence of events which occurred. In Labov's analysis, a defining characteristic of narrative as a form is the temporal sequence of its sentences. That is, the action is invariably told in the order in which it happened. News stories, by contrast, are seldom if ever told in chronological order. Even within the lead paragraph of figure 8.1, result (the military alert) precedes cause (the ambush). Down in the story proper, the time sequence is also reversed. The sequence of events as one of the participants might have told it is:

About 30 of us went by bus for a day at the beach.
On the way back we got to 20 kilometres north of Tegucigalpa.
There some guerrillas ambushed us and shot up the bus with high
   powered rifles.
They wounded six or seven of the soldiers.

Figure 8.1 shows the time structure of events in the story. S2 and
S3 of the news story run these events in precisely the reverse order to
which they happened. The result is placed before the action which
caused it. This is a common principle of news writing, that it is not
the action or the process which takes priority but the outcome. Indeed,
it is this principle which enables news stories to be updated day after
day or hour by hour. If there is a new outcome to lead with, the
previous action can drop down in the story. Our example shows traces
of just such an origin in the dual abstract of its lead paragraph, which
reads like an updating story from the international wires. A previous
story probably carried news of the ambush, and figure 8.1 is a follow-
up which leads with the more recent information of the military alert.

The time structure of the story is very complex. In S1 the latest
occurring event is presented first, followed by its antecedent. S2 and
S3 pick up the action at that antecedent point in time and trace it
backwards as described above. S4 shifts the story into another setting
and timeframe for commentary on what happened, and S5 describes
the final action of the main incident, namely the bus's escape from the
ambush. The last paragraph moves into a third setting and presents
what is in fact temporally the beginning of the events, the group
(possibly) responsible for the ambush.

Where chronological order defines the structure of personal narrative, a completely different force is driving the presentation of the
news story. Perceived news value overturns temporal sequence and
imposes an order completely at odds with the linear narrative point.
It moves backwards and forwards in time, picking out different
actions on each cycle. In one case, at the start of S2, it even repeats
an action – *six or seven soldiers were wounded* – from the previous
sentence. This wilful violation of our expectations that narratives
usually proceed in temporal succession is distinctive of news stories.
It may also have repercussions for how well audiences understand
news stories, as we shall see in chapter 11.

Resolution

The personal narrative moves to a resolution: the fight is won, the
accident survived. News stories often do not present such clearcut

results. When they do, as noted above, the result will be in the lead rather than at the end of the story. In figure 8.1, the nearest thing to a resolution is the general military alert. But this, of course, is only the latest step in a continuing saga. The news is more like a serial than a short story. The criminal was arrested, but the trial is in the future. The accident occurred, but the victims are still in hospital. One kind of news does follow the chronology of the personal narrative more closely: sports reporting. Sport makes good news just because there is always a result. A sports story will lead in standard news fashion with the result of the game and a few notable incidents, but then settle down to chronological reporting of the course of the game.

News stories are not rounded off. They finish in mid-air. The news story consists of instalments of information of perceived decreasing importance. It is not temporally structured, or turned in a finished fashion. One very good reason for this is that the journalist does not know how much of her story will be retained by copy editors for publication. Stories are regularly cut from the bottom up, as I showed in chapter 4, which is a great incentive to get what you believe to be the main points in early.

Coda

Nor is there a coda to the news story. The reason lies in the function which the coda performs in personal narrative. It serves as an optional conclusion to the story, to mark its finish, to return the floor to other conversational partners, and to return the tense from narrative time to the present. None of these functions is necessary in the newspaper, where the floor is not open, and where the next contribution is another story. But the coda does have some parallel in broadcast news. The end of a news bulletin or programme – but not of individual news stories – will usually be explicitly signalled by 'that is the end of the news' or a similar formula. Between broadcast stories there is no discourse marker to mark one off from the other, although intonation or (on television) visual means will be used to flag the change of topic.

Conclusion

Our first approach to the structure of news stories indicates interesting similarities and differences to personal narrative. In news, the abstract is obligatory not optional. Orientating and evaluative material occurs in a similar fashion to personal narratives, but tends to concentrate in the first sentence. The central action of the news story is told in non-chronological order, with result presented first followed by a complex recycling through various time zones down through the story. One characteristic which news and personal narrative share is a penchant for direct quotation. The flavour of the eyewitness and colour of direct involvement is important to both forms.

The Honduras example story also points up four features which are typical of news stories but alien to the face-to-face narrative. First, the personal narrative is just that – *personal*. It relates the narrator's own experience, while the news story reports on others' experiences. The reporter has usually not witnessed these, and first person presentation is conventionally excluded from standard news reporting. Secondly, and consequently, where the personal narrative is told from one viewpoint – the narrator's – in news a range of sources is often cited. In figure 8.1 at least four separate sources are named in the space of six paragraphs. Thirdly, the news revels in giving numbers with a precision which is foreign to conversational stories. In the Honduras story, six sets of figures counting the guerrillas, passengers, casualties, and distance to the location occur in the first two paragraphs. Fourth, the syntax of personal narratives is simple, with mostly main clauses and little subordination. The syntax of news stories can be complex, as S1 and S2 show (although these are unusually long sentences for hard news). We return in the course of these two chapters to examine these characteristics of news stories in more detail.

2 NEWS VALUES

Our analysis above makes it plain that we cannot discuss the structure of news stories independently of their function. We cannot separate news form and news content. The values of news drive the way in which news is presented. We may account for the way news stories are structured only with reference to the values by which one 'fact' is judged more newsworthy than another. News values can be identified through a variety of means such as analysing textbooks which teach news skills or by deduction from what actually appears in the media. They approximate to the – often unconscious – criteria by which newsworkers make their professional judgements as they process stories.

The foundation study of news values is by Galtung and Ruge (1965). Developed on and applied to foreign news in the Scandinavian press, their categories have been found valid and enlightening for a wide range of news types in many countries (for instance, Peterson

1981, Kleinnijenhuis 1989, Leitch 1990). They propose a dozen factors which influence the media's selection of news, foreshadowing by a decade the issues focused in Unesco's New World Information and Communication Order debates. Here I will use these factors as the springboard for my discussion, but add a number of others which experience and analysis indicate to be important. I also modify their terminology where appropriate.

I divide news factors into three classes. The first relates to the content of the news, the nature of its events and actors. The second relates to the news process, and the third group to the quality of the news text. My list does not claim to be complete, but recognizes those factors which can be seen to have a direct impact on the structure of news discourse. Lastly, it should be emphasized that these are *values*. They are not neutral, but reflect ideologies and priorities held in society.

Values in news actors and events

Most of Galtung and Ruge's factors cover the nature of the events and actors in the news. The way these aspects of the news are presented in a story can enhance its newsworthiness. They are also the dimensions on which a story can be judged biased or inaccurate, as we shall see in chapter 10.

NEGATIVITY is what comes to people's minds as the basic news value. Negative events make the basic stuff of 'spot' news. It is a true platitude that news is bad, although it is a difficult question *why* the negative makes news. Involved in negativity are a number of concepts such as damage, injury or death, which make disasters and accidents newsworthy (and unchallengeable subjects for narratives, Labov 1972b: 370). Conflict between people, political parties or nations is a staple of news. Indeed the ultimate in conflict news, war reporting, is one of the earliest historical forms of news and a stimulus for the growth of news media (Boyce, et al. 1978). Deviance is another negative characteristic with proven news interest (Cohen 1973, van Dijk 1988b: 123).

RECENCY (Bell 1983) means that the best news is something which has only just happened. Time is a basic dimension of news stories which we examine in detail in the next chapter (cf. Schudson 1987). Recency is related to Galtung and Ruge's concept of FREQUENCY – how well a story conforms with news work cycles. The day is the basic news cycle for the press and principal television and radio news programmes, while staple radio news works on an hourly cycle. This means that events whose duration or occurrence fits into a 24-hour span are more likely to be reported. So the murder is more newsworthy than the police investigation, the verdict more than the trial.

PROXIMITY means quite simply that geographical closeness can enhance news value. The minor accident is reportable only in the settlement where it happens, not a hundred miles away. The carnival coming to town is news only in the town it comes to. Related is Galtung and Ruge's factor of MEANINGFULNESS – the cultural familiarity and similarity of one country with another, not just the physical distance between them.

The CONSONANCE of a story is its compatibility with preconceptions about the social group or nation from which the news actors come. Thus editors have stereotypes about the manner in which Latin American governments or the British royal family behave. Schank and Abelson (1977) developed the concept of *script* to explain this. People have a mental script for how certain kinds of events proceed. Environmental issues, demonstrations, or superpower summits are all perceived to have a typical pattern which they follow. These events will tend to be seen in terms of the script even when they deviate from expectation. A notable instance has been the inability of Western media to escape from a cold-war framework in reporting the changes in Eastern Europe in 1989–90.

UNAMBIGUITY indicates that the more clearcut a story is, the more it is favoured. If's, but's and maybe's are minimal. The 'facts' are clear, the sources impeccable.

UNEXPECTEDNESS means the unpredictable or the rare is more newsworthy than the routine. Closely related is NOVELTY. 'New' is the key word of advertising, and one of the main factors in news selection. Science is a low-priority news area, but gains coverage when there is a 'breakthrough' to report.

SUPERLATIVENESS says that the biggest building, the most violent crime, the most destructive fire gets covered (Galtung and Ruge's term is THRESHOLD).

RELEVANCE (van Dijk 1988b: 122) is the effect on the audience's own lives or closeness to their experience. Achieving relevance for a story causes much head-scratching and labour in newsrooms. A common angle on economic announcements, political decisions or scientific breakthroughs is to lead with what they supposedly mean for the ordinary reader: more money in the pocket or a better paint for houses. Relevance need not be the same as proximity. Many decisions relevant to New Zealand are made 15,000 km away in Washington, DC.

PERSONALIZATION indicates that something which can be pictured in personal terms is more newsworthy than a concept, a process, the generalized or the mass. Striving for personalization has brought journalists to grief – for instance in the *Washington Post's* Janet Cooke affair. Cooke's feature writing about an eight-year-old drug addict won a 1981 Pulitzer Prize which was withdrawn when it was found the boy did not exist.

ELITENESS of the news actors plays an important role in news decisions. Reference to elite persons such as politicians or film stars can make news out of something which would be ignored about ordinary people. Similarly, the elite nations of the First World are judged more newsworthy than the non-elite nations of the South.

The quality of ATTRIBUTION – the eliteness of a story's sources – can be crucial in its news chances. Highly valued news sources need to be elite on some dimension, particularly socially validated authority (M. Fishman 1980). The unaffiliated individual is not well regarded as a source. In a study of climate change news (Bell 1989) I found that only two out of the 150 sources cited were not backed by affiliation with some organization or institution.

Finally FACTICITY (Tuchman 1978) is the degree to which a story contains the kinds of facts and figures on which hard news thrives: locations, names, sums of money, numbers of all kinds. We saw in the Honduras ambush story above how such facts were favoured.

Values in the news process

Most of Galtung and Ruge's dozen news factors relate to properties of the events and actors which make up the content of the news. The remaining two are continuity and composition, which relate primarily to news gathering and processing. To these I would add four other factors: competition, co-option, predictability and prefabrication.

CONTINUITY says that once something is in the news, it tends to stay there. Politicians and other would-be newsmakers know well that news breeds news. A story run in the newspaper today has a better chance of appearing with another angle tomorrow. Similarly, once one news outlet has a good story, all its competitors want it too.

COMPETITION is the flip side of this coin. The me-too tendency of news media is in paradox with their desire for a scoop. Every news outlet wants an exclusive. Among other things, this means that if the morning paper runs a story, the evening won't unless it is very newsworthy. Stories are also in competition with each other for coverage in the news market. There are slow news days on which a low-value story may get through. And there are 'what-a-stories' (Tuchman 1978) which knock normally certain stories out of the paper. Continuity and competition seem like incompatible values, but they exist side by side in news work. They may operate in the same story when a journalist scoops her rivals with a new angle or exclusive interview on a long-running story.

CO-OPTION means that a story which is only tangentially related can be interpreted and presented in terms of a high-profile continuing story. With the greenhouse effect a long-running story in the world's media, a range of marginally related events can gain news value through association with it – an incident of aircraft turbulence, or the building of a waterfront car park, for example.

COMPOSITION means that in making up a newspaper or broadcast bulletin, editors want both a mixture of different kinds of news and some common threads. If a bulletin is shaping up to be all overseas news, a domestic story may be used which would otherwise be below the threshold of newsworthiness. On the other hand, overseas items are often packaged together in a news bulletin, each supporting the other's news claims.

PREDICTABILITY is important for news operations. If an event can be prescheduled for journalists it is more likely to be covered than if it turns up unheralded. The canny newsmaker uses this knowledge to schedule events around news deadlines. The predictable nature of much news gathering is, of course, in paradox with the high value placed on news as the unexpected.

Finally, there is the factor of PREFABRICATION, mentioned in chapter 4. The existence of ready-made text which journalists can take over or process rapidly into a story greatly enhances the likelihood of something appearing in the news.

Values in the news text

There are also factors in the quality or style of the news text which affect its news value: CLARITY, BREVITY, and COLOUR, particularly in the LEAD or first paragraph. I introduced these in the discussion of the goals of news editing in chapter 4. If a story's writing exhibits these characteristics, editorial decision-makers will favour it above a story which does not exhibit them. The operation of some factors I have listed under the events/actors category above is also closely associated with the manner of their expression in the news text: recency, proximity, unambiguity, personalization, attribution and facticity. How these operate will be a focus of our discussion in the next chapter.

Galtung and Ruge (1965) propose two principles concerning how news factors operate. News factors are not independent but cumulative. That is, a story is more newsworthy if it registers on more than one factor. There is obvious news value in the addition of the elite nation and the negative – superpower conflict – or the negative and the personal – scandal. Secondly, lack of one factor can be compensated for by possessing another. A non-elite nation can get in the news through negativity (coups and earthquakes), consonance (fulfilling Latin American political stereotypes), or having an elite – or at least well publicized – leader (Libya's Colonel Gadaffi).

News factors have a wide applicability in analysing what makes news. They explain, for example, why sport is such a major category of news. Sport meets the frequency criterion – most games are played and concluded in a short, reportable span. Games have a winner, an unambiguous result (cricket is the exception to some of these!). They are consonant with expectations, their script follows a familiar pattern. The game is prescheduled, but its specific outcome remains unexpected. Sport is a continuing activity: games happen daily in season, premier tournaments and competitions continue over several months. Sport involves nations and individuals who are elite in their field. Its personalities are stars. And it even has the negative – sport is organized conflict, there is a loser as well as a winner, there are bad guys who take drugs or abuse the referee. Scoring high on so many factors, it is little wonder that sport receives so much coverage.

3 NEWS AS STORIES

Linguistic research on the nature of news stories saw a great increase during the 1980s. The best and most comprehensive work to date is by van Dijk (1983, 1985c, 1988a, 1988b), who has applied his discourse analysis framework to the study of news. Discourse analysis was a development of the 1970s and 1980s. At a time when mainstream transformational-generative linguistics was confining its attention to language below the level of the sentence, European text linguistics maintained an interest in larger stretches of language. Just as sociolinguists recognized the need to incorporate extra-linguistic information into linguistic descriptions, discourse analysis insisted on the need to look at language structure above the sentence. European discourse analysis draws on cognitive psychology and artificial intelligence as well as text linguistics. It is a framework which was developed widely (for example by van Dijk and Kintsch 1983) before being applied to news.[2]

Other approaches to news stories have focused primarily on the issues of ideological coding, bias and inaccuracy, using quasi-linguistic methods for their analysis. I shall outline these in chapter 10, while noting here that more recently there has been a coming together of the semiotic and discourse approaches to news, to the benefit of both, evidenced in theme issues of communications journals, such as those edited by Mancini (1988b: *European Journal of Communication*) and Scannell (1990: *Media, Culture and Society*).

Discourse analysis of news

In his approach to news discourse van Dijk proposes a 'new, inter-disciplinary theory of news in the press' (1988b: vii). Following a number of earlier presentations (such as 1983, 1985c), *News as Discourse* (1988b) appeared as a major primary theoretical contribution to the analysis of news stories. It is supplemented by a volume of case studies, *News Analysis* (1988a). These are drawn mainly from analysis of a massive sample of international news reporting – 700 stories from 138 selected newspapers in 99 countries – and a study of racism in the European press. Discourse analysis complements some of the studies I have cited earlier in this book on news production (for instance, Tuchman 1978, M. Fishman 1980), and others to be covered in chapter 11 on comprehension of news (Gunter 1987, Lutz and Wodak 1987).

I will present two of what seem to me the most useful of van Dijk's analytical contributions to the study of news discourse, namely macrorules and 'news schemata'. News stories are composed of 'macropropositions' – broadly, topics (van Dijk 1988b: 30ff.). A discourse will usually contain several topics. Topics are structured within the discourse and can be pictured in tree diagrams similar to those used to describe the syntax of sentences. The structure is derived from the discourse by 'macrorules'. These come in three main kinds and reduce the information in a discourse to its gist or kernel – that is, summarizing. There are three types of macrorules:

1 Deletion of information, such as detail of place, age or time. In our story in figure 8.1 the headline places the ambush *in Honduras*. This is reduced from the second sentence description of *20 kilometres north of the capital Tegucigalpa*.
2 Generalization, so that a list of three items such as a dog, a cat and a canary is generalized as *pets*.
3 'Construction' is not unlike generalization, but is applied to verbs rather than nouns, actions rather than things or people. It summarizes a series of actions under an umbrella term. The word *ambush* in the Honduras headline is a cover term for a series of actions: there was a vehicle on a journey which was waylaid and attacked with weapons, wounding some of the occupants.

Such rules of summarization are, not surprisingly, very similar to the processes by which news stories are edited (examined in Bell 1984a and chapter 4 above). By applying such rules, a long text can be reduced to a short one. The rules in fact approximate strategies which newsworkers may use to derive a lead paragraph from detailed story information. So, the second part of the lead in the Honduras story can be summarized from the detail given about the ambush in the next sentence. Macrorules can be applied recursively, yielding ever more succinct summarizations of a text. The subeditor has derived the headline *US troops ambushed in Honduras* from the journalist's lead paragraph which, as we have seen, has itself been reduced from the story as a whole. Place detail is removed, time is omitted ('just recently' is implied by the fact it is news), as are details of numbers of troops or precise manner and results of the ambush. We can note again that in the process the supposed primary information concerning the military alert is omitted from the summarization. An alternative headline of the same length could have been written – *US troops on alert in Honduras* – derived from this first topic of the lead paragraph.

The categories of news analysis

Van Dijk's main contribution in this area is a framework for analysing the discourse structure of news stories. The thematic structure of a story consists of its topics and their organization within the story. This gives the broad semantic structure. Closely parallel is the syntactic structure, which van Dijk terms 'news schemata'.[3] Schemata consist of a set of characteristic categories, organized by rules (van Dijk 1985c: 85). Typical categories to describe a discourse type are those which Labov used for personal narratives. And, as for personal narratives, these categories can be ordered and structured in relation to each other.

News schemata are thus a syntax of news stories, the formal categories into which news can be analysed and their relations to each other. These can be tree diagrammed (as in the figures below) to show the discourse structure of the story. The categories and their organization are known (unconsciously) by the producers and consumers of news. Some categories, such as background or lead, are used by newsworkers to organize their product. Others such as headline are also known to news audiences. Different types of text, like news and personal narratives, have different schemata. Different languages or cultures may have different schemata for similar genres.

Similar to van Dijk's work is earlier research into how people understand stories, conducted in cognitive psychology and artificial intelligence. Rumelhart (1975) develops a 'story grammar', specifying a number of rules which allow a story to be generated and understood. So a story consists of a setting and an episode. Settings consist of a series of stative propositions – 'once upon a time, in a faraway land, there lived a princess who . . .' Episodes consist of an event plus a reaction. These break down into categories such as action, reaction, attempt, plan, application, pre-action, consequence, and so on. He analyses one of Aesop's fables in these terms, complete with syntactic tree diagrams and summarization rules to pare the story down to its semantic kernel. Other researchers in this framework have used a variety of similar categories, for example, setting, event, episode, beginning/development/ending, internal response, attempt, consequence, action, reaction. Pollard-Gott et al. (1979) apply a story grammar framework to analysing a news story, with similar results to those we shall present below.

Comparing these approaches with Labov and van Dijk, it appears there is wide general agreement on most of the categories needed to characterize a range of story types, including news. I will use them to analyse an example story, adapting them and their labels where I believe there is need, and adding some additional categories which seem necessary to fully characterize the structure of news discourse.

Analysing a story's structure

In figure 8.1 we looked at a spot news story from the international news agencies. Figure 8.2 displays a typical example of the other predominant product of the same agencies, diplomatic and political news. The possible component categories of the story's structure are annotated alongside the copy. In figure 8.3, that linear structure is redisplayed as a tree diagram, which reunites the components of different events from where they are scattered throughout the story. The structure as diagrammed in figure 8.3 looks complex, and so it is, but in fact I have here telescoped levels and omitted nodes in order to simplify the presentation as much as possible. The complexity is a true reflection of the structure of such international diplomatic/political stories.

The news text consists of abstract, attribution and the story proper (figure 8.3). The attribution is outside the body copy of the story, and indicates place at the top (*Moscow*, figure 8.2) and source at the bottom (*NZPA-Reuter*). In many papers all three constituents of the attribution would conventionally be presented at the start of the lead paragraph: *Moscow, 31 March, NZPA-Reuter*. Here the time is not stated in attribution, headline or lead, but is explicit within the story – *yesterday* (S2, S12). The NZPA-Reuter attribution means that the story originates from one of the principal international agencies, channelled through London, New York or Paris, and finally Sydney and Wellington. Although most of the action takes place in Lithuania, the story is datelined Moscow. This may indicate a reporter working from Lithuania through a Moscow office. More likely the reporting is in fact being done from Moscow itself. Such off-the-spot reporting is completely standard in international news. Within the story other media are named as sources of specific information – Vilnius radio (S15) and Tass (S19) for Events 5 and 2 respectively. Unusually, and in contrast to the Honduras story, no non-media sources of information are credited.

The abstract breaks down into headline and lead. The headline covers only Event 1, the occupation – the subeditor gratefully picking out the only hard action from a generally verbal story. The lead covers the occupation plus Event 2, the Byelorussian threat, as well as evaluating their effect on the situation. The evaluative clause *stepping up the pressure on rebel Lithuania* generalizes (by 'construction' in the sense of van Dijk above) on the significance of the two separate events reported in the lead. This kind of explicit evaluation is a common device for drawing together the often disparate threads of such a story. There is no expansion or justification of the evaluation within the body of the story.

The story itself covers no fewer than six events:

1   Occupation of the prosecutor's office (S1, S3–4, S6–14);
2   Byelorussian threat to claim territory (S1, S18–19);
3   Estonia's announcement of desired independence (S2);
4   Bush's note to Gorbachev (S5);
5   Occupation of the Communist Party history institute (S15);
6   Withdrawal of deserter amnesty (S16–17).

In figure 8.3 I subsume Events 1, 5 and 6 under a single episode. They share a common setting of place (Vilnius) as well as principal actors (Soviet troops and officials). However, it is not clear from the story how related these happenings are, and further information might lead us to treat them as separate episodes. Events 2 and 4 are related to the main episode only through the general theme of the Lithuanian independence issue. Event 3 is even more remote, drawing parallels between happenings in Estonia and Lithuania. The story as published bears all the hallmarks of a shotgun marriage by the news agency of up to four originally separate stories covering the occupation, the Byelorussian threat, Bush's note, and the Estonian situation.

Events 3–6 are picked up and dropped within a paragraph or so each (figure 8.2). In the diagram I have not specified all the categories required in the analysis. For example, each event implies actors and setting as well as action. Although Events 1 and 2 are treated at greater length, they are delivered by instalments in a manner characteristic of news narrative. A number of devices are used to bring cohesion out of these diverse components. The inclusion of Event 3 is justified (S2) by describing Estonia as *Lithuania's sister Baltic republic*, together with the use of *meanwhile* – a sure signal that a journalist is about to draw a tenuous connection between disparate events (cf. Glasgow University Media Group 1976: 118). Event 4, Bush's note, is said to deal with *the dispute* (S5), the label under which everything is here subsumed. (In fact, the Bush note was covered in an adjacent story in the newspaper.) A time relationship is specified (S6), linking Bush's

Troops take over Lithuanian office

HEADLINE

Event 1

ATTRIBUTION

Place

LEAD
Evaluation S1
Event 1

Event 2

EVENT 3 S2

Previous
episodes S3

EVENT 1 S4

EVENT 4 S5

Action S6
EVENT 1

Context S7

Previous
episodes
S8
Context

Reaction S9

S10

MOSCOW

STEPPING up the pressure on rebel Lithuania, Soviet troops seized a government office in the capital — and neighbouring Byelorussia threatened to claim a slice of the republic if it secedes from the Soviet Union.

The parliament in Lithuania's sister Baltic republic of Estonia, meanwhile, announced yesterday it wanted to break with Moscow too, declaring the beginning of a transitional period that would end in full independence.

Moscow has refused to recognise Lithuania's March 11 declaration of independence.

Instead it has waged what Lithuanians call a war of nerves, with soldiers occupying public buildings and arresting Lithuanian military deserters.

United States President George Bush sent Soviet President Mikhail Gorbachev a note urging peaceful settlement of the dispute.

A few hours later, Interior Ministry troops moved into the public prosecutor's office in the Lithuanian capital Vilnius.

It was the first Lithuanian building to be occupied by Soviet troops since Wednesday, when the Communist Party headquarters was seized.

It was also the first to be taken over from the government as opposed to the party.

Lithuanian President Vytautas Landsbergis went on television yesterday to denounce the move, saying it would bring shame on Moscow.

"We have endured all these years... we will this time as

well," he said.

"What the USSR is doing now will bring only shame in the eyes of all the world."

Earlier yesterday, deputy Soviet prosecutor Alexei Vasilyev told staff at the prosecutor's office that Moscow had relieved their boss, Alturas Paulauskas, from his post.

In his place Mr Vasilyev announced Moscow had appointed Antanas Petrauskas, who quickly told journalists he did not recognise Lithuanian independence.

Control of the prosecutor's office is considered crucial for Moscow to enforce Soviet law which it says still holds sway in Lithuania, including penalties for army desertion.

Vilnius Radio said Interior Ministry troops had also taken over the history institute of the Lithuanian Communist Party.

Chief military prosecutor Alexander Katusev said yesterday a defence ministry amnesty announced on Friday for any Lithuanian deserters who returned to their units was invalid.

They would be considered on a case-by-case basis, he said.

Lithuania was also set upon by its neighbour Byelorussia, where the parliamentary leadership said it would lay claim to Vilnius and six other districts if Lithuania seceded.

"We shall be obliged to insist on the return of Byelorussian land to the Byelorussian Soviet Socialist Republic," the presidium of the republic's Supreme Soviet, or parliament said, according to the official news agency Tass. — NZPA-Reuter

S11

Action S12

S13

Action

S14 Evaluation

Attribution
S15 EVENT 5

S16 EVENT 6

S17

S18

EVENT 2

S19

Attribution

ATTRIBUTION

FIGURE 8.2 Components of an international news agency story, *Dominion Sunday Times*, Wellington, 1 April 1990 (CAPITALS represent major categories, lower-case labels are subordinate categories)

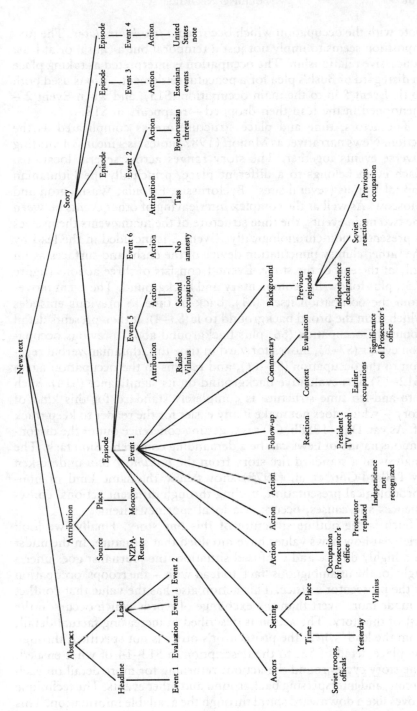

FIGURE 8.3 Structure of Lithuania story from figure 8.2

note with the occupation which occurred *a few hours later*. The jux-
taposition seems to imply not just a temporal but a causal or at least
concessive relationship. The occupation is interpreted as taking place
in disregard of Bush's plea for a peaceful settlement. *Also* is used both
to tie Event 5 in to the main occupation (S15), and when Event 2 –
mentioned in the lead then dropped – reappears in S18.

The actors, time and place structure are as complicated as the
action. News narrative, as Manoff (1987) notes, is a means of knitting
diverse events together. The story ranges across several locations.
Each event belongs to a different place, principally the Lithuanian
capital Vilnius (several sites), Byelorussia, Estonia, Washington and
Moscow. As well as the complex interleaving of other events between
the two main events, the time structure of the main events themselves
is presented non-chronologically. Event 2 is included in the lead by
the rather clumsy punctuation device of the dash, and surfaces again
only at the end of the story. Event 1 consists of three actions (figure
8.3), plus follow-up, commentary and background. The event moves
from the occupation itself (S1), back in time to previous episodes
which form the broad background to it (S3–4). It then presents detail
about the occupation (S6) plus background about previous occupation events (S7–8), moves forward in time to Lithuanian verbal reaction to the occupation (S9–11), and returns to the occupation again
(S12–13) plus evaluative background on its significance (S14). Such
a to-and-fro time structure is completely standard for this kind of
story – which does not make it any easier for the reader to keep track
of. As van Dijk (1988b: 65) says, getting coherence out of the discon-
tinuous nature of news can be a demanding comprehension task. The
analysis of a standard fire story from the *Baltimore Sun* undertaken
by Pollard-Gott et al. (1979) shows how the same kind of non-
chronological presentation, cycling through different actions, consequences and causes, occurs in a local spot news item.

Such is the outline structure of this one story. Finally, we look
briefly at how news values have moulded that structure. In the midst
of a highly diffuse and confused situation, the journalist goes unerr-
ingly for the unambiguous 'fact' to lead with – the troops' occupation
of the prosecutor's office. This action also has the value that conflict
is made more overt than the exchange of words which occurs in the
rest of the story. The action is described in increasing factual detail,
from the lead, where the prosecutor's office is not specified, through
the place detail of S6, to the description in S13–14 of what ensued.
The story cycles round the action, returning for more detail on each
circuit, and interspersing background and other events. The technique
moves like a downward spiral through the available information. This

is in fact described by journalists as the 'inverted pyramid' style –
gathering all the main points at the beginning and progressing through
decreasingly important information.

Spreading the scope of events as wide as possible in the shortest
space, Byelorussia, Estonia and the United States are all called up in
the first five paragraphs. The reference to the United States is of
marginal relevance to the central action of the story, particularly since
there is a detailed story about the Bush note alongside. But the news
value of elite nations and persons – world powers and their
presidents – leads to the events in Lithuania being cast in the light of
superpower relations. The consonance of this story with Western
news stereotypes of Soviet methods is seen in how the occupation is
framed in contrast to Bush's urging for peace. We can also see the news
value of co-option hard at work, bringing diffuse events and locations
under the umbrella of one story. The push for the superlative is clear
in the lexicon selected, especially in the succession of forceful words
in the lead: *stepping up*, *pressure*, *rebel*, *seized*, *threatened*, *secedes*.

4 THE STRUCTURE OF NEWS STORIES

We are now in a position to draw some general conclusions about the
categories and structure of news discourse. Most of the categories
which van Dijk has identified in news discourse – and others in other
story types – are needed, with a few relabellings and additions. A
news text will normally consist of an abstract, attribution and the
story proper (figure 8.4). Attribution of where the story came from
is not always explicit. It can include agency credit and/or journalist's
byline, optionally plus place and time. The abstract consists of the
lead and, for press news, a headline. The lead will include the main
event, and possibly a second event. This necessarily entails giving
some information on actors and setting involved in the event. The lead
may also incorporate attribution (as in the Honduras story), and supplementary categories such as evaluation (see the Lithuania story).

A story consists of one or more episodes, which in turn consist of
one or more events. Events must contain actors and action, usually
express setting, and may have explicit attribution. The categories of
attribution, actors and setting (time and place) need to be recognized
as part of the structure of news stories. They perform the orientation
which Labov (1972b) found in narratives, as well as embedding all
or part of a story as information given by a particular source. These
are also part of the journalist's mental analysis of what goes in a story:
who, when, where, who said?

As well as those elements which present the central action, we recognize three additional categories that can contribute to an event: follow-up, commentary and background (figure 8.4). The Lithuanian story contained all three of these, and all but three of the lower categories of which they can be composed: consequences, expectations, and history.

FOLLOW-UP covers any action subsequent to the main action of an event. It can include verbal reaction, as in the Lithuania story, or non-verbal consequences – for example, if the upshot of the occupation had been demonstrations in Vilnius instead of a presidential speech. Because it covers action occurring after what a story has treated as the main action, follow-up is a prime source of subsequent updating stories – themselves called 'follow-ups'. We can easily imagine a subsequent story where the lead reads *Lithuanian President Vytautas Landsbergis has gone on television to condemn Soviet occupation of* . . . . If the follow-up action had in fact been a demonstration, that would certainly have claimed the lead on a later agency story.

COMMENTARY provides the journalist's or news actors' observations on the action. It may be represented by context, such as the S7–8 information comparing this occupation with previous ones. It may be by explicit evaluation, as in the S14 presentation of the significance of occupying the prosecutor's office. Thirdly, and not exemplified in the Lithuania story, it may express expectations held by the journalist or a news actor on how the situation could develop next.

The category of BACKGROUND covers any events prior to the current action. These are classed as 'previous episodes' if they are comparatively recent. They probably figured as news stories in their own right at an earlier stage of the situation. If the background goes beyond the near past, it is classed as 'history'. Information on the relationship of Lithuania to the Soviet Union during the Second World War was included in stories on other events around this time.

Follow-up and background can have the character of episodes in their own right. That is, episode is a recursive category and can be embedded under consequences, reaction, history or background. If the previous episodes outlined in S3–4 of the Lithuanian story had been more fully expanded, they could easily have incorporated the apparatus of a full episode within them, including categories such as context or evaluation. Similarly, follow-up reaction or consequences can be complex. These are by nature categories which were full stories

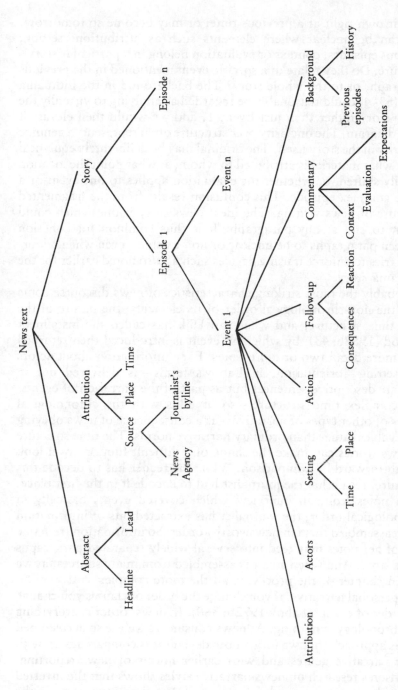

FIGURE 8.4 Outline model structure of news texts. There can be a number of Events or Episodes. Follow-up and Background categories can have Episodes embedded into them. Headline and Lead pick up components from the Story itself. Categories such as Attribution or Setting can be components of either an Event or an Episode

in their own right at a previous time, or may become so tomorrow.

It can be unclear where elements such as attribution, setting, previous episodes, context or evaluation belong in a particular story's structure. Do they relate to a specific event mentioned in the previous paragraph, or to the whole story? The background in the Lithuania story (S3–4) could reasonably be regarded as applying to virtually the whole story rather than just Event 1, and we would then elevate it in the diagram. The unclarity over structure often represents a genuine unclarity in the story itself. The original may be deliberately equivocal about what material is attributed to whom, at what point the location actually shifted, or whether the evaluation applies to one event or a whole complex episode. This confusion results from the fragmented structure of news writing. The ideal news story is one which could be cut to end at any paragraph. It is thus common for cohesion between paragraphs to be unclear or non-existent, even when a journalist tries to enforce it using devices such as *also* noted earlier for the Lithuania story.

Probably the most striking characteristics of news discourse come from the non-chronological order of its elements: the nature of the lead, time structure, and what van Dijk has called the instalment method (1988b: 43), by which an event is introduced then returned to in more detail two or more times. Even information about actors and setting – orientation, in Labov's terms – is delivered not in separate descriptive sentences but as part of the narration of events. The complex time structure – so at odds with the chronological norms of other types of narrative – is a consequence of news obeying news values rather than ordinary narrative norms. The time structure of news stories can make the shape of a difficult film or novel look straightforward by comparison. While the reader has to decode this structure, recall that the journalist had to encode it in the first place. From notes from an interview which covered events basically in chronological order, the journalist has extracted bits of information and reassembled them in newsworthy order. So information from one part of her notes may feed into several widely separated paragraphs of the story. And when a text is assembled from many sources, as we saw in chapter 4, the process is all the more complex.

In personal narrative, if you change the order of clauses you change the order of events (Labov 1972b: 360). In news, order is everything but chronology is nothing. As news consumers we are so accustomed to this approach that we forget how deviant it is compared both with other narrative genres and with earlier norms of news reporting. Schudson's research on news narrative styles shows that the inverted pyramid structure was a development of American journalism in the late nineteenth century. In the 1880s stories covering presidential State of the Union addresses did not summarize the key points at the beginning, but by 1910 the lead as summary was standard (Schudson 1982, 1989). This marks the movement of journalists from being stenographers recording events to interpreters.

Figure 8.5 reprints a story from the *Washington Chronicle* of 10 December 1876. It was a year when – as the centennial issue of the *Washington Post* narrates – 'General Custer was wiped out at Little Big Horn, . . . Wild Bill Hickok shot from behind, . . . and the James gang ambushed'. This clip is a typical spot news story which could run in any local paper today. But it is narrated in absolute chronological order. Where the modern lead would run *A drunken man survived a jump from the Cincinnati–New York express . . .*, the reporter of a century ago begins at the beginning and goes to the end. Even the headline tells a chronological tale. According to Schudson (1978) reporters moved from being recorders or stenographers to interpreters about the turn of the century.

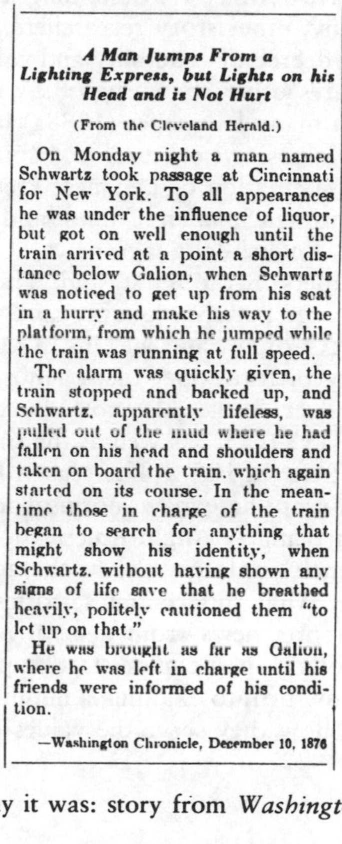

A Man Jumps From a Lighting Express, but Lights on his Head and is Not Hurt

(From the Cleveland Herald.)

On Monday night a man named Schwartz took passage at Cincinnati for New York. To all appearances he was under the influence of liquor, but got on well enough until the train arrived at a point a short distance below Galion, when Schwartz was noticed to get up from his seat in a hurry and make his way to the platform, from which he jumped while the train was running at full speed.

The alarm was quickly given, the train stopped and backed up, and Schwartz, apparently lifeless, was pulled out of the mud where he had fallen on his head and shoulders and taken on board the train, which again started on its course. In the meantime those in charge of the train began to search for anything that might show his identity, when Schwartz, without having shown any signs of life save that he breathed heavily, politely cautioned them "to let up on that."

He was brought as far as Galion, where he was left in charge until his friends were informed of his condition.

—Washington Chronicle, December 10, 1876

FIGURE 8.5 The way it was: story from *Washington Chronicle*, 1876

Story grammarians have concluded that the minimal well-formed narrative must contain setting and action (Pollard-Gott et al. 1979). What constitutes the minimal, well-formed, modern news text? The answer is straightforward: a one-sentence story. Many newspapers publish one-paragraph stories, to fill odd corners or assembled in a column of news briefs. In some broadcast news, many stories may consist of only a single sentence. Because the story is encapsulated in the lead, the lead is a story in microcosm. If we were to analyse the first sentence of the Lithuania story, we would need to specify all the basic structure of Events 1 and 2. This is not surprising. If a lead summarizes a story, we expect it to contain the principal elements of that story. Our process of analysing a news text into its constituent structure produces a summary much like that which the journalist arrives at in writing a lead. The lead-as-complete-story consists minimally of the actors, action and place which constitute a single event. Attributions, abstract, time, and the supplementary categories of follow-up, commentary and background are unnecessary.

The categories I have outlined for describing story structure, drawn from van Dijk, Labov, other story researchers, and my own work, seem to have a high degree of generality and validity. They apply in languages and cultures other than English. Van Dijk's analysis of newspaper stories in many languages (1988a) found few significant differences in news values or structure. In a comparison of different treatments of the assassination of Lebanese President-elect Gemayel in 1982, he found stories in Spanish, Chinese and Swedish all followed a similar pattern to English-language news. There were some differences between papers in the 'First' and 'Third' Worlds. But the greatest differences were between 'quality' and 'popular' papers, for instance within West Germany and the United Kingdom. The popular *Bild Zeitung* (literally 'picture paper') used a more chronological news order for dramatic effect. Burger also notes the distinctiveness of this section of the press (1984: 99), as well as the similarity of broadcast news between countries (p. 105). (The reason for the similarities is clear but beyond our scope here: news norms worldwide are patterned on Western, and particularly Anglo-American, models.)

We still have much to learn about characteristic news structures – for instance, what differentiates stories in the quality and popular press, or sports news from general news. The categories developed above provide an adequate starting point for undertaking such analysis. We now turn to examine a number of these categories in more detail, and how they serve the values of news.

9

Make-up of the News Story

This chapter looks more closely at some of the elements that make up the structure of news stories: leads, headlines, source attributions, news actors, time, place, the use of numbers in the news, and news as talk. Many of these categories connect closely to the journalist's own short-list of what should go in a story, the 'five W's and an H': who, when, where, what, how, why. It is not surprising that a profession's own conscious methods should be reflected in analysis. Indeed Kniffka (1980: 200) goes so far as to suggest that these categories are sufficient to describe the structure of news stories. Further, he claims that they represent the mental processes by which stories are formulated by journalists and understood by readers.

I will not pursue this line here, but note that such categories should themselves be critically analysed for the role they play in the processes of journalism. Manoff and Schudson do just that in an excellent collection of essays (1987) devoted to unpacking what the W's mean in news work. Here we look first at leads and headlines, and then turn to examine what the W's mean for news stories and how they are expressed. My examples are drawn largely from the press. Despite the differences between press and broadcast news, the structures of broadcast news still largely reflect its historical roots in printed journalism. More precisely, my examples come from the average, conservative daily newspaper. Avowedly mass-appeal papers write headlines or structure stories in a different fashion which would require its own study (cf. Burger 1984: 52ff.).

1 THE LEAD

I have already in the last chapter written a lot about leads, their structure and their function in the story as a whole. This is no accident.

The lead is the most distinctive feature of news discourse (not the headline, which I will therefore treat second). Framing the lead is arguably the journalist's primary writing skill, distinguishing the journalistic craft from other forms of professional writing. The lead (or intro) is also the most difficult aspect of news writing for non-journalists to produce.

Cappon (1982) calls his chapter on leads 'the agony of square one'. Journalists hate starting to write as much as anyone. When they do, their aim is to produce leads which are packed with information and news appeal, but as short as possible and clearly understood. Newsworthiness, brevity and clarity are the values of the lead. In chapter 4 I discussed how the copy editors who process journalists' writing also work to achieve these qualities.

The lead is a micro-story. It compresses the values and expertise of journalism into one sentence. Understanding how the lead works is to understand the nature of news stories. In working on a story, even while I am still interviewing a news source, I am mentally searching the material for possible leads. Much of what has been said about the structure of stories applies to the lead. Since the lead may often have to serve as a one-paragraph story, this is not surprising. Just as news values operate to raise the most newsworthy information into the lead, so within the lead itself the most newsworthy is put at the beginning not the end of the paragraph.

The most detailed analysis of the structure and function of news leads is Kniffka's treatment of a single story published in 31 United States newspapers. Analysing reports of the 1972 acquittal of black activist Angela Davis, he found that main actor (Davis) and action (acquittal) were reported in all 31 lead paragraphs (Kniffka 1980: 179). Actor and action were the core of every lead, but no lead was limited to that minimum. Other principal components were specification of the time of the verdict (23 newspapers), or of the charges on which Davis had been tried (24). Few specified place (but this was published immediately above as the dateline). Particularly interesting is the elevation of a descriptive detail to the lead in a majority (19) of the stories. Most of the leads were drawn from news agency copy with wording such as:

> An all-white jury found black militant Angela Davis innocent Sunday of murder-kidnap-conspiracy charges and was given an ovation of cheers and applause in the courtroom.

The description *all-white* is found newsworthy enough to precede both the main actor and the action. Kniffka found that the lead never ran in the form:

* The jury found Angela Davis innocent . . .

If the *all-white* label is not used, a passive verb becomes the most likely alternative form of the lead:

Angela Davis was found innocent Sunday . . .

All other leads were variations on these. All incorporated some reaction to the verdict, and later updates began with reaction from Davis and supporters, comment from the jurors, and similar follow-ups.

Structure of lead paragraphs

Figure 9.1 displays the lead paragraphs from ten international wire service stories, drawn more or less at random from several New Zealand newspapers in April 1990. They reveal several patterns. Note first that actors, main event and place – the journalist's *who*, *what* and *where* – are expressed in all these leads. Agency attribution is usually carried at the end of the story, hence is not shown in figure 9.1. Time is sometimes expressed, and in some papers is carried as dateline (examples 6–8). Stories generated locally by the newspaper itself will not carry dateline or agency attribution, but may go under the journalist's byline.

Secondly, the lead concentrates the news value of the story, in the terms discussed in the previous chapter. Every lead in figure 9.1 majors on negativity, mostly conflict. All but two contain death, violence or the imminent threat of these. Many of the news actors are elite – presidents, prime ministers, kings, leaders, top nations. Consonance with stereotypes of the parties involved is stressed, from Latin American and South African political violence (1, 3, 9) to India–Pakistan border conflicts (6) to West German espionage scandals (5). Continuity with former stories is high, with previous events incorporated into the leads. Facticity is stressed by use of figures (1, 3, 8, 10) as well as detailed reference to person, time and place.

Symbolizing all these values is the lexicon of newsworthiness, principally conflict. In the India lead (6) we find *accuse, evil, tensions, skirmishes, disputed*. In the Jerusalem lead (8): *thousands, thronged, clung, defiantly, disputed*. South Africa (9) out-tops them all: *tough, new, quash, violence, engulfing, immediately, condemned, leftist*.

① US troops ambushed in Honduras

TEGUCIGALPA
UNITED STATES troops in Honduras were put on high alert after at least six American soldiers were wounded, two seriously, in a suspected leftist guerrilla ambush yesterday, United States officials said.

② Troops take over Lithuanian office

MOSCOW
STEPPING up the pressure on rebel Lithuania, Soviet troops seized a government office in the capital — and neighbouring Byelorussia threatened to claim a slice of the republic if it secedes from the Soviet Union.

③ Troops kill 10, says politician

LIMA.— Peruvian army troops killed 10 civilians, including a family of four, after rounding them up in sweeps through Andean villages, a congressman has charged.

⑤ Germans arrest spy

HAMBURG.— A West German cipher clerk has been arrested for passing Nato nuclear-weapons secrets to the Soviet Union in another German spy scandal.

④ Injunction halts council move to honour Mandela

LONDON.— Conservative councillors have gained a High Court injunction blocking moves to grant Nelson Mandela the freedom of their London borough.

FIGURE 9.1 Headlines and lead paragraphs from ten international news agency stories appearing in *The Evening Post*, Wellington, the *Auckland Star* and other newspapers, April 1990

Tensions mount over ⑥ Kashmir dispute

AMRITSAR (India), April 13. — Indian Prime Minister Vishwanath Pratap Singh accused Pakistan today of "evil designs" as tensions between the two countries rose after skirmishes along their disputed border in Kashmir.

⑦

Nepalese Opposition expects to form govt

KATMANDU, April 13. — A veteran Nepalese Opposition leader emerged from a long-awaited meeting with King Birendra today to say he expected a new interim government to be formed by the end of next week.

⑧

Jewish settlement stokes tension

JERUSALEM, April 13. — Thousands of Christian pilgrims thronged the Via Dolorosa in Jerusalem's Old City on Good Friday as Jewish settlers, walkietalkies in hand, clung defiantly to their disputed new home along the route.

Blacks condemn moves to quash political violence ⑨

CAPE TOWN
TOUGH new measures proposed by president Frederick de Klerk to quash the political violence engulfing South Africa's black townships were immediately condemned by leftist black leaders.

Aborigines found dead in jail cells

BRISBANE
TWO Aborigines have been found dead within 24 hours in cells at the Rockhampton Correctional Centre in Queensland.

This is all arguably more value-laden than much of the vocabulary of advertising, a genre which makes none of journalism's claim to objectivity.

Third, while the international agency is always attributed, most leads do not attribute other sources of their information. US officials (1), a Peruvian congressman (3) and Nepalese opposition leader (7) are given as sources of information. Time is sometimes expressed directly as *yesterday*, or *today* (only when the date is given in the dateline: 6, 7). In many examples (2–5) there is no overt time reference. We interpret these as 'reported within the past 24 hours' in the light of the recency criterion, but in fact some of these items could be days-old news and we readers would be none the wiser. Since these are all overseas agency stories, they are always published with explicit place of origin in the dateline, although this does not necessarily coincide with where events occurred. Place is occasionally expressed in the canonical prepositional phrase – *in Jerusalem* (8), *in Queensland* (10). More often we infer a location for events from the description of a main actor – *Peruvian* (3), *West German* (5), *Indian* (6), *Nepalese* (7). Sometimes that inference is misleading. The spy was arrested in Brussels not West Germany (5), according to the story's second paragraph.

Fourthly , all but two of the leads (2, 9) begin with *who* – the main actors. Here the values of personalization and elite actors control order within the lead sentence. The commonness of this pattern can be demonstrated by a glance through any page of a newspaper, and is confirmed in Roeh's study of Israeli radio news (1982: 72). The drive to put the main actors first results in a number of passive-voice sentences (1, 5, 9, 10). News writing lore has it that verbs should be active, but passives are much more common than the prescription implies. Often the only way to get the main news actors at the front of the lead is to passivize the verb. Otherwise minor characters would have to take centre stage, for instance in example 10 – *Prison warders have found two aborigines dead . . .*

But where the people involved in a story are obscure witnesses or givers of information with no news value in their own right, the story may lead on *what* not *who*. And then with a certain kind of *what*. In science reporting, it is the result or its application which leads the story not the process which gave rise to it. The classic chronology of the scientific paper – from problem through method, analysis and results to discussion and conclusion – is overturned for media coverage.

Fifth, most of the leads cover two events not one. The Honduras and Lithuania examples from the last chapter, repeated in figure 9.1, prove to be typical. The discourse structure of the leads is therefore complex, with the events usually linked by a temporal conjunction such as *as* or *after* (*with* plus present participle is also useful). In most cases one event is a sequel to the other (1, 3, 4, 5, 6, 9). This relationship is often expressed by *after* (1, 6). In other cases the previous event is embedded into the main event which it has triggered – *being arrested for [previous event]* (5) or *an injunction blocking moves to [previous event]* (4). In several cases there is a sequence of previous events embedded two-deep. In example 9 we have:

1 black leaders condemn
2 measures proposed by de Klerk to control
3 political violence.

Figure 9.2 diagrams the structure of this lead. It consists of Event 1, the black leaders' condemnation, with its actors and action. Embedded within it is the previous episode, Event 2, the government moves to which black leaders are reacting. Within Event 2 is embedded still earlier episodes to which the government is reacting, the incidents of political violence. The structure of the lead is complex, and it is notable for containing all but one of the main categories in the structure of the story itself. The subsequent six paragraphs, not shown, simply expanded on the actions of the two main events. The only category which has to be added to describe the story as a whole is the setting for Event 2 – *parliament in Cape Town on Monday*.

Where there is a sequence of events, the most recent usually comes first (1, 3, 4, 5, 6). The exception is example 9, where we do not reach the black leaders' reaction until the end of the lead paragraph. In most cases the two events are very close together in time, and the body of the story details both events not just the first. In several examples, the previous episode is a prerequisite to the main event occurring at all and must be mentioned for the story to make sense. That is, the main event in the story is a reaction to a previous main event. So, the black leaders are reacting to the government moves (9), the injunction responds to a council decision (4). In other cases, the two events are related by *and* or *as*, implying co-occurrence (2, 8) or even cause (6). In the case of (6), we have both simultaneity – *as tensions rose* – and sequel – *after skirmishes*.

Sixth, the category of background is expressed in the lead through the embedding of previous events, as we have seen. Commentary is also present, from the evaluative opening clause of the Lithuania

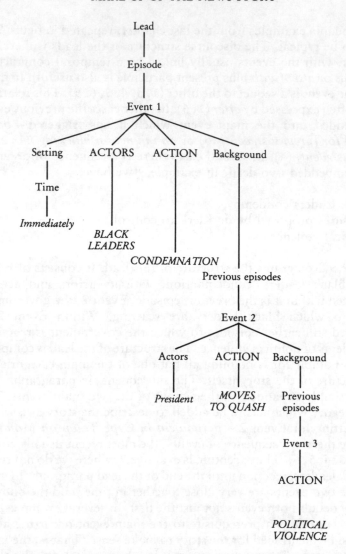

FIGURE 9.2 Structure of lead and headline in an international story — for text see example 9 in figure 9.1 (headline categories in CAPITALS)

example (2) examined in the previous chapter to contextualizing the West German cipher arrest as *another German spy scandal*. We should also note the devices by which a context is evoked without expending words to make it explicit. The phrase *Conservative councillors* in (4) draws on knowledge of the nature of British politics to imply that it was Labour councillors who had passed a motion on Mandela.

I have said that brevity is a particular criterion of the lead. Despite packing in at least two events, most of the leads in figure 9.1 are less than 30 words long. This is the maximum length to which journalists try to work, and I prefer closer to 20 words. The shortest lead I have ever used to begin a story was two words long – *Times change* (in a feature about the development of the technology used for keeping New Zealand standard time). Van Dijk's analysis of international reporting found that in fact the average lead was about 25 words long (1988b: 79).

The tussle between high information content, brevity and clarity (cf. Grice 1975) is not entirely resolved in many of these example leads. Some do give the reader an adequate chance of rapid decoding (3, 4, 5, 10). For the rest, comprehension is jeopardized by the amount of information packed in, the double-deckering of events, and the embedding of background. This complexity seems surprising in the light of the prescription to write simply, but follows from the clash of clarity with maximum content. We must agree with van Dijk's finding that leads can often be syntactically and informationally complex (1988b: 77). (His examples are, however, drawn from elite papers such as the *International Herald-Tribune*, which may not be representative.)

Lead as abstract and beginning

We can regard the lead as basically a summary of a story, deriving its content and structure from the body copy, and so it is. But it is a *directional* summary, a lens through which the point of the story is focused and its news value magnified. This focus may be achieved – as van Dijk notes descriptively (1988b: 57) and Cappon prescriptively (1982: 31) – by raising a colourful detail to the lead. A notable case of this is the phrase *walkie-talkies in hand* in the Jerusalem lead (8). No explanation of the significance of this is advanced in the remainder of the story, so we are left to infer it symbolizes quasi-military alert by the Jewish settlers.

The lead's function is not solely as a stand-alone abstract. In face-to-face narratives, the abstract comes first, then the story itself begins. But the journalistic lead has a dual function. It must begin to tell the story as well as summarizing it. It therefore has to introduce the orientation material which a face-to-face narrator might consign to several separate descriptive sentences – *who*, *when* and *where*. It must provide a springboard for telling the whole story, not just a summary.

And the journalist must do all this labouring under a severe condition: do not repeat yourself.

This can cause problems. The face-to-face narrator will summarize, then repeat the information from the summary in the course of the main narrative. But repetition is a mortal sin in news writing. So it can be difficult to follow a lead which aptly summarizes a story with a second and subsequent paragraphs which do not obviously repeat the lead. The Honduras story in the previous chapter (figure 8.1) is a typical example of failure to solve this problem:

> S1 . . . at least six American soldiers were wounded . . . in a suspected leftist guerrilla ambush . . .
> S2 Six or seven soldiers were wounded when at least three men, believed to be leftist guerrillas, used high-powered weapons in an ambush . . .

Leads also often contain information which never resurfaces in the body of the story. In figure 9.1 all except the last two leads contain information which is unique to the lead and cannot be derived from information in the body copy:

1 United States troops were put on high alert
2 Stepping up the pressure on rebel Lithuania
3 sweeps through Andean villages
4 High Court [injunction]
5 cipher clerk [arrested for] passing Nato nuclear-weapons secrets to the Soviet Union
6 'evil designs'
7 veteran Nepalese Opposition leader . . . long-awaited meeting . . . [King] Birendra . . . interim [government]
8 walkie-talkies in hand

These phrases are of different kinds. Some include colourful detail or quotation (6, 8). Some describe news actors in terms which are not repeated further down the story (5, 7). Others present more detail on the central action (3, 4, 7). In two cases, there is evaluation or context (2, 7) which is not expanded in the body of the story. The West German spy's actual actions are detailed only in the lead, the rest of the published story being given to background (5). And in the most extreme case, the Honduras story (1), the supposed main event is never referred to again in the remainder of the story.

It is thus inadequate to describe the lead as simply a summary of the body of the story. It also part of the story itself, and when it contains material which is not repeated further down, this has to be incorporated in the structure of the story proper. We must conclude that a category which we might normally expect to be filled in the structure of the story proper can be emptied and realized only in the lead. In our analysis of the Lithuania story (figure 8.3), the evaluation category in the lead is effectively of this kind. So we could redraw figure 8.3 to show the evaluation node of the lead as duplicating a second but empty evaluation node within Event 1. Similarly, we would have to say that Event 1 in the Honduras story – the military alert – is transferred *in toto* into the lead, leaving the category empty.

I have concentrated here on leads in just one type of news, the international agency hard news story as published in the press. But we may expect differences in other genres and media. Broadcast stories, for example, are less likely to pack two events into the lead in the way the press does. Local stories can take as known to the reader detail of place or person which the international story may have to carry in the lead. Different types of newspapers use different types of leads according to their assessment of readers' interests.

Features are different again, and allow the writer a more leisurely and less direct approach to the news. The difference is illustrated in the contrast between a hard news story and parallel feature of my own. The hard news story announced the finding of low ozone over New Zealand:

> Low ozone levels have been detected for the second successive summer over DSIR's atmospheric station in Central Otago.

The story was followed a couple of days later by a feature describing the work of the research station which made the measurements. The feature begins descriptively, with no attempt at immediacy:

> A remote site in Central Otago is an international centre of research on the ozone layer.

2 HEADLINES

The distinctive, telegraphic syntax of headlines has drawn a good deal of linguistic attention, for instance in the leading study by Mardh (1980). Here I am interested largely in the discourse structure and function of headlines rather than their syntactic composition.

With much press news drawn from external news agencies and shared with competitors, the headline is a newspaper's opportunity to stamp its individuality on what is otherwise a mass-produced product (Kniffka 1980: 41). Some types of newspaper carry several decks of headlines above stories (van Dijk 1988a: 75 analyses a five-decker from the *New York Times*). In broadcast news, headlines are either absent altogether or collected at the beginning and/or end of longer news programmes.

Headlines appear to be the ultimate in the journalist's drive for summarizing information. This has misled some researchers (for instance, van Dijk 1985c: 84) into seeing the journalistic process as beginning with a headline and working through lead to body copy. That is not what happens. The three components of headline, lead and body copy are presented and read in that order, but were produced in the order lead–body–headline. The lead is where the journalist focuses a story, and the headline is written by other newsworkers. This division of labour arises because the length of a headline is dictated by the constraints of page layout, and page layout is the work of subeditors not journalists. The subeditor derives the headline principally from the lead – which she may in fact edit or rewrite as well.

The journalist's own ultimate abstract is in fact the one-word catchline or slugline by which a story is identified as it is processed through the newsroom. The slugline has to be distinctive enough to separate the story from all other stories which will be handled that day – including updates on the same topic. I do not know how the news agencies slugged the ten example stories used in figure 9.1, but typical sluglines would be AMBUSH (1), INJUNCTION (4), CIPHER (5), PILGRIM or THRONG or SETTLERS (8), TOUGH or CONDEMN (9). A well-chosen slugline is often a good guide to the central news point of its story.

Structure of headlines

As an approach to analysis of headlines, here again are the headlines from figure 9.1:

1 US TROOPS AMBUSHED IN HONDURAS
2 TROOPS TAKE OVER LITHUANIAN OFFICE
3 TROOPS KILL 10, SAYS POLITICIAN
4 INJUNCTION HALTS COUNCIL MOVE TO HONOUR MANDELA
5 GERMANS ARREST SPY
6 TENSIONS MOUNT OVER KASHMIR DISPUTE
7 NEPALESE OPPOSITION EXPECTS TO FORM GOVERNMENT

8   JEWISH SETTLEMENT STOKES TENSION
9   BLACKS CONDEMN MOVES TO QUASH POLITICAL
    VIOLENCE
10 ABORIGINES FOUND DEAD IN JAIL CELLS

Some of these (for example, 3 and 10) are straight summarizations of the main event(s) in their stories' lead paragraph and retain the major categories of the lead. But headlines generally delete structure from the lead. Most of the example leads contained two or even more events. Their headlines generally pare this down to a single main event. Only Event 1 of the Lithuania lead (2) makes it to the headline. In the Honduras story (1), it is the second main event which is headlined, with the first event – military alert – considered weaker news than the ambush.

Unlike the lead, the headline is a stand-alone unit. It simply abstracts the story, it does not have to begin it. While the lead may carry new information which does not recur in the story proper, the headline is entirely derivable from the story. In most cases it can be derived from the lead alone. The Jerusalem headline (8) covers only the second main event of the lead and its actors, although it implies the existence of the other group – Christian pilgrims – by reference to *tension*. This is the only one of our example headlines which cannot be derived solely from the lead. It draws on phrasing from the end of the second paragraph, *stoking Israeli–Palestinian tensions*, focusing on only half the action and actors of the lead and story. Just as the lead may focus on a striking detail, so that detail can carry through to the headline, as Kniffka's example shows (1980: 8):

ANGELA DAVIS SIPS VICTORY CHAMPAGNE

Some of the longer sample headlines (4, 9) successfully summarize the complex structure of the leads from which they derive. In example 9 there are two successive previous episodes embedded under the main event, as we saw in the structural diagram above. Figure 9.2 shows how this headline retains all three action nodes, plus the actors of Event 1. The deleted categories are the time setting (*immediately*) of Event 1, and the actor from Event 2, the South African president. The deleted detail includes description of the actors (*leftist leaders*), qualification of the moves as *tough* and *new* (redundant), and specification of the site of the violence. It is notable how the headline maintains the main structure of the lead, which itself retains almost all the structure of the story. The headline is thus a true abstract of the story.

Previous episodes are culled out of the headline unless they are prerequisite to the main event itself and must be expressed to make it comprehensible. Thus the injunction requires mention of the act it aims to stop (4), the condemnation must mention the action being condemned (9). This suggests that there is a class of the 'previous episodes' category which may need to be obligatorily expressed in a story. On examination it turns out that such previous episodes are typically performative speech acts, and the reaction to them is also a performative. That is, a council motion and an injunction which responds to it are both classic performatives (Austin 1962) where the words perform the deed – passing a motion or imposing an injunction.

Kniffka's (1980) detailed comparison of leads and headlines found a high level of structural correspondence between the two. The subeditor tends to reproduce the syntactic patterns of the lead in the headline. Our examples in large measure confirm this. Headlines, like leads, tend to begin with the main news actors. Only headlines 4 and 6 do not start with mention of actors. However, these two are stories for which the lead *did* in fact begin with actors. And the two leads which did not begin with actors in fact carry headlines with actors first (2, 9). The headline of the complex India/Pakistan story (6) draws on the most generalized component of the lead – *tensions rose*. No actor at all is mentioned, even the Indian prime minister, whose speech dominates both lead and story. This omission seems possible only because the headline relies on the reader's geopolitical knowledge to deduce actors from the mention of the location, *Kashmir*.

Kniffka found that the presence of active or passive voice in the lead was carried over to the headline. However the passive verbs in the spy (5) and South Africa (9) leads are converted to active voice in the headlines, making example 9 in particular an easier sequence to decode. Who is mentioned in first position in a headline, and whether the verb is active or passive, can be ideologically revealing. Van Dijk (1988a: 227) analysed over 400 headlines in the Dutch press reporting the 1985 'Tamil panic', an occasion of racial tensions between the Dutch and immigrant groups. He found that the authorities dominated first position in the headline, with active verbs. When the disadvantaged Tamils were mentioned first, the verb tended to be passive.

Headline rhetoric

Our examples illustrate some of the characteristics of headlines. As one would expect, most headlines abstract the main event of the story.

Some focus on a secondary event or a detail. These are particularly revealing cases. The very fact that a headline features something which the story presents as lesser re-weights the news values in the story. Place is sometimes specified, but never time. Some headlines (for instance, 3) leave location completely unclear, able to be deduced only from the dateline or lead. In other cases, the location which the reader might infer from other components of the headline is misleading (4, 5) or vague (9). Attribution is not usually expressed, unless the news event itself is a speech act (6, 9). The Peruvian headline (3) is unusual in retaining the attribution.

The headline cuts the lead back still further, leaving a core of the main action and its actor, and sometimes previous action and place. So the minimal headline is, to use Kniffka's example:

DAVIS ACQUITTED

Kniffka (1980: 333) found that headlines commonly gave information on the *how* of an event. My finding is that place is the most common third category in the headline, and may even substitute for actor. Evaluation and other commentary categories are absent. But plenty of news values remain expressed, especially in the distinctive, monosyllabic lexicon of headline rhetoric: *troops*, *halt*, *move* (noun), *mount*, *stoke*, *quash*. This formulaic quality provides an open day for satirists such as Michael Frayn. His 'unit headline language' (Frayn 1973: 191) enables newsworkers to assemble headlines by adding monosyllabic, syntactically ambiguous components until they reach:

STRIKE THREAT PLEA PROBE MOVE SHOCK HOPE STORM

Headline structures appear to be very regular across languages. Kniffka confirmed his analysis on both German and American English news texts, finding their leads and headlines structurally identical. The regularity is so consistent that he concludes there is a shared international grammar of lead- and headline-writing (1980: 333).

Finally, headlines are not just a summary but part of news rhetoric whose function is to attract the reader. They use common rhetorical devices such as alliteration, punning, and pseudo-direct quotes, especially in the popular press (Burger 1984: 53, Short 1988). Some topics bring out the repressed word-player in subeditors. My gorse mite story, analysed in chapter 4, produced a clutch of such headlines in the papers that published it:

VORACIOUS MITE TO CONTROL PRICKLY PEST

SHOW OF MITE AGAINST GORSE

MITEY ANSWER FOUND?

MIDGET MITES SET TO GOBBLE GORSE

3 NEWS SOURCES AND ACTORS

Who says

Who says? is one of the primary questions of news work. It should also be a question which is high in the news audience's mind. What credentials does that person having for saying this? How reliable is that news agency? News stories come from two types of sources: media and newsmakers. This agency story from the days of the Vietnam war attributes both:

> Nearly one hundred people were killed or wounded in a pre-dawn rocket attack today on Da Nang air base in the northern quarter of South Vietnam, military sources said, the Associated Press reported.

Attribution serves an important function in the telling of news stories. It reminds the audience that this is an account which originated with certain persons and organizations. It is not an unchallengeable gospel, but one fruit of human perception and production among other conceivably alternative accounts. In theory a news story should be regarded as embedded under a stack of attributions, each consisting of source, time and place:

1 Radio station XA reports in Auckland at 12.00 that
2 NZ Press Association reported in Wellington at 11.00 that
3 Australian Associated Press reported in Sydney at 10.00 that
4 Reuters reported in London at 09.00 that
5 correspondent AB reported in Jerusalem at 08.00 that
6 an Israeli military spokesperson said in Tel Aviv at 07.00 that

Ultimately it is the individual news outlet which by publishing or broadcasting a story is its attributable source, as the first in the list implies. The outlet's principals take responsibility for the successive inputs of their organization's newsworkers, as examined in chapter

3. At the start of the chain is the original newsmaker source (6), and the journalist who wrote the story (5). Bylining makes overt the name of the journalist credited with the story (although it is no guarantee that the journalist actually wrote most of the copy attributed to him).

Each of the four editing steps (2–4) in between is an embedding. As we saw in chapters 3 and 4, most of them remain hidden from the audience. We have seen how newspapers attribute all news agency copy, but broadcast news rarely attributes agencies. One exception is the BBC World Service news, which is distinctive for frequently naming the journalistic sources of its information. When an outlet carries an externally originated story without attribution, it takes tacit responsibility for the content of the story. It says *We tell you here and now that* . . . rather than that someone else is telling you.

There is also a newsmaker component of *who says*: who was the source of this information? News sources are of two broad kinds: suppliers of information which the journalist wants to know, or news actors whose own utterances have news value – announcements, reactions, proposals, and the like. In the second case, the source exercises her role as news actor through speaking.

The source as authority

News is mostly, as we saw in chapter 4, what someone says, either as witness to facts or as news actor. But someone does not mean just *anyone*. The conclusions of sociologists of news production on the nature of news sources are solid (Tuchman 1978, Gans 1979, M. Fishman 1980, Glasgow Group 1980, Sigal 1987). News is what an authoritative source tells a journalist.

Quantitative research on news sources confirms the qualitative conclusions. Nearly half the front page stories (domestic and foreign) in the *New York Times* and *Washington Post* have been found to come from US officials (Sigal 1987). My own study of climate change news in New Zealand (Bell 1989) found that nearly 80 per cent of sources (including most of the scientists) were in local or national government. Ministers, local politicians and officials were cited almost as often as scientists themselves (figure 9.3). Few of them had credentials in the scientific field, and some gave the public wrong information. But they wear a general mantle of authority and are part of the institutional network where journalists expect to get information. The world of journalists' sources is, as M. Fishman argues, 'bureaucratically organized' (1980: 51).

The corollary to this is equally well attested in the research:

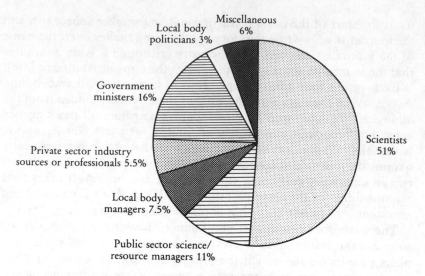

FIGURE 9.3   Amount of New Zealand climate change coverage quoting different source types (percentage of mentions of sources, N = 343)

unofficial news sources are little used (Kress 1983b). Alternative sources tend to be ignored: individuals, opposition parties, unions, minorities, fringe groups, the disadvantaged. Among politicians it is ministers who have overwhelming access to the media. Not one of the political sources on climate change was a backbench or opposition Member of Parliament. Only 10 per cent of sources were women.

The quality of a story's sources affects its news value. The more elite the source, the more newsworthy the story. The converse is also true. Exposure as a news source reinforces the source's authority as well as reflecting it. It is in a journalist's interests to present cited news sources in the most authoritative light. If she feels the source's credentials may be in doubt, she may spell them out in detail. In a story once turned in to me, a journalist inserted into each of his first few paragraphs a fresh piece of evidence expanding on his source's credentials. By the third such qualification, the technique read like a parody – the journalist 'protested too much'. Often a person's full title is too long to fit in the lead and still leave room for the news. Then a generalized label may appear in the lead:

a senior Reagan administration official

On next mention, I gave this source his detailed affiliation, but glossed his rather long, proper title with *head*:

head of the US Department of Agriculture's Foreign Agricultural Service, Mr Thomas Kay

A curious category is that of the unnamed source. Geis (1987: 81) analyses a *Newsweek* article in which no fewer than 17 unnamed sources are mentioned, for instance:

one top-ranking US official
one senior aide
officials throughout the administration
several of Reagan's closest advisors

Different labellings tend to signify different levels of authority (cf. Tunstall 1970b), but it is notable how these labellings claim standing for their anonymous sources. It is also clear that readers cannot assess for themselves the credibility of the sources – or of the story.

There are two cases in which the news value of a story particularly depends on who the source is. The first is when something is news just because someone elite said it. If an ordinary person had said it, it would have had no news value. Talk is news only if the right person is talking. The second case is where there is doubt or contention over 'the facts'. Here a credible source can see a story published when the same information from another source would not get into print.

In spoken English, attribution usually begins a sentence, and broadcast news follows this pattern:

Professor Landsbergis said that if such broadcasts continued his government would stop transmission of Moscow television in Lithuania.

Leitner (1983c) found that 93 per cent of attributions in a sample of British TV news were at the beginning of the sentence. In the press, attribution is often postposed, particularly after a direct quotation:

"Israel is a country aspiring toward peace, but which has always known how to defend itself," acting Prime Minister Yitzhak Shamir said.

Who does

There is a close relationship between authority as a source and standing as a newsmaker (Sigal 1987). The ideal news source is also a news actor, someone whose own words make news. This is why politicians are such prominent participants. They are focuses of both news talk and news action. In the United States, the president is both ultimate news actor and news source. This enables a president in trouble such as Nixon to adopt what Lerman (1983) has termed the 'institutional voice', claiming the mantle of presidency to deflect personal accountability. Roeh's study of radio news in Israel (1982: 154) found two dominant patterns in the news. Out of 600 stories, 68 per cent featured elite persons saying something, and the rest presented non-elite persons doing or being done to. Elite people in the news rarely acted: they talked.

Personalization is a news value in its own right, and we have already seen how leads and headlines are structured to put a news actor first.[1] To understand the criteria by which someone gets in the news, we have only to apply to people the news values presented in the last chapter. One of those values was essentially people-centred – the eliteness of the news actors. For those who are not elite, the surest way is to be a victim of crime, accident or disaster – that is, to have negative or unexpected things happen to you.

In my own studies of how people are referred to in the news I have found this kind of breakdown covers most news actors:

- political figure
- official
- celebrity (e.g. film or music star)
- sportsperson
- professional or other public figure (e.g. lawyer)
- criminal or accused
- human interest figure
- participant (e.g. victim or witness).

Gans's survey of US television and news magazine coverage (1979) found that news actors could be divided into the Knowns and Unknowns. Knowns appeared four times as often as Unknowns. They were (in descending order) the president, presidential candidates, federal, state and local officials, and famous violators of laws or morals (plus a special category for members of the Kennedy family and astronauts). Gans gauges that probably less than 50 individuals, mostly high-placed federal officials, regularly appear in US news.

Virtually everyone who appears in the news is named and labelled. How stories label news actors illuminates news values. News stories do not take time out to describe their characters. The face-to-face narrator may introduce his story with whole sentences of description and characterization. The news story characterizes its actors in passing, within the flow of telling the action. Many commentators have pointed out the significance of how news actors are labelled (see, for instance, Glasgow University Media Group 1980, Davis and Walton 1983a, 1983c, Pilger 1986). It is particularly evident in situations of conflict: one side's *terrorist* is the other side's *freedom fighter*. Schlesinger (1987: 229) records a detailed BBC prescription for who was to be described as *terrorist* and who as *guerrilla*, and when one might turn into the other.

Kniffka found Angela Davis variously labelled *black militant*, *black activist*, *black militant communist*, *black scholar* and *black sister* (1980: 201). In a leading study Davis and Walton (1983c) examined international reporting of the 1978 murder of former Italian prime minister Aldo Moro by the Red Brigades. They found four kinds of labels applied:

- criminal: *gunmen, gang, hit team*
- military: *urban guerrillas, commandos*
- political: *left wing, extremist, Marxist revolutionaries, violent anarchists*
- psychopathological: *fanatics, crazies, evil-minded children, moral morons, willing sadists, inhuman political savages.*

The effect is what Davis and Walton call 'closure': exclusion of this group and their actions from normal society and political life, and hence avoidance of considering their origins and significance in Italian politics.

The syntax of labelling news actors

Here I will examine briefly how the syntax of descriptive noun phrases contributes to this labelling and serves the brevity and news value of a story (Rydén 1975, Bell 1988). In chapter 6, I introduced the rule by which the determiner is deleted from the first, descriptive noun phrase (NP) in apposition with a second, name noun phrase:

the Neighbours star   → Neighbours star
Kylie Minogue   Kylie Minogue

The syntactic change accomplished by the rule is not just determiner deletion. In appositions which retain the determiner, the first NP is primary, and the second parenthetical – indeed newspapers earlier in the century used to (parenthesize) the name. But the rule takes the first, descriptive NP and embeds it into the name NP. The name is no longer parenthetical but head of the whole expression (see Jucker 1989 for an alternative analysis). The syntactic change is reflected in punctuation, with the comma which marked the apposition also lost.

It also brings a subtle but definite semantic change and confers on the descriptive NP something which it did not previously have: titleness. It moves from the category of common count nouns and takes on a status akin to titles such as *President Bush* or *Lord Lucan*. It elevates a description to the rank of a quasi-title, implying that this person belongs to a class as exclusive as heads of state or the nobility. It implies a uniqueness, inviting reinsertion of the definite article, even when we know the aura of exclusivity is unwarranted – as it is for many of these from one February 1990 issue of the London *Daily Mirror*:

little giant Sammy Davis
modern megastar Michael Jackson
veteran actress Shirley MacLaine
boxing champ Mike Tyson
jokers Bill Cosby, Eddie Murphy and Richard Pryor
United Nations official Chris Edley
TV celebrity Tony Danza
royal photographer Norman Parkinson
estranged husband Captain Mark Phillips
Romeo prisoner David McAllister
union chief Eric Hammond
former colleague Colin Wallace
transplant tot Jason Matten
Transport Secretary Cecil Parkinson
acid-tongued interviewer Sir Robin Day
Londoner Dawn Griffiths

For the media a title embodies a person's claim to news value. Elite news actors speak from their standing as president, professor or bishop. The quasi-title embodies the claim of the ordinary person or the newly elite to news fame. The label may be unique and it may stick. Rosenblum (1979: 114) notes how in the mid-1970s 'one news agency desk insisted on adding "former cabaret dancer" to every mention of [Argentinian president] Isabel Peron'. Take the case of a European medical man who practised in New Zealand in the 1970s, was eventually deregistered for not possessing the qualifications he claimed, and moved on to California to repeat the process. His standard label in the New Zealand media in 1974 was:

controversial cancer therapist Milan Brych

In 1980, having been absent from New Zealand and the news for some years, he was reported as under arrest for fraud in California. His label still:

controversial cancer therapist Milan Brych

He was tried in Los Angeles and was demoted in 1983 news reports to:

self-styled cancer therapist Milan Brych

Sentenced a month later, his media downgrading was complete:

bogus cancer therapist Milan Brych

We can see both the decline of Brych's media image as labellings become increasingly negative, and the persistent power of his original quasi-title across a decade and in different countries. The deterioration in titling was paralleled by the shift from *Dr Brych* initially, to *Mr Brych* after his medical qualifications became suspect, and finally to plain *Brych* – the last-name-only reference of the convicted criminal.

The rule of determiner deletion is a development of the twentieth-century media, as its growth decade by decade showed in chapter 7. By 1990 the *Daily Mirror* was categorically deleting all definite and indefinite articles. Along with the increase in the rule, came two other changes. First, there is a shift in who is mentioned in the news. Titles provide us with a record of who is considered newsworthy at different times and why – a social history of celebrity. Until the 1940s, there is a predominance of nobility and military titles in the *Mirror*. These are largely absent now. The quasi-title has replaced the inherited title as a mark of news value. This seems to represent a democratization of the news – a title is conferred on everyone who appears. But paradoxically, if everyone is special, no one is. And the quasi-title is predominantly applied to the newer elites of entertainment, sport or politics.

Second, the structure of the expression has changed. In the *Mirror* before 1950 the appositions were often long, even rambling:

> the dead woman, Mrs Mary Ann Message, a widow, aged about fifty, of Fulham-road, London, S.W.

Since then they have been honed down to the staccato shorthand titling of the 1990 examples above. Here we can see how the rule of determiner deletion serves the goals of news writing, brevity and newsworthiness. It compresses information by preposing modifiers, thus eliminating the articles and prepositions. *The Secretary for the Environment* becomes *Environment Secretary*. At the same time it highlights what is left. The canonical form of name apposition in many media is now a quasi-title noun followed by first and last name and optionally preceded by one or two modifiers – *TV presenter Ed McMann*.

4 TIME AND PLACE IN THE NEWS

Time and place constitute the setting of a news event.[2] They are also an important part of its news value and presentation. As two of the basic W's, they are high on the journalist's list of what to include in a story. Many of the news values outlined in chapter 8 are related to time or place. Most obvious are the recency of a story and frequency, its synchronization with daily news cycles. Unexpectedness, continuity and predictability also contain a time element. Other values relate to place. Geographical proximity is the most obvious, but so also is consonance with stereotypes about a place and its people.

Time and space are also the constraints on the finished news product, leading to the goal of brevity in news writing. The press budgets its news to fit within the physical space of its pages, and broadcasting within the time allotted.

News provides a good site to analyse how time and place setting (and personal reference) are expressed linguistically, because the news story is brief and supposedly self-contained. Setting is conventionally specified on the move during a news story. The journalist tries to set the scene without diverting from the movement of the story. Dwelling on detail of time, place or person is a characteristic of the feature not the hard news story, as this lead from a feature of my own shows:

> On the surface, Mokai is a quiet place.

A marae, a school, and a handful of worn, bare houses are the ghost
of a timber town which, in the 1930s, had four mills and 5000
people.
There are no geysers, no devil's cauldron, no steaming acres of
mud . . .
But below this land lies the hottest geothermal field discovered in
New Zealand and a potentially valuable source of electrical
power.

We saw in the last chapter how time and place can be fragmented
within a story, with several settings encompassed in a short space.
Journalists use syntactic means to reduce the effect of this. *After* and
as are favoured as a means of combining sequential or concurrent
events. The dislocation of time and place between stories is something
which broadcast news is particularly concerned to minimize. Broadcasting tells stories which audiences receive in a real time sequence.
In normal story-telling terms, the constantly shifting setting of a
sequence of 20-second radio news items is eccentric. To increase the
coherence, broadcast news will often express links between the setting
of items. Temporal adverbs such as *meanwhile* are inserted or place
relationships drawn, such as packaging a group of geographically
dispersed items under the catch-all subheading of 'overseas news'.

Where

To illustrate how time and place are expressed in a story, I extract
references from the first six paragraphs of the Lithuania story
presented in figure 8.2 (see p. 166):

	Time	Place
S1		rebel Lithuania
		a government office in the capital
		neighbouring Byelorussia
		the republic
		the Soviet Union
S2	meanwhile	in Lithuania's sister Baltic republic
		of Estonia
	yesterday	Moscow
	beginning	
	transitional period	
	end	

S3   March 11 declaration   Moscow
                              Lithuania
S5   United States
S6   a few hours later   into the public prosecutor's office in
                              the Lithuanian capital Vilnius

The analysis in the last chapter showed the complexity of the time and place structure of this story. The setting shifts across a wide range of locations. Such multiple settings are more obvious on television than in print as visuals show scenes from the different locations. The example shows that while time is usually fairly simply expressed, place specification can be particularly complex, with several embedded prepositional phrases. Some of the references are subject to brief geographical glosses to aid readers' knowledge – *neighbouring Byelorussia, the capital Vilnius*. Others contain contextual or evaluative material – *rebel Lithuania*. As well as pure place names, there are a number of derived, adjectival forms for states such as *Soviet* or *Lithuanian*. When a reference is repeated a variety of proforms are used – *the republic* and *it* standing for *Lithuania* in S1. In keeping with the instalment principle of story structure, more information is given in some repeated references rather than less (S6).

Where is closely allied to *who* in news work. The research of Tuchman (1978) and M. Fishman (1980) on news gathering shows how the journalist's beat or round – their regular ports of call in search of news – constitutes a physical definition of news sources. Rounds consist of contacts within a series of bureaucracies. Locations such as legislature, police headquarters, courts, the town hall function as the focus of news gathering work. So do capital cities, even when the topic is not obviously their sphere. Most of New Zealand's climate change news comes out of the capital, Wellington, because that is where politicians, officials and science managers work and where reportable meetings are held.

Place names often express *who* rather than *where* – the state as political actor rather than as physical territory. This is particularly evident when the capital *Moscow* represents the state as a whole, as in the Lithuania story. Place can also stand for news authority – the Kremlin or Downing Street – or for pigeonhole, a set of stereotypes about a nation and its people (Hallin 1987).

When

Time is a defining characteristic of the nature of news, a major compulsion in news-gathering procedures, and a determinant of the structure of news discourse. Time is so essential to news that I have already covered a good deal about it in earlier sections and chapters. News is by nature a perishable commodity with a limited shelf life. The next edition renders it obsolete. News operates to the rhythm of usually daily deadlines, on which are imposed weekly cycles, with Saturday and Sunday producing differently defined news for publication.

Schlesinger's study of BBC newsroom practices rightly characterizes news work as 'a stop-watch culture' (1987: 83). The drive to deadlines, to get the news first – by a few minutes or even a few seconds – is embedded deep in the news ethos. Getting it first is reason for self-congratulation, and being scooped a cause for mourning. Yet the rush of deadlines is largely self-inflicted. It is a fetish of the profession, as both Schlesinger (1987: 105) and Schudson (1987) note. There is no evidence that the audience really expects such timeliness, but newsworkers expect it of themselves and expect to be evaluated by it. The audience couldn't care who gets the scoop.

And time prescribes the first principle of story structure: lead with the most recent events. After that, story organization is atemporal. It follows other laws than recency – but that very cyclical, instalment time structure is distinctive of news discourse, as we have seen.

The time references listed above for the Lithuania story show how time is anchored in different ways. Some references situate events in absolute/calendar time (*March 11*), others in relation to each other (*meanwhile*, *a few hours later*), still others are deictic with the present as reference point (*yesterday*). As well as through temporal adverbials, time is expressed in every clause by the tense of the verb. Journalists are taught that hard news is basically written in the past tense. Past tense predominates here, but the Lithuania story shows a mix of other tenses: present for evaluation (S15) and comment on previous events (S4); Perfect (S3, S4) and pluperfect (S12, S13) for previous events; conditional for future in indirect speech (S9, S17, S18); and present progressive, future and perfect in direct quotation (S10, S11, S19).

Schudson's perceptive essay on the meaning of time in the news (1987) notes that while the story is written in the past, the headline is in the present (as a glance at figure 9.1 on p. 178–9 shows). Some stories presuppose knowledge of previous events or even distant history for interpretation. The two working horizons of time past for newsworkers are the span of a lifetime, and 'postwar'. The length-of-lifetime horizon also applies to reporting the future. In coverage of possible temperature and sealevel rises under the greenhouse effect, most timeframes were cast as 40 to 60 years, roughly the expected lifespan of a young adult (Bell 1989).

For both journalists and news consumers, the presumption of recency in news is so strong that it has a curious effect: time is rarely specified in headlines, and often not in lead paragraphs. The regular expression of time in press news is past tense (optionally plus time adverbial):

A car bomb exploded at a shopping centre in the Pakistani capital Islamabad yesterday.

Broadcasting leads with the immediacy of present perfect with no time adverbial:

A car bomb has exploded . . .

When place and time are published in the dateline, the story is presented from the reporter's viewpoint not the reader's. So in figure 9.1, examples 6 and 7, we find the dateline *April 13* followed by *today* – which for the reader is in fact yesterday. But the published stories do not retain the place deictic *here* – which in fact would offer less chance of confusing the reader than *today*.

5 FACTS AND FIGURES

This and the next section deal with just two aspects of the *what* of news: how stories use figures as facts, and how news reports the talk of newsmakers. What Tuchman (1978) has called 'facticity' is at the core of news writing. And at the core of facticity are numbers – the most verifiable, quantifiable, undeniable of facts. Said a subeditor who once worked for me: 'Facts are the cornflakes of journalism. There can be no doubt about a fact.'

Tuchman's definition is a little different (1978: 82): 'By "facts" I mean pertinent information gathered by professionally validated methods specifying the relationship between what is known and how it is known.' Journalistic facts are defined by journalists, building up a 'web of facticity'. In standard stories there are standard facts to be included. A fire story will say when and where the fire occurred, how many victims or rescued there were, the number of firefighters or fire engines, how long it took to bring under control, how it is thought to have started, and the estimated cost of the damage. Precisely these ingredients make up this story from an Auckland radio station:

North Shore firemen are battling a scrub fire in the Avenue at Albany.

The blaze has engulfed about ten acres on the hillside overlooking
the main highway north opposite the Wayside Tavern.

Thirty firemen are at the scene, and six fire engines, and two special
appliances have been called in.

It's not known how the blaze started, and so far no property's been
threatened.

This item uses the regular currency of fire reporting, somewhat
devalued by over-use: *battling*, *blaze*, *engulfed*, *at the scene*,
appliances, *threatened*. Such stories could be produced to formula,
setting up a computer macro into which particulars are inserted. The
story also carries four numerals, designed to weight the scale of the
event.

Numbers as rhetoric and information

Typical news numbers include dates, ages, counts of participants
or victims, distances, weights, heights, dollars, percentages, scores,
lengths of time. Journalists use numbers for two main reasons. Figures
undergird the objective, empirical claims of news. But they simultaneously undermine that principle, since they are chosen to express
and enhance the news value of the story. Roeh and Feldman (1984)
have called this 'the rhetoric of numbers' in news. Analysing stories
and headlines in two Hebrew dailies – one popular, one elite – they
found that the popular daily used numbers for rhetorical purposes
rather than to stress its facticity. This is the only explanation for its
bannering across a front page a headline that the state's budget was
to be *4,360,000,000,000* shekels. The string of zeros is there to
emphasize the huge scale of finance, and contrasts with the elite
paper's form of *4360 billion*. The popular paper used numbers in
40 per cent of its headlines, and was particularly fond of embedding numbers in other rhetorical devices such as alliteration or
parallelism – *six planes hijacked in six days*.

Van Dijk (1988b: 90) also regards figures as a rhetorical device, a
means to the end of telling good news stories. Often the audience is
in no position to gauge whether a particular statistic is large, small
or insignificant. In reports of the assassination of Gemayel, the weight
of the bomb (200 kg) was always given (van Dijk 1988a: 114). The
exact size is not important, and different media give different numbers
for such things anyway, but the statistic indicates both precision and
seriousness. However it is not true to conclude that the specific
numbers are therefore of little importance. My climate change study

shows that audiences can absorb precise figures from media input (Bell 1989), and on the basis of that draw conclusions about things which may affect them, such as sealevel rises. When news is high in relevance precise numbers may signify, although when relevance is low, figures may serve just as an indication of general scale of an event (see chapters 10 and 11).

Numbers can take over the news. Some complex areas of news become reduced to being reported in numbers. Thus economic reporting in popular media may be limited to the consumer price index, the share market, and unemployment figures. Sometimes the numbers turn something into news, as in one of our example lead paragraphs from figure 9.1:

Two Aborigines have been found dead within 24 hours . . .

Callously put, Australian media would have been unlikely to regard one dead aboriginal as news. This recalls the oldtime, typically racist adages from newsroom walls: news is what happens to 'one Englishman, 10 Germans, or 1000 Indians'.

Sometimes the numbers get top-heavy. In a story on the squid fishery off New Zealand, I see how I packed one sentence with a few numbers too many for comprehensibility:

Only 4000 tonnes were caught in the four weeks after the season began on December 15, 70 percent down on the 13,000 tonnes taken by this time last year.

Note also the press convention that single digit figures are written out, while double digit and above use numerals.

6 TALKING HEADS

We have already seen how much of news is talk. Some of the discourse categories of news are verbal by definition – reaction, evaluation, expectations. In chapter 4, I showed how all manner of written and spoken inputs are incorporated into news stories, embedding the format of the input into the journalist's text. Here we will be concerned not with these unattributed inputs but with where the news explicitly draws its content from an acknowledged source.

There is a hierarchy of talk in news stories which ranks it according to the degree in which the original verbatim input is reproduced:

1 film and voice of newsmaker (television)
2 voice of newsmaker (radio)
3 direct quotation of newsmaker (press)
4 indirect speech of newsmaker
5 unattributed embedding of newsmaker content.

Comparable hierarchies have been used to analyse speech presentation in the novel, and Short (1988) has applied this to news stories. The application indicates both that the basic fictional framework can be extended to other discourse genres, and also that this extension benefits literary theory. The principal difference between speech presentation in news and in fiction is the dimension of faithful reproduction.

The first three levels of my listing are variations of direct quotation conditioned by the technology of the medium, with the higher medium able to encompass the lower, but not vice versa. That is, television can show the newsmaker on screen and present her actual voice. Such 'talking heads' are anathema to television newsworkers' principles, but they have found them impossible to escape as a major component of their output. Radio as well as television can broadcast the newsmaker's voice as part of a news story. Press and broadcasting reporters can all quote directly, in the flow of their stories, the newsmaker's actual words (although in practice quote marks are hard to flag in broadcasting). But the main method by which all media handle newsmakers' speech is to turn it into indirect speech or to run it unattributed. The Glasgow University Media Group argue that a hierarchy such as the above correlates with the standing of who is speaking (1980: 163, Davis 1985). The more elite the speaker, the more verbatim the presentation is likely to be.

An interaction such as an interview (mostly by telephone) is the main situation from which journalists get their information. Sigal's (1973) analysis of front page stories in the *New York Times* and *Washington Post* shows that 70 per cent of them came from interactions such as press conferences or hearings. Broadcasting allows the news-gathering interaction itself to be presented to the audience. This places before the public the journalistic technique and practice of interviewing, which had been hidden by the technology of print journalism. Displaying the interview for public view has altered conversational behaviour and produced a new interviewing technique suitable for broadcast to the outer, mass audience. The technical requirement for audibility to other parties, for instance, requires the interviewer to eliminate the 'back-channel' exclamations and acknowledgements which are part of a listener's normal response in conversation and which might drown the interviewee's statements.

The speech verb

Talk embedded within a story consists of the talk itself and the attribution to a speaker. The attribution names the source, and may specify time and place, as we saw earlier in this chapter. Here I deal with the main other aspect of attribution – the verb used to describe the act of speech.

Say is the canonical neutral speech verb, along with *tell* for when a listener is specified as direct object, and the useful non-finite form *according to. Say* is by far the most common speech verb in news reporting. In a hard news, action story such as the Honduras example in figure 8.1 (p. 150), all the speech verbs are *say*. Leitner (1983c) found that *say* or *tell* made up 60 per cent of speech verbs on British television news. When talk itself is news, the verbs range much wider. The Lithuania story in figure 8.2 (p. 166) contained:

say (7)
tell (2)
according to
announce (3)
declare (2)
refuse, threaten, insist, denounce

We could call these last three groups in particular 'news performatives', to adapt Austin's (1962) terminology (they were later renamed 'illocutionary acts'). They perform the act which they describe and are characteristic of news as talk. Performatives cannot be true or false. When performed 'happily' – that is by a person with authority to do so – an announcement, denouncement or declaration is a news action. The validity of the respective performatives is precisely what is at issue in Lithuania's *declaration of independence* and the Soviet government's *refusal to recognize it.*

M. Fishman has argued that many bureaucratic documents have a performative character. A will or a lease perform what they say, the bequeathing or leasing of property. And, as Fishman says, 'journalists love performative documents because these are the hardest facts they can get their hands on' (1980: 99). Journalists extend reliance on such documents to other documents and verbal accounts generated by bureaucracies but lacking such legal status. Similarly, journalists love the performatives of politics (particularly elections) or diplomacy, where something happens through someone saying it. If someone with requisite authority says *I announce* or *I denounce*, that is both newsworthy and the saying itself constitutes an indisputable fact. The fusion of word and act is ideal for news reporting. No other facts have to be verified. The only fact is that somebody said something. (And it promises to generate more news by provoking a response of the same kind – verbal reaction.)

As well as often having the status of an action, the speech verb can convey the stance of either speaker or reporter to the statement that follows. The verb can be evaluative, keying the audience in to how to interpret the speaker's statement. Geis (1987: 121) has studied the use of speech verbs in American news magazines such as *Time* and *Newsweek*. He presents one classic case of different verbs (and different versions of the same 'direct' quote) in two reports during the 1984 US presidential campaign:

"I can win this thing on my own," Mondale declared.

US News and World Report

Reporters overheard Mondale muttering, "It looks like I'm going to have to win this on my own."

Time

There is a good deal of connotational difference between the resolve of the first version's *declare* and the aggrieved complaint in *Time*'s word *mutter*. The choice of speech verb precisely reflects and reinforces the different wordings in which the quote has been reproduced. We look in the next chapter at the issue of misquotation.

There is a relationship between who is speaking and the speech verb used, with verb choice assigning news value to the source. Several studies have found systematic differences between the use of *say* for the speech of a range of 'credible' sources such as management or the US government, versus *claim* for unions and the Soviet government (Glasgow University Media Group 1980: 184, Leitner 1983c, Geis 1987, Short 1988).

Direct quotes

Direct quotation serves three main purposes in news reporting. First, a quote is valued as a particularly incontrovertible fact because it is the newsmaker's own words (Tuchman 1978: 96, Roeh 1982: 55). It is strong evidence in the potential libel suit which is always lurking in the journalist's subconscious, especially if the quote is on tape and can be played back.

A second function is to distance and disown, to absolve journalist and news outlet from endorsement of what the source said. The disowning may be because of the meaning of what the source said, such as a manifestly one-sided labelling like *terrorist*, or because the wording is regarded as stylistically inappropriate, such as a collo-quialism. The contracted forms *don't* and *they're* would normally appear in the press only in a direct quotation. Quotes bring alien forms into the news story. Most obviously, this is the only place where first or second person pronouns occur. Indirect quotation converts first and second persons to third. The absence of first person from news stories is in complete contrast to conversational narratives (which are usually told about the speaker).

Journalists and copy editors sanction in newsmaker quotation linguistic forms which they would not write themselves or reproduce in indirect speech. This also applies, as we saw in chapter 6, in varying degrees to all incoming wordage which newsworkers may use, including agency copy. Distancing is particularly obvious when individual words are picked out by 'scare quotes', for instance in one of the lead paragraphs in figure 9.1:

> Indian Prime Minister Vishwanath Pratap Singh accused Pakistan today of "evil designs" as tensions between the two countries rose after skirmishes along their disputed border in Kashmir.

Direct quotes may signify 'so-called' (Tuchman 1978: 96):

> Egypt and Jordan today agreed that the Palestine Liberation Organization should attend the Geneva Middle East peace con-ference at what they call the appropriate stage.

In the agency copy from which this derived (Bell 1984a), *at the appropriate stage* was in quotation marks. In the above broadcast ver-sion a verbal gloss was inserted. In broadcast news direct-quoting an isolated phrase in the newsmaker's voice is not possible. Something like a minimal complete utterance has to be produced. The converse of quotation as disowning is that non-attribution can imply the news outlet's agreement. Some official sources are regarded as so incon-testable that they are not even named explicitly when their informa-tion is used (Kress 1983b).

The third function of direct quotation is to add to the story the flavour of the newsmaker's own words. Quotes (not 'quotations', in news terminology) are supposed to be brief, pithy, colourful, to add something which a version in reported speech would not. I snapped up this gem from the unlikely context of an interview with a senior US official about the effects on New Zealand trade of US disposal of its stockpiles of agricultural products:

> "Whenever there is a shoot-out along the main street, some innocent passers-by are apt to get hurt," he said.

In practice quotes are rarely better than the story around them, which can result in the scarcely quotable being quoted.

Indirect speech

Direct quotation is the exception not the rule in news stories. Predominantly, journalists turn what their sources say into indirect speech.[3] This puts the journalist in control of focusing the story, able to combine information and wordings from scattered parts of an interview. It also explains why stories rarely lead with a direct quote. There are few quotes where the source's words focus the story clearly and succinctly enough for the journalist to use them as lead in preference to his own formulation.

In the press, indirect speech is signalled by tense concord – use of past tense for indirect speech after the past tense speech verb. This holds even when the statement is not attributed within the immediate paragraph:

> Junior Government Whip Judy Keall said the issue was health rather than politics.
> Those who raised the question of civil rights had a problem.
> "There is the whole question of passive smokers' rights," she said.

The use of past tense flags the second paragraph as part of what Keall said, particularly when it is sandwiched between two explicitly attributed sentences. However, in practice past tense concord is very difficult to apply consistently and correctly sentence after sentence (and is therefore one of the most difficult things for journalists to learn). Past tense concord can be used to distinguish indirect speech from the journalist's own present tense description. But concord can also be ambiguous with past tense used for genuine description of past events (Short 1988: 72):

Rotherham District Hospital later said Mr Scargill was being
detained overnight.
He was not seriously hurt but was being treated for arm, leg and
head injuries.

Nevertheless in print news, present tense in indirect speech is supposedly reserved for features, although my impression is that past
tense concord is on the wane. In broadcast news, present tense is the
common form for both the speech verb and the indirect speech:

Spokesperson Gary Betteridge says there's no immediate danger of
excessive exposure to ultraviolet rays because of ozone
irregularities and he says the latest measurements are useful in
helping develop a warning system.

The equivalent press story would have used past tense throughout.
Broadcast copy editors regularly convert past tense in agency stories
to present (Bell 1977: 195), so that tense concord hardly ever applies.
Use of the present is assumed to help create the impression of
immediacy.

Finally, interviews do not just consist of answers by newsmakers
but also of questions from journalists. There is now a good deal of
research into the characteristics of broadcast news interviews as a
genre in their own right (Blum-Kulka 1983, Heritage 1985, Jucker
1986, Greatbatch 1988). Within broadcast news the interaction
within an interview is quite commonly seen or heard, but occasionally
the press also summons up the context of a newsmaker's utterances.
Clayman (1990) has examined the significance of those occasions on
which print stories display the interactional context from which a
newsmaker is quoted. He found that stories (drawn from the *Los
Angeles Times*) which, for instance, ran the reporter's question as well
as the newsmaker's answer did so largely to signal interactional
resistance. They show the news source as hesitating to reply, refusing
to answer, giving non-answers, or admitting something only under
repeated questioning.

How an interview becomes a story still needs investigation. The pattern by which the interview unfolds is story-driven. The journalist is
already turning an interview into a story before it has started. I come
to an interview with a handful of main questions which seem likely
to bring out the main story. While the interview is in progress I am
searching for the story in what the source is telling me. I find myself
already mentally focusing and editing the material into story shape.

I am automatically weighing its news value, especially to identify possible lead paragraphs to start the story with. After the interview, I go back through my notes to clarify, correct and amplify them. I mark the main points, and begin to write using the most promising lead.

The whole field of news as talk throws up some of the most interesting and under-researched questions of news discourse. What linguistic forms and intonations do broadcasters use to signal that an insert of newsmaker speech follows? What is the nature of news performatives? What are the patterns of tense use in reporting speech? What are the relationships between source status and the choice of speech verb?

The elements of news stories discussed in this chapter beg for further research, but they are just some of those which invite linguistic analysis. Such analysis will enlighten the nature of news stories and how they express news values. They will also illuminate the nature of the linguistic categories and frameworks themselves. For I have in writing this chapter exercised precisely the practices I have been describing – selecting, quoting, sourcing, citing numbers, and the like – but in the rather different genre of academic prose. The tight, explicit nature of news offers us something of a laboratory for examining aspects of discourse structure which occur more widely.

10

Telling It Like It Isn't

The media are means of communication, and most of what I have covered so far in this book assumes the media communicate successfully. We have studied the communicators and how they produce media messages (chapters 3 and 4), the nature of the news text they produce (chapters 8 and 9), and the audience and their relationship to communicators and media content (chapters 5 to 7). Yet our discussion has made it obvious that miscommunication is not only possible but inherent. The news story is controlled by news values. It is not a neutral vehicle, nor is news production a neutral process, despite the journalist's century-old creed of objectivity (Schudson 1978). In this chapter we focus on where the news is misreported. In the final chapter, we see how audiences understand – and misunderstand – what they receive from the media.

1 APPROACHES TO MEDIA MISCOMMUNICATION

Miscommunication includes concepts such as misrepresentation, misunderstanding, inaccuracy, distortion and misreporting (Bell 1991b). In her work on miscommunication in face-to-face interaction, Humphreys-Jones defines it as 'incorrect understanding by one person of the intention underlying the output of another' (1986: 108). Misunderstanding is a hearer-based concept, oriented to perception. But miscommunication may be sited at other points of the communication situation. I differentiate *misunderstanding* by the audience from *mis-presentation* by the communicator. It is possible for hearers to misunderstand something which was clearly and accurately expressed. We can assess whether miscommunication has occurred by comparing the propositional content of a message either with what the communicator declares herself to have meant by it, or with what the hearer declares himself to have understood. In these two chapters, I present material gathered through both these approaches.

Two aspects of the structure of mass communication promote the chance of miscommunication. First, the lack of audience feedback means that the communicator has no means of knowing if she has been misunderstood. Second, the number of newsworkers through whom a story must pass multiplies the sites at which miscommunication may occur. The extent to which the media misrepresent – or audiences misunderstand – content has been a focus of concern since media research began. Three research traditions are especially relevant. While differing in their methods, they all share a broad concern with how media content relates to some sense of 'reality', particularly where there is a mismatch between reality and media content.

Content analysis

Analysis of media content has a long tradition in communication research, with such studies typically motivated by a search for bias in media messages. Content analysis had its heyday from the 1930s to 1960s. Much of the basic research was conducted as part of the US war effort, initially in the Second World War and later in the Cold War period. It was ideologically driven and concentrated on Nazi and Soviet 'propaganda' (for instance, Lasswell et al. 1949).

Since Berelson (1952) summarized content analysis research and provided its classical definition, there have been several basic texts in the area (Pool 1959, Budd et al. 1967, Holsti 1968, Krippendorff 1980). The research was traditionally quantitative or pseudo-quantitative, relying on coding aspects of content into a number of discrete categories and counting their frequency. Most content analysis has been devoted to news, but it also covered other media genres including soap operas, comic strips, cartoons and advertisements. The periodical *Journalism Quarterly* has been the traditional forum for such research, and even runs to content analysis of content analyses (Gerlach 1987). Typical topics include coverage of Iran in US news, the portrayal of corporate crime in the media, how death is handled in children's literature, or how the nuclear accident at Chernobyl was covered.

Content analysis remains a basic part of many studies. It is best when supplemented by other methods or a researcher's own qualitative insights, for example in Gans's perceptive study of US news (1979).

Critical linguistics

'Critical linguistics' is the label applied to methods developed by a number of British and Australian linguists (for example, Fowler et al. 1979, Kress and Hodge 1979, Kress 1983a, 1983b). Their work is concerned to analyse how underlying ideologies are embodied in linguistic expression. They examine how syntactic rules serve and reveal ideological frameworks, often using news texts for data. This research is at its strongest in the direct comparison of different media accounts of the same event, demonstrating how language is a vehicle of covert interpretation in supposedly neutral reporting.

However, the approach has two main deficiencies, one linguistic and the other sociological. First, it presumes that there is a clearly definable relation between any given linguistic choice and a specific ideology (Kress 1983a). The belief that there is ideological significance in every syntactic option, and that we can identify uniquely what it is, is hard to sustain (cf. Clayman 1990). Such a conscious view of linguistic processes seems too strong even when a rule is subject to a deliberate, focused editing choice of the kind I present later in this chapter. Secondly, the approach imputes to newsworkers a far more deliberate ideological intervention in news than is supported by the research on news production which we have covered in previous chapters.

These two presuppositions result in a conspiracy theory of newsworkers' application of syntactic rules such as nominalization and agent deletion in passives, with large ideological conclusions drawn from equivocal data. While this strand of work addresses central issues in news discourse and is an antidote to neutralist research, the analysis is inadequate to support the conclusions.

Semiotics

What I term the 'semiotic' approach derives from structuralist advances in literary criticism in Europe (for example, Barthes 1968). These have spread into communication research in Britain, particularly through work at the Birmingham Centre for Cultural Studies (for instance, Hall et al. 1980), and increasingly to the United States. The hallmark of this approach is a close reading of media texts, particularly with a view to identifying and decoding the ideological frameworks which underpin media messages. The journal *Media, Culture and Society* publishes frequent papers in this framework, and there are introductory texts which apply these methods to a whole medium such as television or a genre like news (Hartley 1982). The semiotic approach is increasingly replacing American-style content analysis as the primary way in which communications researchers analyse media messages. It differs from traditional content analysis in being qualitative rather than quantitative. Its focus is on subsurface rather than overt content, and it concentrates on the likelihood of different audiences giving different readings to the same text (Scannell 1990).

It is obvious that a study of news stories and other media genres can benefit from literary-critical techniques – and that linguistic methods and insights can in turn benefit literary studies. There is evidence of increasing cross-fertilization between the two fields, for instance in the rediscovered work of Mikhail Bakhtin (for instance, 1986), and the application of linguistic techniques to literary analysis (see Leech and Short 1981) and non-literary texts (Short 1988).

The Glasgow University Media Group drew on both semiotic and traditional content analysis methods and produced some of the best known – although by no means the best executed – studies of media texts (1976, 1980). Initially concentrating on industrial reporting in British television news, they found that on a number of measures the coverage could be adjudged as biased. They have since studied defence news (Glasgow Group 1985), in coverage of both nuclear weapons and the peace movement, and the Falklands/Malvinas war of 1982. The methodology of their early work was regrettably easy to fault both linguistically (Leitner 1983d) and sociologically (Schlesinger 1980, 1987: 47), as well as drawing fire from the British television channels studied. This left their case vulnerable to counter-attack (see Harrison 1985). But the Glasgow Group's work remains stimulating and suggestive even though the specifics of the analysis are less than convincing.

A convergence of approaches

I have sketched these three approaches too briefly to do them justice, but we can see they tend to share a common problem – lack of sound basic linguistic analysis. The language analyses have often been at best naive or at worst wrong. Secondly, because the main goal of most studies has been to establish the existence of bias or ideological loading, they have often leapt past the groundwork to premature conclusions about the significance of sometimes poorly described linguistic patterns.

It is here that the discourse analysis framework has much to offer, despite its terminological problems and attempts to encompass everything under its umbrella. Van Dijk's work, while lacking nothing in ideological commitment (1988a: 289), shows what direct attention to formal analysis of the news text can provide. Setting aside premature attempts to decode what underlies the language, insights are gained in the process of rigorous linguistic analysis.

As research continues, the semiotic and discourse analysis approaches are drawing closer together. The term 'discourse' is used in both. In linguistics it is reserved for largely formal analysis above the level of the sentence, parallel to syntax within sentences. In semiotics it covers the ideology as well as its expression. The convergence is evidenced in a number of collections and special issues of journals (Mancini 1988b, Scannell 1990) and explicit comparisons of the various frameworks (Montgomery 1986, Beniger 1988, Mancini 1988a, Bruck 1989). It promises increasing insights into the nature of news stories and how they are vehicles of interpretation and miscommunication. In the remainder of this chapter, I present some of my own research on misreporting and misediting of news.

2 MISREPORTING: THE CLIMATE CHANGE CASE

We have seen how news values drive the way journalists write their stories. Here we look at cases where that drive has tipped over into misreporting – that is, where the source believes that what she said has not been faithfully communicated. This data is drawn from my study of climate change news in New Zealand (Bell 1989, 1991b). Under 'climate change' are grouped two largely distinct issues: the depletion of the ozone layer, and the greenhouse effect and its impacts. A scientific topic is particularly apt for studying the issue of news miscommunication. The methods, timeframes and values of science differ widely from those of journalism (cf. Friedman et al. 1986, Nelkin 1987). The news cycle is 24 hours at most – the cycle of scientific research is often years. News seeks for facts as definite and unqualified as possible: the findings of science are often in news terms almost qualified to death.

In research on science popularization, Dubois (1986) and Adams-Smith (1987, 1989) have examined the process by which papers from scientific journals are turned into news stories. Here the journalist acts as text processor, as we saw in chapter 4, but the technical subject matter makes her role of translator and interpreter more obvious. Medical terms are translated, conclusions picked up from the end of the scientific paper and used as the news lead. The paper is given the hard-news flavour of an event, released *today* even though it has been awaiting publication for months. Adams-Smith (1987) shows how the values of recency and relevance motivate the way in which one medical news story was framed. The result was a headline – *Breast feeding is contraceptive* – contrary to the sense of the source paper.

Research on misreporting

My study was in two complementary parts, covering both media reporting and public understanding of the issue (see chapter 11). The principal method of assessing news accuracy is that pioneered by Charnley (1936, cf. Singletary 1980, Tillinghast 1983). Clips of stories are sent back to sources cited, along with a questionnaire asking them to identify any inaccuracies. The method has one main drawback. Sources are not disinterested parties in their judgements of reports about themselves. What a source holds to be error, the journalist might regard as just point of view. The technique of surveying sources is not perfect. It is, however, better suited to coping with science news, which is less concerned with self-image and advancement than, for example, party political news. We use the journalist's retelling of a source's information in the form of a published story as the means to identify misreporting, with the source as judge of the accuracy of that retelling.

All daily media coverage of the climate change issue in New Zealand was collected for six months in 1988 – a total of 360 press and broadcast stories. We mailed to local professional and scientific sources the stories in which they were cited, accompanied by questionnaires (Bell 1989). A five-point scale was used as the basic measure of accuracy, ranging from 1 'absolutely accurate' to 5 'extremely inaccurate'. Sources rated 29 per cent of stories absolutely accurate, and 55 per cent slightly inaccurate, with 16 per cent in the higher inaccuracy levels. So while over 80 per cent of stories are rated no worse than slightly inaccurate, a significant minority of stories misreported the source more or less severely. In one full-page feature, sources found no fewer than 23 inaccuracies.

Sources were asked to identify inaccuracies under six headings. Scientific/technical inaccuracies were present in about a third of

TABLE 10.1 Numbers of inaccuracies of different classes in New Zealand news about climate change, and percentage of stories (N = 201) in which different classes of inaccuracy occurred

	Number of inaccuracies	Percentage of stories
Inaccurate headline*	22	12.1
Inaccurate lead paragraph	17	8.5
Scientific/technical inaccuracy	139	34.3
Non-scientific inaccuracy	72	31.8
Misquotation	110	33.7
Omission	64	24.6
Exaggeration	81	26.0
Distortion	54	19.5

* For headline category, only press clips counted.

stories – technical terms misused, wrong figures given, scientific facts confused (table 10.1). Non-scientific inaccuracies (such as mis-spelled names, misnamed organizations and wrong dates) also occurred in about a third of the stories, as did misquotations. About a quarter of stories had significant omissions or exaggerations, and one fifth had distortions of emphasis.

Overstatement in headlines and leads

Given that leads and headlines are micro-stories, it is not surprising they contain a microcosm of the problems of misreporting. Our sources found inaccurate headlines in 12 per cent of the press clips (table 10.1). Only 8 per cent of lead paragraphs were assessed as inaccurate. Many stories which have inaccuracies in the body copy compound those with a headline which takes the story from bad to worse:

EXPERT PREDICTS SEA WALL FOR CITY

Rising sea levels will force Wellingtonians to choose within the next few years between building sea walls or moving parts of the city inland, Wellington rotarians were told yesterday.

Gary Betteridge, the DSIR spokesman on climatic change, said sea levels here were expected to rise on average by up to 1.2 metres by the middle of next century.

The lead annuls the ambiguities of scientific scenarios with the definite future *will*. It brings the time scale nearer: *the next few years* in the lead does not mesh with the 60-odd years of the next paragraph. The second paragraph also brings the place closer to home: *here* is used to apply a global average to New Zealand. The headline caps it with the unambiguous *predicts*, reinforced by the claim of source credentials, *expert*. The opening of this story is a textbook case of news values pushed beyond their warranted limits – negativity, proximity of place and time, unambiguity and relevance.

The urge to get the most out of a story is again exemplified in a case compounded by editing changes. The lead paragraph in a television news item (with the same unhappy source as above) ran:

> New Zealand *can expect* more of the weather conditions which have battered the country over recent months, according to a DSIR scientist . . .
> Unusual weather this year may just be a temporary aberration, but *scientists believe* it's more likely to be the greenhouse effect.

The source commented that this came close to misrepresenting what he said. The journalist had during interview tried to push him to make a greenhouse-effect interpretation of current weather conditions (which had included a devastating cyclone). The source had explicitly refused. The journalist got the interpretation in anyway by using the generalized *scientists believe* attribution. Still more problematic was the version run on the main news programme earlier the same evening:

> A DSIR scientist *is predicting* more of the weather which has battered the country over recent months . . .
> A simple change in weather patterns can't be ruled out, but *Dr Betteridge believes* the evidence points to the greenhouse effect.

Here *predict* replaces *expect*, and the specific source is attributed rather than' scientists in general. The source rejected this version as a definite overstatement.

Negativity is a prime news value which operated in this lead paragraph from a radio news item:

> Predictions of increasing world temperatures look like bringing only headaches for New Zealand's stock farmers.

Positive benefits can be expected as well as negative impacts – and some were covered later in the story. Negativity is again a factor in this broadcast lead paragraph:

A group of scientists has come up with a hit list of places around
New Zealand they say will be submerged by the greenhouse
effect.

The source said it was the journalist who pressed the scientists to name
places. The naming serves both facticity and relevance – some
audience members live in those places and will be personally affected.

Exaggeration as exemplified above was one obvious area of scientific inaccuracy. The second was confusion between the greenhouse
effect and ozone depletion. The two phenomena are largely distinct,
occurring through different processes and at different heights in the
atmosphere, although involving some of the same gases. The most
common confusion was to present ozone depletion as the cause of the
greenhouse effect. Often this took the form of a story entirely concerned with one phenomenon carrying a headline or illustration about
the other. These problems clearly result not from any inclination to
exaggerate but from the newsworker's goal of clarifying things for the
reader. A story on the dangers to eyesight from ultraviolet rays ran
under the headline *Greenhouse effect threatens eyesight* and began:

> More New Zealanders will develop cataracts as a result of the holes
> in the ozone layer – the Greenhouse effect – unless they ade-
> quately protect their eyes.

Misquotation

We have seen in the previous chapter how inaccurate direct quotes and
choice of speech verb can jeopardize faithful reporting. The high principle of direct quotation for journalists is that a quote consists of the
actual words spoken by the newsmaker (see Cappon 1982: 71, cf.
Short 1988). Yet misquotation is one of the most common complaints
of news sources, with 34 per cent believing they have been misquoted
(table 10.1). Van Dijk found that direct quotes from written sources
were often summaries not verbatim (1988b: 132). The most severe
case of misquotation in this study was a feature published in several
newspapers where a source quoted at some length denied having provided most of the quotes or anything like them. He believed the journalist had probably obtained information from a colleague (with the
same first name) and then wrongly attributed it to the published
source.

Broadcasting has its own variation on misquotation and this, too,
occurred in our study. The technology makes it possible to edit a strip

of talk so that it sounds like continuous speech but in fact has had phrases or sentences removed. Broadcasters argue – with some justification – that *not* cleaning up infelicities in a quotation can do a disservice to the verbally less skilled newsmaker. Another issue is the broadcast practice of repatching questions and answers, so that a question receives an answer which was originally given to another, albeit similar, question. This practice has surfaced as evidence in libel suits against television news (Geis 1987: 157).

Misattribution

Journalists draw on a variety of sources, spoken and written, and rework them into a unified story. In the process, the boundaries between who said what, and what is the journalist's own input, are regularly blurred. This was the primary problem our sources had with attribution and it happens in two kinds of cases. First, it may occur in a story which cites more than one source. The text does not make it clear which source a particular piece of information comes from, because the attributions are some distance away in other paragraphs. Secondly, the information may be general background, context or evaluation from the journalist himself. It is not directly, within the same sentence, sourced to a particular person. But because it occurs in a sequence which *is* sourced to that person, he or she appears to be the source of this information also.

This is a familiar issue to journalists (one of the problems identified occurred in a story taken from a press release I had written). It is not easy to mark general background off from a source's specific statement without repetitive attribution. But there is also a payoff for the journalist in this ambiguity. No explicit attribution is made, so the journalist is covered against an accusation of misquoting, but the background paragraph does appear to carry a source's authority.

Too much, too near and too soon

The journalist's basic 'facts' of *when, where* and *how much* are the site of much misreporting. Scientific or technical inaccuracies were the most frequent identified by our sources (table 10.1). Many were problems with numbers, or with scope of time or place.

Inaccurate reporting of units of measurement occurred several times, particularly with variations on 'metres'. The sealevel around New Zealand was reported to be already rising at 1–2 centimetres per year when the source had (correctly) said millimetres. One story had the source predicting annual rainfall increases of 8 centimetres rather than millimetres. Another referred to a glacier as starting at a height of 2700 *kilo*metres above sealevel, not metres. Another story had a source say in direct quotation that the amount of carbon dioxide in the atmosphere would increase 20-fold in the next 50 years: the scenario is for a two-fold increase. These inaccuracies do not occur at random. If they did, we would expect units both smaller and larger than the correct level. But all these exaggerate and none reduce, clearly prompted by enhancing the news value of the story.

There are a number of 'facts' about climate change which occur frequently in the news and on which there has been some scientific consensus: the site and timing of the ozone hole, and scenarios for temperature and sealevel rises under the greenhouse effect. We identified all mentions of these in the six months of news coverage in order to assess how accurately media reporting reflects the balance of scientific opinion. All mentions of the ozone hole correctly placed it over Antarctica – with a couple of stories mentioning the lesser Arctic hole. The record is not quite so good on timing. Most clips timed the hole correctly in spring, but several wrongly put it in winter. One compounded the confusion by explaining that the hole occurred *each spring (July)*!

For scenarios of possible temperature rises under the greenhouse effect, the reported figures were overwhelmingly within the ranges suggested by scientists (see Bell 1989 for detail). Getting the numbers right is, however, not the only issue in such reporting. Two other factors come into play: the time and place scope of the scenario, and the way in which the statement is framed – its illocutionary force. About a third of the mentions of temperature rise were cast in the form of predictions, expectations or certainties. In some cases, temperature figures were treated as predictions even though they had been explicitly used as 'what if' assumptions in order to calculate possible sealevel rises. The problem here is less one of actual exaggerated figures than of setting correct figures within an inadequately hedged context.

Inaccuracies of time and place scope invariably make things sound closer to here and now than they are. Place scope was a problem in the broadcast item which said *Seven of New Zealand's eight warmest years have been in the 1980s*. The meteorologist quoted the figure as a general southern hemisphere average, not specific to New Zealand. Figures for other parameters were on occasions treated as specific to New Zealand when they were global – or sometimes even northern hemisphere – averages.

The actual figures reported for sealevel rises were also overwhelmingly accurate, with most mentions at the lower rather than upper end

Huge rise in seas predicted

THE west Antarctic ice sheet will melt as the greenhouse effect continues, raising sea levels by eight metres, according to the latest scientific research.

Glaciologists have said a 4 degrees celsius rise in global temperature would lead to the melting of this ice sheet.

The climate research section of the National Aeronautics and Space Agency in the United States has predicted a global temperature rise of 4.2C by 2050.

Victoria University geologist Peter Barret, who heads the New Zealand Antarctic Survey, said yesterday that cities like London and Calcutta "could go" within a hundred years.

Dr Barrett said the errors in climatic predictions were getting smaller, and the only question now was how fast the west Antarctic ice sheet would melt.

"It'll probably take two or three hundred years, assuming things progress in an orderly fashion," he said.

But some scientists had warned that climatic change as a result of the greenhouse effect would not happen smoothly.

"At least one well established New York scientist is saying that there may be points, thresholds, if you like, and once they're exceeded, things might in fact happen quite quickly," Dr Barret said.

FIGURE 10.1 Overstatement through displacing timeframe: opening paragraphs of lead story in Wellington's *The Dominion* newspaper, 20 December 1988

of scientific scenarios. But here time scope was an occasional problem. In two cases, huge rises were mentioned – 30 metres and 60 metres – without indication that they presupposed centuries-long melting of polar icecaps. This makes the story more newsworthy by bringing the distant future closer.

The problem of omitting timeframes was encapsulated in a story which was the front-page lead in Wellington's morning daily (figure 10.1). It spoke of eight metre rises resulting from melting of polar icecaps. No timeframe is specified in the lead paragraph (and the attribution is very generalized). The third paragraph implies a period of 60 years – which would represent four-fold exaggeration of the upper scientific scenarios. Only in the sixth paragraph does it become clear that a time-span of two to three hundred years is required to melt the icecaps. The distance of six paragraphs between the figure of eight metres and the true timeframe – together with mention of another, much shorter timeframe in the intervening paragraphs – is a sure recipe for readers to conclude that the huge rises are imminent. We shall see below in our analysis of public understanding that this is precisely what seems to have happened.

According to the journalist who wrote the story, the timeframe was in her original lead paragraph, but was taken out by a subeditor. She did not consider this deletion a problem because the timeframe was included later. The source of the story disagreed. As analyst, I also disagree, particularly since the subeditor compounded his version of the lead by raising the stakes still higher in the headline. The example reminds us that journalists are – like researchers – in competition with their colleagues for publication. This journalist was pleased to have got her story on the front page rather than worried about editing problems.

3 MISEDITING INTERNATIONAL NEWS

In chapter 4, I analysed how newsworkers edit stories on the production line with four goals in mind: clarity, brevity, language standardization, and news value. We have just seen an example of how the drive for news value can push editors into unwarranted interference in a story. In this section I present findings drawn from my own study of editing of international news (Bell 1983, 1984a).

In assessing misreporting we are subject to a source's or some other judge's version as a yardstick. In editing analysis we have the surer authority of the input copy against which to compare the edited output copy. We treat the input copy as a canonical text, making identification of semantic mismatch much surer. For the purpose of editing analysis, the input story is treated as reality, an adequate and accurate representation (which is of course an idealization).

Editing can be described by a series of editing rules (chapter 4). Copy editors work to an accuracy condition: no editing rule may be applied if its effect is to make the meaning of the output story in any way non-congruent with that of the input. The output can contain less information than the input, but not incompatible information. Deletion or unwarranted alteration of a major story constituent such as an event, actors, time, place or attribution may well result in an inaccurate output version.

Some 150 errors were found in the editing of 290 international news agency stories (for detail of method, see Bell 1984a). I found five classes of editing inaccuracy – falsification, over-assertion, overscope, refocus and addition.

Falsification

Falsification occurs when information in the output copy is not congruent with input copy. The most extreme case of falsification in this study saw *not* being deleted, so that the output said the polar opposite of the input:

> The spokesman could not   → *denied*
> say how many people had
> died but *did not deny* a
> report by a journalist who
> claimed more than 1500 had
> perished.

Two independent recipient copy editors were misled by the double negative in *did not deny*. It is more newsworthy to have someone deny something than confirm it.

Strengthening consonance of a story with national stereotypes led to some unwarranted changes in this copy:

> Federal authorities were today   → Emergency law is being
> taking emergency measures   enforced . . .
> to aid flood victims.

Receiving this story about severe floods in Brazil, the copy editor presumably could not credit that a South American government might help its citizens rather than coerce them.

The time and place deictics which occur in the lead paragraphs of international stories – *here* and *today* – are traps for the unwary. Copy editors can be tempted to enhance the recency of slightly stale news by taking liberties with the time specification. I have seen stories where time adverbials have been updated from *last night* to *today* to *late today* as they were edited first by an agency and then by a recipient radio station, with each version claiming greater recency as the events in fact receded into the past.

Over-assertion and over-scope

Here the illocutionary force (assertive strength) of a statement is increased beyond the warrant of the input copy. Where falsification is something contrary to the evidence of input copy, over-assertion is a change which further evidence could prove to be warranted, but such evidence is currently lacking. Individual words, phrases or sentences can be intensified, making a story sound better than it really is.

This can happen in two main ways. First, a copy editor may intensify an expression, for instance by inserting a word such as *all* or *only*. Secondly, over-assertion can result from deleting linguistic hedges, the devices which tone down the illocutionary force of what is asserted. These paragraphs come from an Australian Associated Press-Reuter story about how a piece of wing broke from an aircraft approaching Mascot airport in Sydney. Three copy editors from different stations or agencies independently started to chop out the hedges from the AAP version:

AAP	Mr W.A. Norton of Dent Street, Lindfield, saw the incident on his way to work. He said the jet continued towards Mascot without any apparent problem.
→ ZB	The jet continued to Mascot without any apparent problem.
→ GNS	The aircraft apparently landed without any trouble.
→ PA	The jet landed without any trouble.

The input version is a sourced eyewitness account which sticks to what Mr Norton actually saw. His words *continued, towards* and *apparent* make no commitment to whether the aircraft eventually landed safely. But the editor for radio station ZB replaced *towards* with *to*, indicating that the aircraft had arrived. The General News Service editor had the aircraft actually *land*. And the Press Association editor even took out *apparent*. This series of deletions is possible only because the initial eyewitness attribution has been removed from all three versions. If Mr Norton's account had been kept, it would be clear he was in no position to say that the aircraft landed safely, since he was many kilometres away from the airport on the other side of Sydney harbour.

One of the most common and least desirable forms of over-assertion is through attribution deletion. Attribution deletion serves news value. It reduces ambiguity by eliminating viewpoint, making reality seem monolithic rather than multisided. Attribution is most obviously needed when there are reports from sharply opposed groups. A single event commonly produces two incompatible crops of statistics from belligerent parties, as Knightley's classic history of war reporting shows (1975). But it is essential for the audience to know which side is the source in order to interpret what they hear. The copy editor deleted the attribution from this story:

> Israeli naval units tonight raided three Lebanese ports sinking about ten vessels in each of them, *the Israeli military spokesman announced*.

Other (unused) reports gave the Lebanese count: 21 vessels sunk. Neither may be correct, but we have the need and right to know the sources.

Attribution can also source the news origin of a story, as we saw in chapter 9. News agency attributions are regularly deleted by copy editors, particularly in broadcast news. But they do serve an important function. For many countries, all staple international news comes through a single agency. The audience can hear a story on breakfast radio, read a confirming account in the morning paper, and watch it again on television news that evening. The multiple and apparently independent versions make the story seem unfaultable, but they may all come from a single input story received by all media. Explicit attribution would at least make this fact accessible to the audience.

Copy editors have the same problems as their journalist colleagues in handling the time or place scope of sources' statements. Over-scope is the commonest form of this, mistakenly broadening the scope of a linguistic unit beyond the warrant of the input copy. Shifting or deleting time or place adverbials can redefine unacceptably the scope of what is being said, as we saw in figure 10.1 above. The story about widespread floods in Brazil gave a possible death toll of 1500 in one city. By deleting the name of both city and state, the copy editor made a disaster which affected at least seven Brazilian states seem less serious than it was. On the other hand, the declaration of a disaster zone in the same story was made to appear more widespread than the input copy warranted. New Zealand copy editors would not treat so casually the geography of a more distant but better known region such as Western Europe.

Refocus and addition

In refocus information is deleted or reordered so that the balance of a story becomes non-congruent with that in the input copy. This is the kind of imbalance, distortion or omission which news sources often complain of (cf. table 10.1 on p. 218 above). It is virtually impossible to prove, but becomes a little more visible when it results from active editing choices. Reordering a story to find a better lead is a standard copy editing task but one which offers wide opportunity for error.

Information addition is surprisingly common in copy editing. It usually inserts background or explanatory detail (cf. Rosenblum 1979), but occasionally the new information is inaccurate. One copy editor betrayed exasperation at the inconclusiveness of a rain-interrupted cricket match in Guyana. The lead paragraph of the input story said that play had been *held up at the start of the final day*. This was rewritten as:

> In the West Indian city of Georgetown the final day of the Fourth Test between the West Indies and England has been *washed out by rain, resulting in a draw*.

Giving the result is unambiguous and fits the event into the time cycle of radio news. But unfortunately for the copy editor's attempts to pre-judge the outcome, the match did restart – had in fact already done so before this story was received in Wellington. Two hours later the same editor blithely sent through an update saying the game was underway again.

Technical linguistic failure presumably plays a part in most editing

error, with the copy editor misunderstanding, possibly through haste
or lack of geographical, political or other knowledge. But if that was
all that was going on, we would expect editing inaccuracies to be scattered at random. This is not the case. Virtually every editing inaccuracy I found served to enhance the news value of the story,
particularly for unambiguity, negativity, consonance, superlativeness, recency or proximity. And inaccuracy not only alters stories in
patterned ways, it also occurs in particular types of news. From the
few examples I have given above, it will be no surprise that news about
nations of the South was much more inaccurately edited than that
about the United States or Western Europe (Bell 1983). News about
Brazil, Argentina and Ethiopia had an average of one serious editing
error per story. Such a finding is consistent with the many studies
which have shown imbalances in news flow and presentation between
the North and the South (for instance, Peterson 1981, Stevenson and
Shaw 1984).[1]

The study of editing inaccuracy has the advantage of limiting its
range to comparing input and output texts. It examines not selection
between equal alternatives but the active intervention of the copy
editor in the meaning of stories. This makes the force of the patterns
which emerge all the more striking.

11

(Mis)understanding the News

The importance of the audience has been one of the main themes throughout our discussion of news language. We have examined the structure of the audience (chapter 5) and their influence on the style of news language (chapter 6). Still more dominant has been the notion of the news story. We have examined the production of news stories (chapters 3 and 4), their characteristics (8 and 9) and their shortcomings (10). In this chapter we bring these strands together, and examine how audiences comprehend the news stories they receive.

While much relevant research has investigated misreporting of media messages, there has been less interest in how the audience understand and misunderstand these messages. There have been studies concerned, for instance, with whether satirical programmes whose clear aim is to question racial stereotyping (such as the US comedy, *All in the Family*) may be used to reinforce rather than reduce such attitudes (Vidmar and Rokeach 1974). One of the findings of media effects research is that audiences tend to hear what they want to hear, interpreting content in terms of their own viewpoints.

We must distinguish from the outset between non-comprehension and miscomprehension. Non-comprehension means that an audience member either derived no meaning from a media message or did not even recall it. Miscomprehension means that someone derived from the text meanings it did not really contain. Later in this chapter I present findings from my own research on audiences' comprehension of climate change news. Comprehension and non-comprehension represent the extent to which the public recalls or forgets information about climate change. Miscomprehension is the amount of inaccuracy or confusion in the information which they do recall. Most research has focused on degree of recall, although it often appears that researchers thought they were examining understanding not just memory. Much less research exists on the accuracy or otherwise of what audiences do remember – miscomprehension. As Jacoby and Hoyer (1987) indicate, one can recall something one has miscomprehended, and miscomprehend something recalled.

Comprehension plays a part in news production as well as news reception. As we saw in examining the structure of how news is produced, newsworkers function first as comprehenders of their sources' information before they reformulate those understandings into news stories. Their primary role is as listeners, and misperception is the first pitfall to which news reporting is subject.

1 RECALL AND COMPREHENSION

The research indicates a generally low degree of recall of information received through the media. Some of the research is sponsored by advertising interests (for instance, Jacoby and Hoyer 1987), most of the rest focuses on news. Several of the leading researchers summarize work in the area in the course of presenting their own contribution. Gunter (1987) is particularly comprehensive, but see also Robinson and Levy (1986), Jacoby and Hoyer (1987) and van Dijk (1988b).

Findahl and Hoijer (1981) found that 25 per cent of basic information heard in radio news broadcasts in Sweden was recalled. Van Dijk (1988b) cites an unpublished 1980 study by Larsen, who found that a maximum of 20 per cent of propositions in radio news were recalled. A proposition is a separate piece of information in the story – a 'fact' in journalistic terms. Information gained through reading the newspaper sticks much better than from broadcast news (Gunter 1987).

Lutz and Wodak's large-scale study suggested that perhaps only 30 per cent of Austrian listeners comprehended the news, despite high consumption, for example through having the radio on constantly (Wodak 1987). Recall of the main facts in two stories examined in depth ranged from 6 to 34 per cent of subjects (Lutz and Wodak 1987). They also played radio news stories to informants and requested them to retell the stories. They identified the ten core pieces of information contained in each text, and examined the extent and accuracy with which these were reproduced. Scoring each piece of information at 1 point, the average was 4.02 (out of 10) on immediate retelling, down to 3.26 when subjects were requestioned half an hour later.

Jacoby and Hoyer (1987) conducted a massive project into the comprehension of advertising and editorial copy in magazines, interviewing over 1300 respondents. Each respondent read four communications and then answered six questions on each. Some 63 per cent of answers were correct, 21 per cent incorrect, and 16 per cent were don't know's. The level of 63 per cent comprehension is much higher than in other studies, as were the same researchers' findings in another project on television comprehension (70 per cent). However, Robinson and Levy (1986) argue that the public absorbs more information than earlier studies had indicated. They found that aided recall using key words (very like the newsworker's slugline) as prompts produced much higher recall than unaided. Nevertheless, only a third of the audiences in both the United States and United Kingdom understood the central point of stories from the evening television news.

Van Dijk (1988b) surveyed a random sample on recall of four stories from Dutch newspapers. He counted the number of propositions per story and the amount recalled. A detailed analysis of one item which contained 83 propositions found that 35 of those propositions were recalled by no one at all. Another sample was interviewed a month later, and only a quarter to a third could answer questions after the time lapse. The core of hard news facts such as figures and dates were not recalled with the passage of time. These results are compared with a laboratory experiment in which students read a newspaper and were then asked to recall one story. Their amount of recall was about twice as high as that in the field study on the same day as publication.

Factors affecting recall

The research indicates that recall of broadcast news can be as low as 5 per cent of the information and rarely exceeds 30 per cent even on immediate questioning. In general we might expect that the low level of linguistic redundancy in news writing, packing maximum information into minimum words, could well result in low recall or comprehension (cf. Burger 1984: 258). Only a little research looks at how the structure of news stories affects recall or comprehension. Classic hard-news techniques of telling stories – *who, what, when, where* in the first paragraphs – result in better recall (Thorndyke 1979, Wodak 1987). Adding information concerning the actor or place in the story lifted recall of the whole story from 25 per cent to between 30 and 40 per cent (Findahl and Hoijer 1981). Presenting causes or consequences within a story increases comprehension, presumably because of its attempt at integrating and motivating the information.

Different elements in the story are recalled differentially. Larsen is cited by van Dijk as finding that setting was remembered better than the actual topic – *who* and *where* was remembered rather than *what*. Main events (42 per cent) are remembered more than causes (34 per cent), which are remembered more than consequences (26 per cent: van Dijk 1988b).

Some of the news values presented in chapter 8 promote recall by news consumers as well as selection by newsworkers. The negative or the spectacular is better recalled. Personalization of news in notable individuals and presentation of unique events led to stories being better recalled. But Robinson and Levy (1986) found no correlation between comprehension and news values such as conflict, proximity, relevance, and consonance. Television news techniques such as use of humour or violent footage may well be distracting rather than an aid to recall.

Most of the research on news comprehension covers broadcasting, and some of its findings are peculiar to the broadcast format. First items in a news bulletin are remembered better than following items, with recall recovering for the final items (Gunter 1987, Lutz and Wodak 1987). Robinson and Levy (1986) found that last items are recalled best of all. However, these were the typical send-the-viewers-off-with-a-smile stories which are high on human interest anyway, making it hard to separate the effect of position from news value. The form in which broadcast news is structured is radically abnormal compared with most methods of giving information, with a dozen or more unrelated items crammed in sequence into a few minutes. In order to reduce the fragmented nature of the bulletin, broadcast news practice tends to group thematically-linked stories (for instance, overseas or industrial stories) into a package, presumably as an aid to comprehension. The technique has been criticized for its potential to pre-set an interpretative slant on a story. However, several studies show that it also makes stories less memorable rather than more so.

Previous knowledge is the single biggest factor in news recall, whether this is tested by the day, by the week, or over a long period (Robinson and Levy 1986). Many separate studies show that those in the know are in a position to know more, that news is for the already initiated (Findahl and Hoijer 1981).

The audience is not monolithic nor does it bring the same presuppositions to bear on media content. Recall is affected by demographic factors such as age, education, occupation, gender and class (Gunter 1987). Jacoby and Hoyer (1987) found a trend for older people to misunderstand more. Those with more education or higher income miscomprehended less. Wodak (1987) found significant class and sex differences in recall, favouring males and the middle class.

Other strands of research focus on the different ways in which different audiences comprehend the same content. The possibility of differential readings of a media message is central to semiotic approaches. In particular Morley (1983) has shown how different sectors of society produce quite different readings of what they receive from the media. Researching understandings of a popular BBC current affairs programme among working-class viewers, he found that a group of apprentices tended to accept the perspectives offered in the programme. Trade union activists gave antagonistic readings, while a group of black students 'did not so much produce an oppositional reading as refuse to "read" it at all' (Morley 1983: 115). The programme made no connection at all with the concerns of the black students' own culture.

The audience write their script

Comprehension can be viewed as either (or both) a bottom-up or top-down process. Bottom-up processing involves working from the individual bits of information one receives towards a more general understanding. In top-down processing the receiver works from previous knowledge or understanding (often termed 'schemata' or 'scripts') in coming to grips with new information. While in practice both processes are likely to be operating, two converging strands of research on top-down processing cast particular light on how audiences understand news. Work in cognitive psychology and artificial intelligence has examined how hearers understand stories (for instance, Woodall et al. 1983, Gunter 1987). Van Dijk (1988b) has applied his general model of discourse comprehension (van Dijk and Kintsch 1983) to news comprehension – using a *Newsweek* story as the primary example.

There are two particularly important kinds of schemata which receivers bring to the process of comprehension: cognitive schemata, which provide background information about the world, and formal schemata, knowledge of the conventional structures of news stories. The formal schemata mean that news consumers bring to the understanding of news the kinds of categories and structures which we outlined in chapter 8. They know that stories consist of headlines, lead paragraphs, episodes, reaction, commentary and so on, even though they could not verbalize that knowledge. And they use those categories to decode the stories.

Related to the cognitive schemata are pre-existing mental scripts by which people interpret new information in the light of quite general and fixed preconceived frameworks. Scripts are the knowledge we base on a standard sequence of events which we have experienced many times and use to interpret new occurrences (Schank and Abelson 1977). In daily life, we have a script for how a meal in a restaurant or a trip by public transport or a birthday party generally proceeds. In news comprehension, scripts enable audiences to fill out the content of a news story from their own prior knowledge, and relate the new information to what they already know. Some degree of prior knowledge is a precondition of being informed by the news at all.

Information from items with similar scripts can be easily confused. For instance, audiences have a mental script concerning the pattern of demonstrations or civil unrest. Both Findahl and Hoijer (1981) and Jensen (1988) found that information about such events became confused with what were perceived as similar events taking place elsewhere but reported in the same bulletin. Nearly a quarter of the audience confused details between two stories about demonstrations in different countries. This process may increase over time, so that there is an increasing 'meltdown' effect of information from one story merging into another (Woodall et al. 1983).

Story structure and comprehension

Some researchers have tried to gauge how different story structures affect news comprehension. Thorndyke (1979) took stories from the *New York Times* and *Los Angeles Times*, hypothesizing that recall could be inhibited by the canonical news order which puts the 'important' information first rather than following chronological sequence. He rewrote the stories in a condensed version deleting what was deemed to be non-essential information but keeping the basic structure. A narrative version reworked the condensed version into chronological order, and a topical version grouped information under subheadings. Subjects read the stories, and then attempted to reproduce the information. By number of propositions recalled, the original version was lowest for comprehension (19 per cent of propositions), and the other three versions higher and similar to each other at 25 per cent. However, when only the main points of the original version were counted (that is, those which were included in the condensed version) 22 per cent were recalled, compared with 12 per cent for the propositions which were deleted to make the condensed version. This indicates that recall is best for the principal elements of structures such as actors and action, as diagrammed in chapter 8.

In a second experiment, Thorndyke (1979) took narrative and condensed versions and added an outline version, including numbering and subheadings. Backgrounders or features were best recalled from narrative and outline. Spot news was best recalled from the condensed version – which is the nearest to the standard press hard news format.

Lutz and Wodak (1987) used actual radio news bulletins recorded from Austrian state radio. Each item was also rewritten in two different ways which were believed to be more comprehensible. The first rewrite simplified syntax and content progression. It became a little more like a narrative than an inverted-triangle news story, but was a similar length to the original. The second rewrite aimed at greater semantic coherence, clarifying connections and contradictions. It changed the original much more radically, using short sentences and producing a much shorter story.

The amount of recall was measured crudely by the number of words students used in retelling the story. On average, the reformulated versions produced longer retellings than the original – 30 per cent more for the more radically rewritten second reformulation. While the lower-educated students benefited slightly from the reformulated versions, the high school students benefited much more. This finding of an increasing knowledge gap is not unique. Educational television programmes such as *Sesame Street* have been shown to benefit middle-class children more than the disadvantaged children they were primarily designed to help.

Lutz and Wodak also found that different techniques of news presentation did affect comprehension in a detailed analysis of three particular stories and their rewritten versions. The number of dead in riots in Tunisia was best remembered when carried in the lead sentence (34 per cent recalled it), compared with the second sentence (27 per cent) or the middle of the story (20 per cent). Where contradictory claims were made about casualties by the opposing sides in the Iran/Iraq war, 33 per cent of subjects mentioned the contradiction when it had been made explicit in the story, compared with only 6 to 9 per cent in the versions where the contradiction was not pointed out.

These two studies provide some more detailed evidence on how story structure and elements, as outlined in chapters 8 and 9, affect comprehension. The results are equivocal on whether the cyclical time sequence of standard news writing is harder to comprehend, or whether chronological order is easier. It does, however, seem that information is better remembered if carried in the lead paragraph, and that the major levels of structure such as those diagrammed in figures 8.3 and 8.4 are better remembered. We now need quite rigorously controlled testing which varies elements of the news story systematically and measures their comprehension in more sophisticated ways.

News comprehension research also casts light on the nature of story structure. Lutz and Wodak (1987) tested the form in which subjects retold news stories, asking them to write a lead paragraph themselves. They found that only the middle-class students reproduced a standard news format. Even when lower-class subjects retold a lot of the desired information, they did not do so in accepted news style. By contrast over half the middle-class students were able to reproduce news writing. Both comprehension of the news, and productive capability in news formats, appear to be strongly social-class conditioned. This compares interestingly with the known skill of lower-class speakers as tellers of personal narratives (Labov 1972b). Middle-class narratives by contrast (Horvath 1990) are often about third parties rather than the speaker's own experience – just as the news is.

Further evidence for the conventional nature of news scripts and their formulaic structures comes from attempts to have computers 'understand' news stories. DeJong (1982) describes a computer programme which scans and summarizes stories from the United Press International news service wire. The programme possesses 60 'sketchy scripts' for news situations such as demonstrations, earthquakes, accidents or crimes. It scans the UPI stories to recognize the elements of scripts and paraphrase them. The events in its sketchy script for demonstrations show interesting presumptions of physical violence and the ordering of who attacks whom:

1 The demonstrators arrive at the demonstration location.
2 The demonstrators march.
3 Police arrive on the scene.
4 The demonstrators communicate with the target of the demonstration.
5 The demonstrators attack the target of the demonstration.
6 The demonstrators attack the police.
7 The police attack the demonstrators.
8 The police arrest the demonstrators.

The programme may find much of the information it needs in the lead paragraph, but reads the whole story and can pick up core information which is carried only in later paragraphs. Run for a trial week on actual UPI copy, the programme recognized and understood a majority of the stories for which it had sketchy scripts. It was unable to handle stories written in convoluted syntax, or where a conventional event was described in unconventional terms – for example when summit talks were described in terms of the two leaders embracing. The ability of a computer to generate a script for common news stories reinforces our contention that much news writing follows a conventional format.

2 THE PUBLIC MISUNDERSTAND CLIMATE CHANGE

Most of the research covered above has concentrated on recall rather than comprehension, and on non-comprehension rather than miscomprehension. Only Morley (1983) attempts to identify the nature of audiences' misunderstanding of media content. In my own study of public understanding of climate change, I focus both on the degree of non-comprehension and on the site and nature of miscomprehension.

As a complement to the study of misreporting of climate change described in the last chapter, I conducted a pilot-scale survey of the level of public understanding of the issue soon after the period of the news sample (Bell 1989, 1991b). Informants representing a cross-section of society ($N = 61$) were asked what they knew about climate change, and where they got their information. The sample was designed to approximate the composition of the New Zealand population on five demographic parameters: age, gender, ethnic group, occupation, and urban or rural residency.

Informants were asked six questions covering the nature, causes and effects of ozone depletion, and the same for the greenhouse effect. Every piece of information offered by interviewees was categorized. The degree of non-understanding – how much interviewees did or did not know – was measured by scoring the answers to each question out of ten, compared with a model answer of core information for each question. Points were given for each piece of relevant and accurate information, such as that refrigerants are a source of ozone-depleting chlorofluorocarbons. This gave an index of an individual's knowledge about greenhouse and ozone, ranging from 0 to 60 (for detail of methodology, see Bell 1989).

The scoring system produced indexes which seemed to represent fairly informants' degree of knowledge about climate change. The index identifies the amount informants knew or did not know. It does not 'take off marks' for wrong information given. It is an index of understanding and non-understanding not of misunderstanding, except in-so-far as misunderstood/incorrect facts do not receive points. The nature of any misunderstandings (how accurate interviewees' information was) was identified through qualitative analysis, for instance of what informants thought were the causes of ozone depletion. It proved impossible to quantify misunderstanding in any useful way (a problem which Lutz and Wodak also found). But on to this qualitative analysis we were able to build a number of quantitative measures.

Almost everyone knew something about climate change, although the degree of understanding was not high. Of our small cross-section of New Zealand society, 93 per cent knew about ozone depletion and 80 per cent about the greenhouse effect. Knowledge about the greenhouse effect was lower (9.1 out of the possible 30 for the three survey questions) than for ozone depletion (10.4). The simple fact that greenhouse means warming is well known, the nature of ozone depletion less so. The causes of ozone depletion are much better known than the causes of the greenhouse effect. Nearly half the sample knew nothing at all about the causes of greenhouse warming. People knew a good deal about the impacts of both ozone depletion and the greenhouse effect, but often attributed rising temperatures to ozone depletion.

The research looks not at how people understand particular media messages presented to them in an experimental situation but how they understand a range of media inputs received naturally over time. We can do this because of two factors of which this project took advantage. First, the media are the sole source of information on this issue for most of the population. All informants who knew anything about the issue cited the principal daily media as a source of their information. Newspapers and television were both sources for three-quarters of the sample, and radio for nearly half. Only a few informants also mentioned friends as sources, whereas with most public issues we would expect personal experience and friends to be important inputs. Secondly, New Zealand's comparative isolation means that access to media originating outside the country is limited. *Time* magazine was the only foreign medium cited with some frequency. We thus have an almost experimental situation in which assessment of the public's understanding of the issue is broadly equivalent to an assessment of how they understand the media input.

Understanding ozone

Few informants had any clear idea of what the ozone hole is, or indeed of the nature of ozone or the ozone layer, but nearly half the sample knew that ozone filters ultraviolet light. The term 'ozone hole' clearly conjured up unhappily literal connotations in some people's minds, shown by references such as 'the hole coming down from the sky'.

Many knew the hole occurs over Antarctica, and a few even mentioned the lesser Arctic ozone hole. This closely reflects the balance of media mentions of the hole. From our six-month sample of reporting on climate change, we had culled all news mentions of where the ozone hole occurred. 97 per cent put the hole over Antarctic, plus a couple of mentions of the Arctic hole. In our public survey several people placed the hole over New Zealand itself, a mistake which cannot be attributed to media coverage within our sample period.

While New Zealanders were relatively clear about *where* the ozone hole occurs, they had no accurate idea about *when* it happens. Only ten people offered any information about the timing of the phenomenon, and none of those timed it accurately in spring. They said either that it was there all year, or that it occurred in summer – an error which did not occur in media coverage. No informant responded with the one inaccurate timing which the media did report – that the hole occurs in winter.

There is a complete mismatch between media coverage and the public's understanding here. There is no recall among our cross-section of the New Zealand public of the large number of media references to springtime. That information seems to have been overwhelmed by another factor in the public mind. My interpretation is that people are aware summer is the time of naturally decreasing ozone and increasing UV radiation over New Zealand, and have extrapolated that to Antarctica. This confirms the indications of research cited earlier in the chapter that *where* may be better recalled than *when*. It also cautions against expecting automatic reflection in the public mind of facts reported in the media (and consequently against holding the media responsible for all public misunderstandings of scientific matters). This particular misunderstanding is largely the public's own work, deduced from their own experience of decreased summertime ozone over New Zealand itself.

A second mismatch between news input and audience understanding arises with the causes of ozone depletion. The balance of media mentions of products which result in ozone loss closely reflects the actual ozone depleting potential of New Zealand usage (figure 11.1).

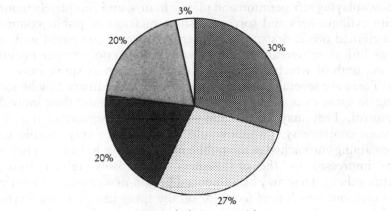

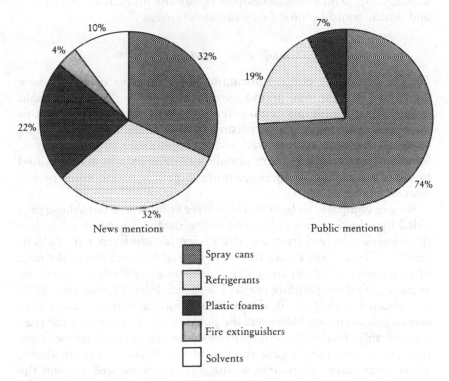

FIGURE 11.1 Distribution of New Zealand consumption of ozone depleting substances, and distribution of mentions of the substances in news reporting, compared to the public's mentions

But the graphs also show the public are exaggerating spray cans, downplaying refrigeration and plastic foams, and completely ignoring fire extinguishers and solvents. Three quarters of public comments attributed ozone destruction to aerosol sprays, compared with only one fifth to refrigeration and a few per cent to polystyrene manufacture, both of which contribute almost as much as spray cans.

There are several possible explanations. Consumers may be focusing on spray cans as the product which is most under their individual control. They may be drawing on long-term memory of the 1970s ozone controversy – which would be a case of a very specific script remaining entrenched in the public mind for over a decade. They may be impressed by the obviousness of aerosols' release into the atmosphere. They may be influenced by non-news media content such as cartoons which tend to major on the spray can as a visual symbol of ozone problems. In any case, we are clearly dealing here with a mental script which was developed before the immediate news input and which could be modified only slowly over time.

High noon, high tide

On the greenhouse effect, informants were asked to specify by how much and in what time period temperature and sealevel rises might occur. Most informants could offer no specific figures. This lack of information seems at first surprising in view of the amount of media coverage the issue had received and its importance to people's lives. However, in the light of the minimal recall of news information found by other researchers, it is perhaps more surprising that so many people offered figures at all.

We can compare the figures which were volunteered with those provided by scientists and publicized in the media. I used as a baseline the scenarios derived from the 1985 scientific conference in Villach, Austria. These figures were routinely quoted by scientists at the time of this study, 1988, as the current consensus. Villach indicated an average global temperature rise of 1.5 to 4.5 degrees Celsius by 2030. As indicated in chapter 10, the media's reporting of temperature rises was largely accurate. However, the public tended to magnify the rises considerably. Half of those informants who offered both temperature rises and a time period gave the top of the Villach range or above. There were three informants whose answers were well beyond the upper limit, and in one case the overestimation was by a factor of 9 (1–2 degrees per year).

The miscomprehension of these facts contrasts strikingly with the journalist's emphasis on including figures in a story (cf. chapter 9). Looking in more detail at how informants reported figures, we can see that people process such information, reframing it in rounded figures rather than photocopying it. The public has absorbed the temperature rise information received through the media, and recalled it in a different and exaggerated form compared with that in which it was received. The actual Villach figures were often reported in the media yet none of these specific numbers is volunteered by informants, not even the 40-year time period, the most frequent in media reports. Instead time periods are converted to the major round numbers (10, 20, 50, 100, 150 years).

Exaggeration was even more striking with sealevel rises (figure 11.2). The Villach scenario was for a possible 20 to 140 centimetre rise in 40 years. Also graphed in figure 11.2 is the much more conservative scenario of 20 to 60 centimetres in 60 years, published less than a month before our survey in a study by the Royal Society of New Zealand. Of fourteen informants who gave both sealevel rise and timeframe, two offered figures in the low range of the Villach scenario, three in the mid range, and one informant near the upper limit. The other eight informants all gave figures beyond even the most extreme Villach scenario, often magnified many times.

We must conclude that public exaggeration considerably exceeds anything for which the balance of media reporting can be held directly responsible. Out of some 120 mentions of temperature/sealevel rises in the news sample, only one (temperature) rise was exaggerated. The public are not dealing here with obscure scientific parameters but everyday units such as degrees of temperature and metres of height. These should indicate the improbability of a temperature of 100 degrees in 40 years' time, or of a sealevel rise of ten metres in a similar period, which would put most of New Zealand's cities deep under (boiling?) water.

But although the majority of news coverage was accurate, there was one notable instance of exaggeration outside the strict six-month sample. About a month before the public survey, the story discussed in the previous chapter (figure 10.1 on p. 223) appeared in *The Dominion*, the morning daily in the public survey area. It carried the figure of an eight-metre rise in its lead paragraph. It is beyond coincidence that one of the informants volunteered eight metres as her estimate, since one would have rather expected a rounded figure of five or ten metres. It seems that extreme figures may take hold in the public mind, while the conservative figures are lost without trace. None of the estimates offered by informants is within the Royal Society's upper

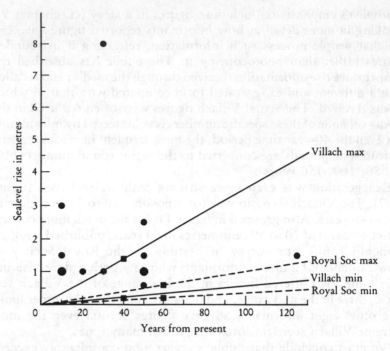

FIGURE 11.2   Estimates of possible sealevel rises by 14 members of the New Zealand public, plotted against the upper and lower scenarios from the 1985 Villach conference and from the 1988 Royal Society of New Zealand report

scenario (figure 11.2), although these had been well publicized shortly before the survey (and after the exaggerated *Dominion* story).

This may be just part of a general human tendency to exaggerate what is remembered from media content. The research on news recall indicates that the negative or the spectacular is better remembered. There is also a small study by Wales et al. (1963) on the accuracy of people's recall of news and advertising copy. Many more informants recalled content in exaggerated than in minimized form. There is also another factor described in the last chapter: the problem of news stories presenting figures as certainties rather than scenarios or possibilities. It seems plausible that an exaggerated certainty in expressing figures may be reflected in people's minds as exaggeration of the figures themselves. Our survey showed that the public seem quite sure climate change is going to happen – probably surer than the scientists themselves. Rating the likelihood on a five-point scale, half the informants thought such changes were absolutely certain, another quarter thought they were likely, and the remainder either thought changes were possible or did not know. Regardless of its origin, the exaggeration does matter. People who magnify in their own minds scenarios for temperature or sealevel rises may well – when the huge rises do not occur – turn against the scientists and journalists whom they regard as the source of those messages.

The greenhouse layer and the ozone effect

Besides exaggeration, the second main area of misunderstanding was confusion over the science. A large majority of informants confused ozone depletion and the greenhouse effect in some way. Untangling such misunderstandings is by nature difficult, but the main sites of people's confusion seem to be:

- There is a single greenhouse/ozone phenomenon rather than two largely distinct phenomena
- The greenhouse effect includes ozone depletion
- Ozone depletion is a (or the) cause of greenhouse warming
- Greenhouse impacts result from ozone depletion.

These misunderstandings are more than an academic question. People who link high ultraviolet radiation with high temperatures may fail to avoid exposure to UV at a time when temperatures may not be high but UV is. And if people are incorrectly attributing greenhouse impacts to ozone depleting causes there may be less incentive to tackle the real causes of greenhouse warming. The confusion leaves New Zealanders vulnerable to mis-associating causes and effects, reducing the motivation to avoid the real effects and solve the real causes.

The ozone/greenhouse confusion is also a classic case of meltdown between events with similar mental scripts (Woodall et al. 1983). This is promoted because both occur in the atmosphere, about which most of us know little, and both have come to public prominence at the same time. More widely, audience members probably have a general script for environmental issues against which incoming information is interpreted. There was a good deal of evidence from our survey that informants related pollution in general and phenomena such as acid rain to greenhouse or ozone problems. Jensen (1988) calls such generalized interpretations 'super-themes'. In his in-depth study of viewers' understanding of a Danish television news broadcast, the salience of environment as a super-theme was shown by informants projecting an environmental interpretation on to two stories to which it was marginal, as well as on to two centrally environmental topics.

Most informants in our survey said they found the media presented information about climate change in a way they found easy to understand. Given the generally low level of knowledge revealed by our survey, this question probably elicited answers which reflect informants' concern for their self-image rather than their real difficulties. Several commented that one needed to know about the issue before the coverage could be understood. This perception reflects exactly the finding that those who already know something are in a position to add to their knowledge, but those who know nothing at all do not learn from new information. News functions, as Lutz and Wodak's title has it, as 'information for the informed'.

Conclusion

Several of the researchers who have concentrated on news comprehension have worked within media organizations and contributed their findings to influence the way in which news is presented (for instance, Gunter for Britain's Independent Broadcasting Authority, and Robinson and Levy at the BBC). Their recommendations include separating similar stories within a bulletin to avoid confusion through meltdown, slowing down pace, increasing linguistic redundancy, focusing on human interest angles, and explaining technical or specialist terms.

The findings and recommendations of the climate change project have been communicated to both media and scientists in New Zealand, and influence my own continuing work as a science journalist and media consultant. I believe newsworkers should take into account the ways in which a story is open to be misunderstood, and write in a manner which minimizes misunderstanding. This may require, for instance, going for the bottom-of-the-range figure rather than the top. Such writing of course goes against long-entrenched news values on which journalists have been trained to operate – getting the most out of a story. But such values are called into question when they lead to misreporting or misunderstanding. We can recommend, from the findings in this and the previous chapter, a number of caveats for news staff: ensure that headlines are not overstated, that qualifications on statements are maintained, and that time or place scope is specified. Such steps would reduce the incidence of misreporting. However, real change depends on long-term reshaping of the values which drive the way news stories are gathered, structured and presented.

Notes

CHAPTER 1 MEDIA AND LANGUAGE

1 Trudgill (1983b) is the easiest of the introductory texts, addressed to the interested lay person rather than the student. Introductions for students include Hudson (1980) and Downes (1984). Fasold's two-volume text (1984, 1990) is the most detailed and comprehensive. Collections which bring together foundational papers in sociolinguistics include Hymes (1964), J. Fishman (1968), Gumperz and Hymes (1972), Pride and Holmes (1972) and Baugh and Sherzer (1984). Newmeyer (1988) collects papers commissioned to present a state-of-the-art overview of the field. Leading journals are *Language in Society*, *International Journal of the Sociology of Language*, *Journal of Language and Social Psychology*, *Language and Communication* and *Language Variation and Change*. The European strand of discourse analysis which I draw on in this book lacks a good introductory text. Van Dijk (1985b) is a four-volume *Handbook of Discourse Analysis* with contributions from a wide range of the approaches which have called themselves discourse analysis. Journals include *Text*, *Discourse Processes*, *Journal of Pragmatics* and the recent *Discourse and Society*.

2 The American and European traditions of mass communications research originated and developed along quite different lines, with cross-fertilization occurring only recently. McQuail (1987) is a standard introduction to mass communication theory which ranges widely across both traditions. One of the best approaches to the American tradition is through the readers which collect together key papers, for example Schramm (1960), Nafziger and White (1963), Dexter and White (1964), Schramm and Roberts (1971), Janowitz and Hirsch (1981). Halmos (1969), Tunstall (1970a) and Christian (1980) are British collections of articles. Principal journals include *Journal of Communication*, *Journalism Quarterly*, *Media, Culture and Society*, *European Journal of Communication*, *Communication Research*, *Gazette*, and *Media Information Australia*.

CHAPTER 2   RESEARCHING MEDIA LANGUAGE

1   There is an intermediate class of copy – advertising dressed up as news. This may occur in an advertising supplement, where display advertising is mixed with 'editorial' copy, which is in fact promotion for the adjacent advertisers. A second possibility is where an advertisement uses typeface and layout similar to a publication's editorial copy. In most countries this material has to be flagged 'advertisement'. Myers (1983) offers an interesting commentary on the function which such imitation serves in magazines.

2   Other subgroups of copy, which do not fit cleanly into any one category, I usually separate out as potentially different. The 'fat caption', for example, is a brief story without a headline and attached directly to an accompanying photograph. Newsbriefs are only one or two sentences long, usually gathered into a column under a general headline.

3   Having worked as journalist for a number of government departments and as editor of a news service, I have frequently seen local journalists' bylines on what was virtually word for word a story I or one of my staff had written and distributed. I have even had my stories published bylined as from a paper's 'Own Correspondent'.

CHAPTER 3   THE PRODUCTION OF NEWS LANGUAGE

1   I describe in the present the Medialink system when I was editor in 1986–7. Medialink was a small news service operated by the New Zealand Ministry of Agriculture and Fisheries and covering primary industries news. It had a staff of six and owned the country's largest news network, distributing electronically to most New Zealand daily newspapers and broadcast media, and to many specialist publications. Medialink was closed by the ministry in 1987.

2   Goffman's long paper 'Radio talk' (in Goffman 1981) is one of the most worthwhile studies of media language, although its central themes are not directly relevant to my concerns in this book. As well as its overt focus on announcers' errors and what they reveal about their 'footing', it contains a wealth of insight into the nature of media communication.

3   Much conflict within and about the news media in fact focuses on occasions when proprietors decide to act in professional editorial roles. In particular, conflicts between publicly owned media organizations and their ultimate principal, the state, are a commonplace. Disputes have arisen regularly between the BBC and the British government over coverage of events such as the Falklands/Malvinas war (Harris 1983, Glasgow University Media Group 1985) or longer-running issues, particularly the nuclear debate (Aubrey 1982, Glasgow Group 1985) and Northern Ireland (Pilger 1986, Schlesinger 1987).

4   To include the full range of press animator roles, I describe the system as it was before August 1988, when *The Dominion* became one of the first New Zealand newspapers to convert to direct computer input by journalists. At that point, the jobs of typesetters, proofreaders and compositors (11–14 in figure 3.2) were redundant for news production. Typesetting functions were performed through journalists' direct input of copy, page subeditors did the final camera-ready page make-up formerly the work of compositors, and there was no formal proofreading.

5   News agencies are often referred to as 'wire services' because for the first century of their existence their copy was carried on telegraph wires. I will call the networks on which copy flows the 'wire system', even though it is now carried on computer data lines.

CHAPTER 4   AUTHORING AND EDITING THE NEWS TEXT

1   Hess (1984) provides an insightful and readable account of the work of press offices and officers in US federal agencies. Many government departments issue hundreds of press releases a year.

2   To complete the embedding process, the statements in the final press release were attributed to the director of the agency in which the scientists worked. He had made no input to generating the release, but originated a couple of the late amendments.

3   Although I have not cast my analysis in his framework, my first two editing functions are very like Grice's Maxims of Conversation, category of Manner (1975): 'avoid obscurity, avoid ambiguity, be brief, be orderly.' It should not surprise us that the principles for making a good conversational contribution are comparable to those which emerge from analysis of producing good news stories.

4   I use the (American) term 'lead' for the first paragraph or 'intro' of a story. In British and New Zealand terminology, the lead is the main point of a story, and the intro is its expression in a first paragraph. 'Lead' is also the term used for the main front-page story in a newspaper or first story in a broadcast bulletin.

CHAPTER 5   THE AUDIENCE FOR MEDIA LANGUAGE

1   Burger's text *Sprache der Massenmedien* (1984) is probably the best existing overview of media language, but unavailable in English.

2   In Bell (1984b: 177) I analysed this incident treating embedded and mass audiences as one. The framework proved inadequate, showing the need to recognize multiple layers as well as multiple roles for media communication.

CHAPTER 6   STYLIN' THE NEWS: AUDIENCE DESIGN

1   Audience design parallels closely the principles of the Soviet literary theorist and philosopher of language, Mikhail Bakhtin (whose work I was unaware of when first propounding audience design). Bakhtin's theories are founded on the dialogic nature of speech and literature: 'For the word (and, consequently, for a human being) nothing is more terrible than a *lack of response*' (Bakhtin 1986: 127). For someone to speak is to respond and be responded to: 'An essential (constitutive) marker of the utterance is its quality of being directed to someone, its *addressivity*' (Bakhtin 1986: 95).

2   I am indebted to Andreas Jucker for fruitful comparison of his and my findings and interpretations, and for permission to cite his data. Although he interprets the linguistic structure differently from me, our independent findings of audience correlation are strikingly parallel.

3   YAR was excluded from figure 6.3 because its data was largely from the additional sample. Note that the data for newscaster PB on news station YA, and SD on station ZB, came from the additional sample, and therefore did not contribute to the means graphed in figure 6.3.

CHAPTER 7   TALKING STRANGE: REFEREE DESIGN IN MEDIA
LANGUAGE

1   Compare my notion of referee design again with Bakhtin (1986: 126): 'The author of the utterance, with a greater or lesser awareness, presupposes a higher *superaddressee* (third), whose absolutely just responsive understanding is presumed, either in some metaphysical distance or in distant historical time (the loophole addressee)'.

2   A third, privately owned channel started up in late 1989. With broadcasting deregulation, other contenders are proposing additional channels in the near future.

3   I use the labels 'Upper', 'Middle' and 'Lower' New Zealand in preference to the trichotomy imported from Australia of Cultivated, General and Broad (Mitchell and Delbridge 1965, cf. Bayard 1987). The Australian classification is of doubtful applicability to New Zealand, and in any case I am dealing here with media language only, which does not necessarily correspond to everyday speech. The term 'Upper British' means RP or an acceptable approximation of it, and 'Lower British' other urban and rural dialects of England, especially London-based.

CHAPTER 8   TELLING STORIES

1   In the days of wire despatches both the place and date were carried on the dateline. Most of the elements surrounding news copy are named after

the line above the body copy on which they traditionally occurred – headline, catch-line, date-line, by-line. 'Datelined Moscow' means the story was 'filed' – written and supplied to the news agency – from Moscow. The slugline is named for the 'slugs' of hard metal type used in the original letterpress technology before the advent of offset printing and computer typesetting.

2 Discourse analysis means many things to many people, and includes a British tradition quite distinct from continental text linguistics. This is not the place for a general critique of the European brand of discourse analysis, but one point is necessary background to my presentation here. Although van Dijk's is the most able and enlightening linguistic analysis of news stories, the approach suffers from cumbersome terminology, unclear and inconsistent categorizations, and opaque exposition. Being not at all sure I understand the theoretical framework, I will not attempt to outline it here as a whole but select those aspects which offer the best insights into the structure of news stories. I hope that in the process I do not do injustice to the framework.

3 Van Dijk differentiates the thematic and schematic as two levels, the semantic and the syntactic, but writes that they are closely related (1985c: 69). The two are given many of the same category labels, and both can be represented as tree diagrams. Van Dijk's own thematic (1988a: 77) and schematic (p. 95) analyses of a story from the *New York Times* use virtually the same categories. The theoretical difficulty of keeping syntax and semantics separate is even more difficult at the discourse level than below the sentence. I will therefore describe news stories in terms of a single set of discourse categories and their structures.

CHAPTER 9 MAKE-UP OF THE NEWS STORY

1 Personification can shade into anthropomorphism (Sigal 1987), at its most extreme in the language of war making. Nuclear weapons have from the beginning been domesticated by names. The bombs dropped on Hiroshima and Nagasaki were nicknamed *Little Boy* and *Fat Man* (Chilton 1982). The flip side of this is depersonalizing the enemy through labels such as *gook* or *Hun*. A third accompanying feature is the ascent into abstraction to describe the waging of war, so bombing becomes *protective reaction*.

2 Geis's analysis of political reporting (1987: 100) identifies three components of setting: time and event, with event subdivided into place and the event proper. He labels the whole expression a 'situation adverb'. An event is typically a meeting, speech, interview or the like. This is particularly likely to be mentioned in reports of news-as-talk, but seems less necessary for other kinds of news. Note also Verschueren's (1985) 'metapragmatic' analysis of speech events embedded into the *New York Times*'s reporting of an international crisis.

3 Turning an interview into a story is at the heart of the journalist's craft and is not an automatic skill. As a self-taught journalist, my first stories consisted of the verbatim contents of a recorded interview, cut, reshuffled and interspersed with the questions.

CHAPTER 10 TELLING IT LIKE IT ISN'T

1 The South's long-standing grievance against the Western news agencies was aired in Unesco through the 1970s, and led to the MacBride Report (1980). Unesco adopted its New World Information and Communication Order to address these and similar problems in other areas of communication. This was a major factor in the eventual decision of the United States to withdraw from Unesco.

References

Adams-Smith, Diana E., 1987. 'The process of popularization – rewriting medical research papers for the layman: discussion paper.' *Journal of the Royal Society of Medicine* 80: 634–6.

1989. 'Medical knowledge for the masses: New Zealand newspaper versions of published medical articles.' *New Zealand Family Physician* Autumn: 66–8.

Altheide, David L., 1974. *Creating Reality: How TV News Distorts Events.* Beverly Hills/London: Sage.

Aubrey, Crispin (ed.), 1982. *Nukespeak: The Media and the Bomb.* London: Comedia.

Austin, J. L., 1962. *How to Do Things with Words.* London: Oxford University Press.

Baetens Beardsmore, Hugo (ed.), 1984. *Language and Television (International Journal of the Sociology of Language* 48), Amsterdam: Mouton.

Bakhtin, M. M., 1986. *Speech Genres and Other Late Essays.* Austin: University of Texas Press.

Barthes, Roland, 1968. *Elements of Semiology.* New York: Hill and Wang.

Baugh, John and Joel Sherzer (eds), 1984. *Language in Use: Readings in Sociolinguistics.* Englewood Cliffs, NJ: Prentice-Hall.

Bayard, Donn, 1987. 'Class and change in New Zealand English: a summary report.' *Te Reo* 30: 3–36.

Bell, Allan, 1977. 'The language of radio news in Auckland: a sociolinguistic study of style, audience and subediting variation.' Unpublished PhD thesis. Auckland: University of Auckland. (Ann Arbor, Michigan: University Microfilms International, 1979.)

1982a. 'Radio: the style of news language.' *Journal of Communication* 32/1: 150–64.

1982b. 'This isn't the BBC: colonialism in New Zealand English.' *Applied Linguistics* 3/3: 246–58.

1983. 'Telling it like it isn't: inaccuracy in editing international news.' *Gazette* 31/3: 185–203.

1984a. 'Good copy – bad news: the syntax and semantics of news editing.' In Peter Trudgill (ed.), *Applied Sociolinguistics*, London: Academic Press, 73–116.

1984b. 'Language style as audience design.' *Language in Society* 13/2: 145–204.

1985. 'One rule of news English: geographical, social and historical spread.' *Te Reo* 28: 95–117.

1986. 'Responding to your audience: taking the initiative.' Paper presented to the Minnesota Conference on Linguistic Accommodation and Style-Shifting, Minneapolis, Minnesota.

1988. 'The British base and the American connection in New Zealand media English.' *American Speech* 63/4: 326–44.

1989. 'Hot news – media reporting and public understanding of the climate change issue in New Zealand: a study in the (mis)communication of science' (Project Report to the Department of Scientific and Industrial Research and Ministry for the Environment). Wellington: Victoria University, Department of Linguistics.

1990. 'Audience and referee design in New Zealand media language.' In Allan Bell and Janet Holmes (eds), *New Zealand Ways of Speaking English*, Bristol: Multilingual Matters, 165–94.

1991a. 'Audience accommodation in the mass media.' In Howard Giles, Justine Coupland and Nikolas Coupland (eds), *Contexts of Accommodation: Developments in Applied Sociolinguistics*, Cambridge: Cambridge University Press.

1991b. 'Hot air: media, miscommunication and the climate change issue.' In Nikolas Coupland, Howard Giles and John M. Wiemann (eds), *The Handbook of Miscommunication and Problematic Talk*, Newbury Park, CA: Sage, 259–82.

Beniger, James R., 1988. 'Review essay: information and communication – the new convergence.' *Communication Research* 15/2: 198–218.

Berelson, Bernard, 1952. *Content Analysis in Communication Research*. Glencoe, Ill.: Free Press.

Blom, Jan-Petter and John J. Gumperz, 1972. 'Social meaning in linguistic structure: code-switching in Norway.' In John J. Gumperz and Dell Hymes (eds), *Directions in Sociolinguistics*, New York: Holt, Rinehart and Winston, 407–34.

Blum-Kulka, Soshana, 1983. 'The dynamics of political interviews.' *Text* 3/2: 131–53.

Boyce, George, James Curran and Pauline Wingate (eds), 1978. *Newspaper History from the Seventeenth Century to the Present Day*. London: Constable; Beverly Hills: Sage.

Boyd-Barrett, Oliver, 1980. *The International News Agencies*. London: Constable.

Brown, Gillian, 1977. *Listening to Spoken English*. London: Longman.

Brown, Penelope and Stephen C. Levinson, 1987. *Politeness: Some Univer-*

sals in Language Usage (2nd edn). Cambridge: Cambridge University Press.

Brown, Roger and Albert Gilman, 1960. 'The pronouns of power and solidarity.' In Thomas A. Sebeok (ed.), *Style in Language*, Cambridge, MA.: MIT Press, 253–76.

Bruce, Bertram, 1981. 'A social interaction model of reading.' *Discourse Processes* 4: 273–311.

Bruck, Peter A., 1989. 'Strategies for peace, strategies for news research.' *Journal of Communication* 39/1: 108–29.

Brunel, Gilles, 1970. 'Le français radiophonique à Montréal' ('The French of radio in Montreal'). Unpublished MA dissertation. Montreal: University of Montreal.

Budd, Richard W., Robert K. Thorp and Lewis Donohew, 1967. *Content Analysis of Communications*. New York: Macmillan.

Burchfield, Robert W., Denis Donoghue and Andrew Timothy, 1979. *The Quality of Spoken English on BBC Radio*. London: British Broadcasting Corporation.

Burger, Harald, 1984. *Sprache der Massenmedien* (Language of the Mass Media). Berlin: Walter de Gruyter.

Burns, Tom, 1977. *The BBC: Public Institution and Private World*. London: Macmillan.

Cappon, Rene J., 1982. *The Word: An Associated Press Guide to Good News Writing*. New York: Associated Press.

Cedergren, Henrietta and David Sankoff, 1974. 'Variable rules: performance as a statistical reflection of competence.' *Language* 50/2: 333–55.

Charnley, Mitchell V., 1936. 'Preliminary notes on a study of newspaper accuracy.' *Journalism Quarterly* 13/4: 394–401.

Chilton, Paul, 1982. 'Nukespeak: nuclear language, culture and propaganda.' In Crispin Aubrey (ed.), *Nukespeak: The Media and the Bomb*, London: Comedia, 94–112.

Christian, Harry (ed.), 1980. *The Sociology of Journalism and the Press* (*Sociological Review* Monograph 29). Keele: University of Keele.

Clark, Herbert H., 1987. 'Four dimensions of language use.' In Jef Verschueren and Marcella Bertuccelli-Papi (eds), *The Pragmatic Perspective: Selected Papers from the 1985 International Pragmatics Conference*, Amsterdam/Philadelphia: John Benjamins, 9–25.

Clark, Herbert H. and Thomas B. Carlson, 1982. 'Hearers and speech acts.' *Language* 58/2: 332–73.

Clayman, Steven E., 1990. 'From talk to text: newspaper accounts of reporter–source interactions.' *Media, Culture and Society* 12/1: 79–103.

Cohen, Stanley, 1973. *Folk Devils and Moral Panics*. St Albans: Paladin.

Collum, Danny Duncan, 1989. 'The art of commerce.' *Sojourners* 18/11: 32.

Corbett, Greville and Khurshid Ahmad, 1986. 'A computer corpus of Australian English.' *Australian Journal of Linguistics* 6/2: 251–6.

Coupland, Nikolas, 1980. 'Style-shifting in a Cardiff work-setting.' *Language in Society* 9/1: 1–12.

1984. 'Accommodation at work: some phonological data and their implications.' *International Journal of the Sociology of Language* 46: 49–70.

1985. ' "Hark, hark, the lark": social motivations for phonological style-shifting.' *Language and Communication* 5/3: 153–71.

Coupland, Nikolas, Justine Coupland, Howard Giles and Karen Henwood, 1988. 'Accommodating the elderly: invoking and extending a theory.' *Language in Society* 17/1: 1–41.

Crisell, Andrew, 1986. *Understanding Radio*. London: Methuen.

Cutlip, Scott M., 1954. 'Content and flow of AP news – from Trunk to TTS to Reader.' *Journalism Quarterly* 31/4: 434–46.

Danielson, Wayne A., 1963. 'Content analysis in communication research.' In Ralph O. Nafziger and David M. White (eds), *Introduction to Mass Communications Research*, Baton Rouge: Louisiana State University Press, 180–206.

Davis, F. James and Lester W. Turner, 1951. 'Sample efficiency in quantitative newspaper content analysis.' *Public Opinion Quarterly* 15/4: 762–3.

Davis, Howard, 1985. 'Discourse and media influence.' In Teun A. van Dijk (ed.), *Discourse and Communication: New Approaches to the Analysis of Mass Media Discourse and Communication*, Berlin: de Gruyter, 44–59.

Davis, Howard and Paul Walton, 1983a. 'Death of a premier: consensus and closure in international news.' In Howard Davis and Paul Walton (eds), *Language, Image, Media*, Oxford: Basil Blackwell, 8–49.

(eds), 1983b. *Language, Image, Media*. Oxford: Basil Blackwell.

1983c. 'Sources of variation in news vocabulary: a comparative analysis.' In Gerhard Leitner (ed.), *Language and Mass Media (International Journal of the Sociology of Language* 40), Amsterdam: Mouton, 59–75.

Davison, W. Phillips, 1983. 'The third-person effect in communication.' *Public Opinion Quarterly* 47/1: 1–15.

DeJong, Gerald, 1982. 'An overview of the FRUMP system.' In Wendy G. Lehnert and Martin H. Ringle (eds), *Strategies for Natural Language Processing*, Hillsdale, NJ.: Lawrence Erlbaum, 149–76.

Dexter, Lewis Anthony and David Manning White (eds), 1964. *People, Society and Mass Communications*. Glencoe: Free Press.

van Dijk, Teun A., 1983. 'Discourse analysis: its development and application to the structure of news.' *Journal of Communication* 33/2: 20–43.

(ed.), 1985a. *Discourse and Communication: New Approaches to the Analysis of Mass Media Discourse and Communication*. Berlin: de Gruyter.

(ed.), 1985b. *Handbook of Discourse Analysis* (4 vols). Orlando: Academic Press.

1985c. 'Structures of news in the press.' In Teun A. van Dijk (ed.), *Discourse and Communication: New Approaches to the Analysis of Mass Media Discourse and Communication*, Berlin: de Gruyter, 69–93.

1988a. *News Analysis: Case Studies of International and National News in the Press*. Hillsdale, NJ.: Lawrence Erlbaum.

1988b. *News as Discourse*. Hillsdale, NJ.: Lawrence Erlbaum.

van Dijk, Teun A. and Walter Kintsch, 1983. *Strategies of Discourse Comprehension*. New York: Academic Press.

Donsbach, Wolfgang, 1983. 'Journalists' conceptions of their audience.' *Gazette* 32/1: 19–36.

Dorian, Nancy C., 1981. *Language Death: The Life Cycle of a Scottish Gaelic Dialect*. Philadelphia: University of Pennsylvania Press.

Downes, William, 1984. *Language and Society*. London: Fontana.

Dubois, Betty Lou, 1986. 'From *New England Journal of Medicine* and *Journal of the American Medical Association* through the Associated Press to local newspaper: scientific translation for the laity.' In T. Bungarten (ed.), *Wissenschaftssprache und Gesellschaft* (*Scientific Language and Society*), Hamburg: Akademion, 243–53.

Epstein, Edward Jay, 1973. *News from Nowhere: Television and the News*. New York: Random House.

Ervin-Tripp, Susan M., 1972. 'On sociolinguistic rules: alternation and co-occurrence.' In John J. Gumperz and Dell Hymes (eds), *Directions in Sociolinguistics*, New York: Holt, Rinehart and Winston, 213–50.

Espinosa, Paul, 1982. 'The audience in the text: ethnographic observations of a Hollywood story conference.' *Media, Culture and Society* 4/1: 77–86.

Evans, Harold, 1972. *Newsman's English* (*Editing and Design*, vol. 1). London: Heinemann.

Fasold, Ralph, 1984. *The Sociolinguistics of Society*. Oxford/New York: Basil Blackwell.

1990. *The Sociolinguistics of Language*. Oxford/Cambridge, MA.: Basil Blackwell.

Fenby, Jonathan, 1986. *The International News Services*. New York: Schocken Books.

Ferguson, Charles A., 1959. 'Diglossia.' *Word* 15/2: 325–40.

Fill, Alwin F., 1986. 'Divided illocution.' *International Review of Applied Linguistics* 24/1: 27–34.

Findahl, Olle and Birgitta Hoijer, 1981. 'Media content and human comprehension.' In Karl Erik Rosengren (ed.), *Advances in Content Analysis*, Beverly Hills/London: Sage, 111–32.

Fishman, Joshua A., 1965. 'Who speaks what language to whom and when.' *La Linguistique* 2: 67–88.

Fishman, Joshua A. (ed.), 1968. *Readings in the Sociology of Language*. The Hague: Mouton.

Fishman, Mark, 1980. *Manufacturing the News*. Austin: University of Texas Press.

Fowler, Roger, Bob Hodge, Gunther Kress and Tony Trew, 1979. *Language and Control*. London: Routledge and Kegan Paul.

Frayn, Michael, 1973. 'Unit headline language.' In Stanley Cohen and Jock Young (eds), *The Manufacture of News: Social Problems, Deviance and the Mass Media*, London: Constable, 191–4.

Friedman, Sharon M., Sharon Dunwoody and Carol L. Rogers (eds), 1986. *Scientists and Journalists: Reporting Science as News*. New York: Free Press.

Gal, Susan, 1979. *Language Shift: Social Determinants of Linguistic Change in Bilingual Austria*. New York: Academic Press.

Galtung, Johan and Mari Holmboe Ruge, 1965. 'The structure of foreign news.' *Journal of Peace Research* 2/1: 64–91.

Gans, Herbert J., 1979. *Deciding What's News*. New York: Pantheon.

Garrison, Martin B., 1979. 'The video display terminal and the copy editor: a case study of electronic editing at the *Milwaukee Journal*.' Unpublished PhD dissertation. Illinois: Southern Illinois University at Carbondale.

Geis, Michael L., 1987. *The Language of Politics*. New York: Springer-Verlag.

Gerlach, Peter, 1987. 'Research about magazines appearing in *Journalism Quarterly*.' *Journalism Quarterly* 64/1: 178–82.

Gieber, Walter, 1956. 'Across the desk: a study of 16 telegraph editors.' *Journalism Quarterly* 33/4: 423–32.

Giles, Howard, Anthony Mulac, James J. Bradac and Patricia Johnson, 1987. 'Speech accommodation theory: the first decade and beyond.' In Margaret L. McLaughlin (ed.), *Communication Yearbook 10*, Beverly Hills: Sage, 13–48.

Giles, Howard and Peter F. Powesland, 1975. *Speech Style and Social Evaluation*. London: Academic Press.

Glasgow University Media Group, 1976. *Bad News*. London: Routledge and Kegan Paul.

1980. *More Bad News*. London: Routledge and Kegan Paul.

1985. *War and Peace News*. Milton Keynes: Open University Press.

Goffman, Erving, 1974. *Frame Analysis*. New York: Harper and Row.

1981. *Forms of Talk*. Philadelphia: University of Pennsylvania Press.

Greatbatch, David, 1988. 'A turn-taking system for British news interviews.' *Language in Society* 17/3: 401–30.

Grice, H. P., 1975. 'Logic and conversation.' In Peter Cole and Jerry L. Morgan (eds), *Speech Acts*, New York: Academic Press, 41–58.

Gumperz, John J. and Dell Hymes (eds), 1972. *Directions in Sociolinguistics*. New York: Holt, Rinehart and Winston.

Gunter, Barrie, 1987. *Poor Reception: Misunderstanding and Forgetting Broadcast News*. Hillsdale, NJ.: Lawrence Erlbaum.

Guy, Gregory R., 1980. 'Variation in the group and the individual: the case of final stop deletion.' In William Labov (ed.), *Locating Language in Time and Space*, New York: Academic Press, 1–36.

Haarman, Harald, 1984. 'The role of ethnocultural stereotypes and foreign languages in Japanese commercials.' *International Journal of the Sociology of Language* 50: 101–121.

1986. *Language in Ethnicity: A View of Basic Ecological Relations*. Berlin: Mouton de Gruyter.

Hall, Stuart, Dorothy Hobson, Andrew Lowe and Paul Willis (eds), 1980. *Culture, Media, Language*. London: Hutchinson.

Hallin, Daniel C., 1987. 'Where? Cartography, community and the Cold War.' In Robert Karl Manoff and Michael Schudson (eds), *Reading the News*, New York: Pantheon, 109–45.

Halmos, Paul (ed.), 1969. *The Sociology of Mass-Media Communicators* (*Sociological Review* Monograph 13). Keele: University of Keele.

Harris, Robert, 1983. *Gotcha! The Media, the Government and the Falklands Crisis*. London: Faber and Faber.

Harrison, Martin, 1985. *TV News: Whose Bias?* Hermitage, Berkshire: Policy Journals.

Hartley, John, 1982. *Understanding News*. London/New York: Methuen.

Hartley, John and Martin Montgomery, 1985. 'Representations and relations: ideology and power in press and TV news.' In Teun A. van Dijk (ed.), *Discourse and Communication: New Approaches to the Analysis of Mass Media Discourse and Communication*, Berlin: de Gruyter, 233–69.

Heritage, John, 1985. 'Analysing news interviews: aspects of the production of talk for an overhearing audience.' In Teun A. van Dijk (ed.), *Discourse and Dialogue* (*Handbook of Discourse Analysis*, vol. 3), London: Academic, 95–119.

Hess, Stephen, 1984. *The Government/Press Connection: Press Officers and their Offices*. Washington, DC: Brookings Institution.

Hester, Al, 1971. 'An analysis of news flow from developed and developing nations.' *Gazette* 17/1: 29–43.

Holmes, Janet, 1986. 'Functions of *you know* in women's and men's speech.' *Language in Society* 15/1: 1–21.

Holsti, Ole R., 1968. 'Content analysis.' In Gardner Lindzey and Elliot Aronson (eds), *The Handbook of Social Psychology*, vol. 2, Reading, MA.: Addison-Wesley, 596–692.

1969. *Content Analysis for the Social Sciences and Humanities*. Reading, MA.: Addison-Wesley.

Horvath, Barbara M., 1990. 'Talking in texts.' Paper presented to the New Zealand Seminar on Language and Society, Victoria University, Wellington.

Howitt, Dennis, 1982. *The Mass Media and Social Problems*. Oxford: Pergamon.

Hudson, R.A., 1980. *Sociolinguistics*. Cambridge: Cambridge University Press.

Humphreys-Jones, Claire, 1986. 'Make, make do and mend: the role of the hearer in misunderstandings.' In Graham McGregor (ed.), *Language for Hearers*, Oxford: Pergamon, 105–26.

Hymes, Dell (ed.), 1964. *Language in Culture and Society*. New York: Harper and Row.
— 1974. *Foundations in Sociolinguistics: An Ethnographic Approach*. Philadelphia: University of Pennsylvania Press.
Jacoby, Jacob and Wayne D. Hoyer, 1987. *The Comprehension and Miscomprehension of Print Communications: An Investigation of Mass Media Magazines*. Hillsdale, NJ.: Lawrence Erlbaum.
Janowitz, Morris and Paul M. Hirsch (eds), 1981. *Reader in Public Opinion and Mass Communication* (3rd edn). New York: Free Press.
Jensen, Klaus Bruhn, 1988. 'News as social resource: a qualitative empirical study of the reception of Danish television news.' *European Journal of Communication* 3/3: 275–301.
JICNARS, 1980. *National Readership Survey 1980*. London: Joint Industry Committee for National Readership Surveys.
Jones, G. and A.J. Meadows, 1978. 'Sources and selection of scientific material for newspapers and radio programmes.' *Journal of Research Communication Studies* 1/1: 69–82.
Jones, Robert L. and Roy E. Carter, Jr, 1959. 'Some procedures for estimating "news hole" in content analysis.' *Public Opinion Quarterly* 23/3: 399–403.
Jucker, Andreas H., 1986. *News Interviews: A Pragmalinguistic Analysis (Pragmatics and Beyond 7/4)*. Amsterdam/Philadelphia: John Benjamins.
— 1989. 'Stylistic variation in the syntax of British newspaper language.' Unpublished MS. Zurich: University of Zurich.
Klapper, Joseph T., 1960. *The Effects of Mass Communication*. Glencoe, Ill.: Free Press.
Kleinnijenhuis, Jan, 1989. 'News as olds: a test of the consonance hypothesis and related news selection hypotheses.' *Gazette* 43/3: 205–28.
Kniffka, Hannes, 1980. *Soziolinguistik und empirische Textanalyse: Schlagzeilen- und Leadformulierung in amerikanischen Tageszeitungen* (Sociolinguistics and Empirical Text Analysis: Headline and Lead Formulation in American Daily Newspapers). Tübingen: Niemeyer.
Knightley, Phillip, 1975. *The First Casualty*. London: Andre Deutsch.
Kress, Gunther, 1983a. 'Linguistic and ideological transformations in news reporting.' In Howard Davis and Paul Walton (eds), *Language, Image, Media*, Oxford: Basil Blackwell, 120–38.
— 1983b. 'Linguistic processes and the mediation of "reality": the politics of newspaper language.' In Gerhard Leitner (ed.), *Language and Mass Media (International Journal of the Sociology of Language* 40), Amsterdam: Mouton, 43–57.
Kress, Gunther and Robert Hodge, 1979. *Language as Ideology*. London: Routledge.
Krippendorff, Klaus, 1980. *Content Analysis: An Introduction to its Methodology*. Beverly Hills/London: Sage.
Kumar, Krishan, 1975. 'Holding the middle ground: the BBC, the public and

the professional broadcaster.' *Sociology* 9/1: 67–88.

Labov, William, 1966. *The Social Stratification of English in New York City.* Washington, DC: Center for Applied Linguistics.

1972a. *Sociolinguistic Patterns.* Philadelphia: University of Pennsylvania Press.

1972b. 'The transformation of experience in narrative syntax.' In William Labov, *Language in the Inner City,* Philadelphia: University of Pennsylvania Press, 354–96.

1984. 'Field methods of the Project on Linguistic Change and Variation.' In John Baugh and Joel Sherzer (eds), *Language in Use: Readings in Sociolinguistics,* Englewood Cliffs, NJ.: Prentice-Hall, 28–53.

Labov, William and Joshua Waletzky, 1967. 'Narrative analysis: oral versions of personal experience.' In June Helm (ed.), *Essays on the Verbal and Visual Arts (Proceedings of the 1966 Annual Spring Meeting of the American Ethnological Society),* Seattle: University of Washington Press, 12–44.

Lambert, Wallace E., 1967. 'A social psychology of bilingualism.' *Journal of Social Issues* 23/2: 91–109.

Lasswell, Harold D., 1960. 'The structure and function of communication in society.' In Wilbur Schramm (ed.), *Mass Communications,* Urbana: University of Illinois Press, 117–30.

Lasswell, Harold D., Nathan Leites et al., 1949. *Language of Politics.* New York: Stewart.

Lazarsfeld, Paul F., 1948. 'The role of criticism in the management of mass media.' *Journalism Quarterly* 25/2: 115–26.

Lealand, Geoff, 1988. *A Foreign Egg in our Nest? American Popular Culture in New Zealand.* Wellington: Victoria University Press.

Leech, Geoffrey N., 1966. *English in Advertising.* London: Longmans.

Leech, Geoffrey N. and Michael H. Short, 1981. *Style in Fiction: A Linguistic Introduction to English Fictional Prose.* London/New York: Longman.

Leitch, Shirley, 1990. *News Talk: Media Stories on Unemployment.* Palmerston North: Dunmore Press.

Leitner, Gerhard, 1980. ' "BBC English" and "Deutsche Rundfunksprache": a comparative and historical analysis of the language on the radio.' *International Journal of the Sociology of Language* 26: 75–100.

1983a. *Gesprächsanalyse und Rundfunkkommunikation: Die Struktur englischer phone-ins* (Conversational Analysis and Radio Communication: The Structure of English Phone-in Programmes). Hildesheim: Georg Olms.

(ed.), 1983b. *Language and Mass Media (International Journal of the Sociology of Language* 40). Amsterdam: Mouton.

1983c. 'Reporting the "events of the day".' Unpublished MS. Berlin: Free University.

1983d. 'Review article' of Glasgow University Media Group 1980, *More Bad News.* In Gerhard Leitner (ed.), *Language and Mass Media (Interna-*

tional Journal of the Sociology of Language 40), Amsterdam: Mouton, 107–20.

1983e. 'The social background of the language of radio.' In Howard Davis and Paul Walton (eds), *Language, Image, Media*, Oxford: Basil Blackwell, 50–74.

1984. 'Australian English or English in Australia: linguistic identity or dependence in broadcast language.' *English World-Wide* 5/1: 55–85.

Lerman, Claire Lindegren, 1983. 'Dominant discourse: the institutional voice and control of topic.' In Howard Davis and Paul Walton (eds), *Language, Image, Media*, Oxford: Basil Blackwell, 75–103.

Levinson, Stephen, 1988. 'Putting linguistics on a proper footing: explorations in Goffman's concepts of participation.' In Paul Drew and Anthony Wootton (eds), *Erving Goffman: Exploring the Interaction Order*, Cambridge: Polity Press, 161–227.

Lipski, John M., 1985. 'Spanish in United States broadcasting.' In Lucia Elias-Olivares, Elizabeth A. Leone, Rene Cisneros and John R. Gutierrez (eds), *Spanish Language Use and Public Life in the United States*, Berlin: Mouton, 217–33.

Lutz, Benedikt and Ruth Wodak, 1987. *Information für Informierte: Linguistische Studien zu Verständlichkeit und Verstehen von Hörfunknachrichten* (Information for the Informed: Linguistic Studies on the Comprehensibility and Comprehension of Radio News). Vienna: Verlag der Österreichischen Akademie der Wissenschaften.

MacBride, Sean et al., 1980. *Many Voices, One World* (Report by the International Commission for the Study of Communication Problems). Paris: Unesco; London: Kogan Page; New York: Unipub.

McEntegart, Damian and R. B. Le Page, 1982. 'An appraisal of the statistical techniques used in the Sociolinguistic Survey of Multilingual Communities.' In Suzanne Romaine (ed.), *Sociolinguistic Variation in Speech Communities*, London: Edward Arnold, 105–24.

McIntyre, Ian, 1988. 'Fall of the smoke blower.' *The Times*, 18 June 1988.

McQuail, Denis, 1969a. *Towards a Sociology of Mass Communications*. London: Collier-Macmillan.

1969b. 'Uncertainty about the audience and the organization of mass communications.' In Paul Halmos (ed.), *The Sociology of Mass-Media Communicators* (*Sociological Review* Monograph 13), Keele: University of Keele, 75–84.

1987. *Mass Communication Theory: An Introduction* (2nd edn). London: Sage.

Mancini, Paolo, 1988a. 'Simulated interaction: how the television journalist speaks.' *European Journal of Communication* 3/2: 151–66.

(ed.), 1988b. *The Analysis of News Texts* (*European Journal of Communication* 3/2). London: Sage.

Manoff, Robert Karl, 1987. 'Writing the news (by telling the "story").' In Robert Karl Manoff and Michael Schudson (eds), *Reading the News*, New York: Pantheon, 197–229.

Manoff, Robert Karl and Michael Schudson (eds), 1987. *Reading the News*. New York: Pantheon.

Mardh, Ingrid, 1980. *Headlinese: On the Grammar of English Front Page Headlines*. Lund: CWK Gleerup.

Matthewson, Lisa, 1989. 'Conversational behaviour of television viewers.' Unpublished MS. Wellington: Victoria University.

Milroy, Lesley, 1980. *Language and Social Networks*. Oxford: Basil Blackwell.

1987. *Observing and Analysing Natural Language: A Critical Account of Sociolinguistic Method*. Oxford: Basil Blackwell.

Mintz, Alexander, 1949. 'The feasibility of the use of samples in content analysis.' In Harold D. Lasswell, Nathan Leites et al., *Language of Politics*, New York: Stewart, 127–53.

Mitchell, A.G. and Arthur Delbridge, 1965. *The Speech of Australian Adolescents*. Sydney: Angus and Robertson.

Mody, Bella, 1986. 'The receiver as sender: formative evaluation in Jamaican radio.' *Gazette* 38: 147–60.

Moeran, Brian, 1984. 'Advertising sounds as cultural discourse.' *Language and Communication* 4/2: 147–58.

Montgomery, Martin, 1986. 'Language and power: a critical review of *Studies in the Theory of Ideology* by John B. Thompson.' *Media, Culture and Society* 8/1: 41–64.

1988. 'D-J talk'. In Nikolas Coupland (ed.), *Styles of Discourse*, London/New York: Croom Helm, 85–104.

Morley, David, 1983. 'Cultural transformations: the politics of resistance.' In Howard Davis and Paul Walton (eds), *Language, Image, Media*, Oxford: Basil Blackwell, 104–117.

Myers, Kathy, 1983. 'Understanding advertisers.' In Howard Davis and Paul Walton (eds), *Language, Image, Media*, Oxford: Basil Blackwell, 205–23.

Nafziger, Ralph O. and David M. White (eds), 1963. *Introduction to Mass Communications Research*. Baton Rouge: Louisiana State University Press.

Nelkin, Dorothy, 1987. *Selling Science: How the Press Covers Science and Technology*. New York: W.H. Freeman.

Neuwirth, Kurt, Carol M. Liebler, Sharon Dunwoody and Jennifer Riddle, 1988. 'The effect of "electronic" news sources on selection and editing of news.' *Journalism Quarterly* 65/1: 85–94.

Newmeyer, Frederick J. (ed.), 1988. *Language: The Socio-cultural Context* (*Linguistics: The Cambridge Survey*, vol. 4). Cambridge: Cambridge University Press.

Pateman, Trevor, 1983. 'How is understanding an advertisement possible?' In Howard Davis and Paul Walton (eds), *Language, Image, Media*, Oxford: Basil Blackwell, 187–204.

Payne, Arvilla C., 1980. 'Factors controlling the acquisition of the Philadelphia dialect by out-of-state children.' In William Labov (ed.),

Locating Language in Time and Space, New York: Academic Press,'
143–78.

Peterson, Sophia, 1981. 'International news selection by the elite press: a case study.' *Public Opinion Quarterly* 45/2: 143–63.

Philo, Greg, 1987. 'Whose news.' *Media, Culture and Society* 9/4: 397–406.

Pilger, John, 1986. 'Media games.' In John Pilger, *Heroes*, London: Pan, 473–539.

Pitt, David (ed.), 1977. *Social Class in New Zealand*. Auckland: Longman Paul.

Platt, John T. and Heidi K. Platt, 1975. *The Social Significance of Speech*. Amsterdam: North-Holland.

Pollard-Gott, Lucy, Michael McCloskey and Amy K. Todres, 1979. 'Subjective story structure.' *Discourse Processes* 2/4: 251–81.

Pool, Ithiel de Sola (ed.), 1959. *Trends in Content Analysis*. Urbana: University of Illinois Press.

Pool, Ithiel de Sola, Harold D. Lasswell and Daniel Lerner, 1970. *The Prestige Press: A Comparative Study of Political Symbols*. Cambridge, MA.: MIT Press.

Pool, Ithiel de Sola and Irwin Shulman, 1959. 'Newsmen's fantasies, audiences, and newswriting.' *Public Opinion Quarterly* 23/2: 145–58.

Pride, J. B. and Janet Holmes (eds), 1972. *Sociolinguistics: Selected Readings*. Harmondsworth: Penguin.

Righter, Rosemary, 1978. *Whose News? Politics, the Press and the Third World*. London: Burnett.

Robinson, John P. and Mark R. Levy, 1986. *The Main Source: Learning from Television News*. Beverly Hills: Sage.

Roeh, Itzhak, 1982. *The Rhetoric of News in the Israel Radio: Some Implications of Language and Style for Newstelling*. Bochum: Studienverlag Brockmeyer.

Roeh, Itzhak and Saul Feldman, 1984. 'The rhetoric of numbers in front-page journalism: how numbers contribute to the melodramatic in the popular press.' *Text* 4/4: 347–68.

Rosenblum, Mort, 1979. *Coups and Earthquakes*. New York: Harper and Row.

Rumelhart, David E., 1975. 'Notes on a schema for stories.' In Daniel G. Bobrow and Allan Collins (eds), *Representation and Understanding*, New York: Academic Press, 211–36.

Rydén, Mats, 1975. 'Noun-name collocations in British English newspaper language.' *Studia Neophilologica* 47/1: 14–39.

Sachsman, David B., 1976. 'Public relations influence on coverage of environment in San Francisco area.' *Journalism Quarterly* 53/1: 54–60.

Scannell, Paddy (ed.), 1990. *Texts and Audiences* (*Media, Culture and Society* 12/1). London: Sage.

Schank, Roger C. and Robert P. Abelson, 1977. *Scripts, Plans, Goals and Understanding*. Hillsdale, NJ.: Lawrence Erlbaum.

Schlesinger, Philip, 1980. 'Between sociology and journalism.' In Harry

Christian (ed.), *The Sociology of Journalism and the Press* (*Sociological Review* Monograph 29), Keele: University of Keele, 341–69.

1987. *Putting 'Reality' Together: BBC News* (2nd edn). London: Methuen.

Schmidt, Rosemarie and Joseph F. Kess, 1986. *Television Advertising and Televangelism: Discourse Analysis of Persuasive Language* (*Pragmatics and Beyond* 7/5). Amsterdam/Philadelphia: John Benjamins.

Schramm, Wilbur (ed.), 1960. *Mass Communications*. Urbana: University of Illinois Press.

Schramm, Wilbur and Donald F. Roberts (eds), 1971. *The Process and Effects of Mass Communication* (revised edn). Urbana: University of Illinois Press.

Schudson, Michael, 1978. *Discovering the News: A Social History of American Newspapers*. New York: Basic Books.

1982. 'The politics of narrative form: the emergence of news conventions in print and television.' *Daedalus* 111/4: 97–112.

1987. 'When? Deadlines, datelines and history.' In Robert Karl Manoff and Michael Schudson (eds), *Reading the News*, New York: Pantheon, 79–108.

1989. 'The sociology of news production.' *Media, Culture and Society* 11/3: 263–82.

Selting, Margret, 1983. 'Institutionelle Kommunikation: Stilwechsel als Mittel strategischer Interaktion' ('Institutional communication: style shift as a means of strategic interaction'). *Linguistische Berichte* 86: 29–48.

1985. 'Levels of style-shifting – exemplified in the interaction strategies of a moderator in a listener participation programme.' *Journal of Pragmatics* 9/2–3: 179–97.

Shipley, Linda J. and James K. Gentry, 1981. 'How electronic editing equipment affects editing performance.' *Journalism Quarterly* 58/3: 371–4, 387.

Short, Michael, 1988. 'Speech presentation, the novel and the press.' In Willie Van Peer (ed.), *The Taming of the Text: Explorations in Language, Literature and Culture*, London: Routledge, 61–81.

Sigal, Leon V., 1973. *Reporters and Officials*. Lexington, MA.: Heath.

1987. 'Who? Sources make the news.' In Robert Karl Manoff and Michael Schudson (eds), *Reading the News*, New York: Pantheon, 9–37.

Singletary, Michael, 1980. *Accuracy in News Reporting: A Review of the Research* (*ANPA News Research Report* 25). Washington, DC: American Newspaper Publishers Association.

Solomon, Martha, 1978. 'Jimmy Carter and *Playboy*: a sociolinguistic perspective on style.' *Quarterly Journal of Speech* 64/2: 173–82.

Soloski, John, 1989. 'News reporting and professionalism: some constraints on the reporting of news.' *Media, Culture and Society* 11/2: 207–28.

Sparks, Colin, 1987. 'The readership of the British quality press.' *Media, Culture and Society* 9/4: 427–55.

Sparks, Colin and Michelle Campbell, 1987. 'The "inscribed reader" of the

British quality press.' *European Journal of Communication* 2/4: 455–72.

Stempel, Guido H. (III), 1952. 'Sample size for classifying subject matter in dailies.' *Journalism Quarterly* 29/3: 333–4.

Stevenson, Robert L. and Donald Lewis Shaw (eds), 1984. *Foreign News and the New World Information Order*. Ames, Iowa: Iowa State University Press.

Tannen, Deborah, 1988. 'The commingling of orality and literacy in giving a paper at a scholarly conference.' *American Speech* 63/1: 34–43.

Thakerar, Jitendra N., Howard Giles and Jenny Cheshire, 1982. 'Psychological and linguistic parameters of speech accommodation theory.' In Colin Fraser and Klaus R. Scherer (eds), *Advances in the Social Psychology of Language*, Cambridge: Cambridge University Press, 205–55.

Thomas, Jenny, 1986. 'The dynamics of discourse: a pragmatic analysis of confrontational interaction.' Unpublished PhD thesis. Lancaster: University of Lancaster.

Thorndyke, Perry W., 1979. 'Knowledge acquisition from newspaper stories.' *Discourse Processes* 2/2: 95–112.

Tillinghast, William A., 1983. 'Source control and evaluation of newspaper inaccuracies.' *Newspaper Research Journal* 4: 13–24.

Troesser, Michael, 1983. 'Rundfunkmoderation bei Beteiligungssendungen – im Spannungsfeld zwischen Offenheit und Kontrolle' ('The role of the moderator in radio participation programmes – reconciling openness and control'). In Gerhard Leitner (ed.), *Language and Mass Media* (*International Journal of the Sociology of Language* 40), Amsterdam: Mouton, 77–91.

Trudgill, Peter, 1972. 'Sex, covert prestige and linguistic change.' *Language in Society* 1/2: 179–96.

1974. *The Social Differentiation of English in Norwich*. London: Cambridge University Press.

1981. 'Linguistic accommodation: sociolinguistic observations on a sociopsychological theory.' In Carrie S. Masek, Roberta A. Hendrick and Mary Frances Miller (eds), *Papers from the Parasession on Language and Behavior*, Chicago: Chicago Linguistic Society, 218–37.

1983a. *On Dialect*. Oxford: Basil Blackwell.

1983b. *Sociolinguistics: An Introduction to Language and Society* (2nd edn). Harmondsworth: Penguin.

1986. *Dialects in Contact*. Oxford: Basil Blackwell.

Tuchman, Gaye, 1978. *Making News: A Study in the Construction of Reality*. New York: Free Press.

Tunstall, Jeremy (ed.), 1970a. *Media Sociology*. London: Constable.

1970b. *The Westminster Lobby Correspondents*. London: Routledge and Kegan Paul.

Twentieth Century Fund, 1981. *Annual Report*. New York: Twentieth Century Fund

Verschueren, Jef, 1985. *International News Reporting: Metapragmatic Metaphors and the U-2 (Pragmatics and Beyond 6/5).* Amsterdam/Philadelphia: John Benjamins.

Vestergaard, Torben and Kim Schrøder, 1985. *The Language of Advertising.* Oxford: Basil Blackwell.

Vidmar, Neil and Milton Rokeach, 1974. 'Archie Bunker's bigotry: a study in selective perception and exposure.' *Journal of Communication* 24/1: 36–47.

Wales, Max, Galen Rarick and Hal Davis, 1963. 'Message exaggeration by the receiver.' *Journalism Quarterly* 40/3: 339–41.

Westley, Bruce H. and Malcolm S. MacLean, Jr, 1957. 'A conceptual model for communications research.' *Journalism Quarterly* 34/1: 31–8.

White, David Manning, 1950. 'The "Gatekeeper"; a case study in the selection of news.' *Journalism Quarterly* 27/4: 383–90.

Wodak, Ruth, 1987. ' "And where is the Lebanon?" A socio-psycholinguistic investigation of comprehension and intelligibility of news.' *Text* 7/4: 377–410.

Woodall, W. Gill, Dennis K. Davis and Haluk Sahin, 1983. 'From the Boob Tube to the Black Box: television news comprehension from an information processing perspective.' *Journal of Broadcasting* 27/1: 1–23.

Wright, John W. (II) and Lawrence A. Hosman, 1986. 'Listener perceptions of radio news.' *Journalism Quarterly* 63/4: 802–8, 814.

Yaeger-Dror, Malcah, 1988. 'The influence of changing group vitality on convergence toward a dominant linguistic norm: an Israeli example.' *Language and Communication* 8/3–4: 285–305.

Index